WAKE UP, America!

M. Sebastian Thomas

WAKE UP, America!

M. Sebastian Thomas

Subjects: 1-Social Care 2- Family Life 3- Marriage 4- United States 5-Culture

Published by IngramSpark

Cover Design and Typesetting: Araceli Chavez

ISBN 979-8-9906282-1-2

Library of Congress Control Number: 2024912996

Printed in the United States of America

DEDICATION

This book is dedicated to my grandchildren

PREFACE

During the late 1970s, when I was teaching at Desalles University in Center Valley, Pennsylvania, occasionally students would miss class and then subsequently do poorly on the tests. I would ask those students to come to my office. When they come, I tell them to improve their grade. They would give excuses such as girlfriend or boyfriend problems. I tell those students that if they do not improve, then I will have to contact their parents. In most cases, the student will be shaken and beg me not to call their parents. Such students promise to work harder.

Two decades later, in the 1990s, in one of my classes at St. Francis University in Loretto, PA, one of my students performed poorly and, as usual, I asked him to come to my office. I wanted to speak with him about missing classes and earning poor grades on tests. I told him that I may call his parents. The student did not care. The student told me, "Go ahead." He said, "I don't care for them. I don't live with them. They do not care for me. For holidays, I go to my grandparents' home." Such replies were common at that time. Upon inquiry, I learned that the parents of that student were either separated or divorced.

I asked myself, "What is happening?" At this rural, Catholic college, such lack of contact between parents and students should not be a common phenomenon. If this is happening here, then what is happening at other colleges and universities? What are the student and parent relationships in larger colleges and universities or bigger cities?

I also noticed that the divorce rate in America was increasing among the entire population. I can't watch this and sit idle, I thought. I must do something.

What must I do? I will write a book. Hence, the purpose of writing this book is to: (1) share my observations about the massive number of broken families in America, (2) share the significant causes I identify, (3) predict the consequences of the disintegration of the traditional nuclear family in America, and (4) offer concrete solutions for the United States and the rest of the world- especially my grandchildren.

TABLE OF CONTENTS

PART 1

WAKING
THE DRAGON

An Introduction to the Most Pressing Problem

Facing America Today

CHAPTER 1
WHY I WRITE THIS BOOK

*"He who does not prevent a crime
when he can, encourages it."*
- SENECA

Let's go back in time to August 26, 1963. On that day, I was sitting in an airplane. A lady sitting close to me said, "We have arrived." I looked down and saw New York City spread out before me. It was 4:30 in the morning.

At the Idlewild Airport (now John F. Kennedy International Airport), the immigration officer examined my papers and then said two pleasant words: "Good luck." I took a Greyhound bus from NYC to Pittsburgh, Pennsylvania where I was admitted in to the MBA program at Duquesne University. When I arrived, I was picked up by my host family (arranged by the Pittsburgh Council for International Visitors). I would be staying at their house for a couple of days as I waited for the semester to start at Duquesne University.

When we reached their home in Allison Park, I walked into the host family's home; I was exhausted, but I paused long enough to notice that the TV was 'on.' The television news was reporting about Dr. Martin Luther King's march in Washington D.C., which took place earlier that day. I had arrived in America.

I love the United States of America. America gave me many opportunities. It has given me a place to learn, earn, grow, and raise a family. I am grateful to this nation. I could not enjoy the life I live without the education and employment opportunities available in this nation. I love my children, grandchildren, and the future generations to come. It is for them, and all the future generations of this nation, that I write this book.

I was born and grew up into an adult in an Eastern culture, specifically India. In my 20s, I came to America and witnessed the cultural changes of the 1960s, the Vietnam War era. During that time, I married my wife, who also grew up in the same Eastern culture of India. From the 1960s into the start of the 21st century, my wife and I have lived in America. We reared two children in America and now have eight grandchildren. In thirty years, I worked at four different universities in Pennsylvania. Over these years, I have observed that the core of the nation—nuclear families— are disintegrating. What is a nuclear family? Generally, the nuclear family means a father (male) and mother (female) plus their biological children. It can include adopted children or a father/mother who remarries after the death of their first spouse. If the nuclear family fails, then the nation will fail. I do not want to see this nation fail.

Based on my observations and life experiences in America over the past fifty-seven years, I act upon my moral obligation to transmit my knowledge and insight to others. We are amidst a "family catastrophe" in the social culture of America. Our failure to acknowledge and address the situation will yield long-term consequences that shall affect all future generations. The current indications of the impending family catastrophe in America are like the warnings ignored by the Roman empire 2,000 years ago, which ultimately led to its downfall.

By writing this book, I choose not to be complacent and indifferent. Instead, I make the decision, as a loving person, to do my part to prevent the erosion of family values and help restore them in America. In this book, I set forth the causes and consequences of the disintegration of the nuclear family in America and offer necessary and concrete solutions. The need to protect marriage and the nuclear family is more urgent today than ever before. I issue a warning that failure to stabilize and support strong nuclear families will lead to an impending decay and downfall of this nation. Effective remedies must be identified and implemented immediately. The current state of affairs in American family life is much more severe than stormwater flooding over land, wildfires burning forests, unmaintained highways, uncertain stock markets, or a terrorist bombing. While all those events are severe and disabling, they pale in comparison to the destruction and disintegration of the nuclear family.

CHAPTER 2

AN UNWELCOME CHANGE

Over the years, our lifestyles have undergone many drastic changes, most of which are improvements. Take the case of transportation. Two hundred years ago, people moved from place to place by walking or by using a horse buggy. Road conditions were poor, and traveling was a time-consuming affair. Then came trains, planes, and automobiles. The early automobiles could not be driven beyond 25 to 35 miles per hour. Then came the standard shift, then the automatic shift. Then came efficient engines and the Global Positioning Symstem (GPS). Then came well-paved highways with wide lanes and cars easily driving fifty-five to seventy-five mph. Trains and planes have undergone similar improvements. While the quality of traveling has increased and the ease of traveling has increased, its basic purpose of transportation has remained the same.

One hundred years ago, those who wanted to enjoy music had to make the effort to listen to music performed live at a concert. Then came the gramophone and the turntable, and music could be recorded and listened to later. Then came the radio. Then came the CD. Then the iPod. Today, we can listen to the highest quality music essentially anywhere on the globe on demand in the privacy of our own wireless earbuds. While the quality of recorded music and the ease of listening to it has increased, the fundamental goal of entertainment and pleasure has remained intact.

Two hundred years ago, food had to be freshly purchased, cooked, and consumed every day. There was no refrigeration. Fruits and vegetables could only be obtained during their natural growing season. Today, we can buy food at any number of grocery stores and gas stations. It is easy to store, pack, and refrigerate it. Foods from around the world can be obtained in your neighborhood. Many fruits and vegetables can now be obtained all year. However, the basic purpose of food has not changed: we consume food to nourish ourselves.

In these areas of our life—transportation, entertainment, and nourishment—drastic changes have occurred. Our technology and capabilities have improved so that we obtain higher quality and more convenience. However, we have kept the basic purpose of these social experiences intact. They still serve the same role now as they did generations before.

However, when it comes to family life there has not been improvement but deterioration. We have gone from intact nuclear families to broken families, from sex inside marriage to pre-marital sex, from dating for marriage to dating to mate, from low STD prevalence to epidemic STD prevalence, and from family-centric life to self-centric life. I would not call this an improvement but a cultural reversal. In other areas of our lives, we have advanced our technologies to fulfill the same essential roles as before. But today, American family lives are in shambles. The basic tenets of the nuclear family are gone. Members of American families no longer fulfill the same roles they once did. We must ask ourselves, why is it that family lives have not improved in the last 100 years? Why have we advanced in so many other areas of our lives except this one? Why is it that in the past five decades, with many improvements in America, the fundamental social building block- the nuclear family- is falling apart?

Five decades ago, if I asked someone whether it is OK to have a divorce, they would have said 'No way.' Four decades ago, the answer would be 'No' to 'Maybe.' Three decades ago, the answer would be 'Maybe' to 'Yes.' Two decades ago, the answer would be 'Yes.' Today, the answer is 'Absolutely.' In many American cities today, it seems that if you have not divorced at least once in your life, you are outside the norm. Before, you would get invited to Silver Wedding anniversaries (25 years) and Golden Wedding anniversaries (50 years) and maybe even the rare Platinum Wedding anniversary (75 years). Today, if a married couple makes it to their 10th or 20th wedding anniversary, people sigh with relief and say the marriage survived. In fact, the average length of a marriage in the US is now a mere 8 years (Vuleta, 2021).

Five decades ago, if I asked a woman 'Do you have children?' and she said 'Yes,' and then I asked her 'Are you married?', she would punch me in my face. Or if I asked 'Are you married?' and she said 'No,' and then I asked her 'Do you have children?', she would also punch me in my face. Today, you can ask these questions in this way and you won't get any reaction, because women having children out of wedlock has become normal. As of May 2022, a little more than 40% of children born in the US were from unmarried mothers (CDC National Center for Health Statistics).

In the 1970s and 80s, when I was teaching as a Professor, sometimes a student would be absent from several classes or submit poor work. I would then ask them to come to my office and warn them that I was going to notify their parents about their poor work and class absences. The student would typically grow concerned, even scared, and beg me not to contact their parents. They would then promise to attend class regularly and improve their studies—and in many cases, the students did actually improve. However, in the late 90s and into 2000, when I sat down with a student to discuss the same sort of performance, the student was not concerned. Instead, they would say, "Go ahead and tell my parents, I don't care. I don't live with my parents anyway" or, even worse, "I don't have any parents. For the holidays, I am going to my grandparents' house or my friend's house." This change in response from the students reflects a problem. It reflects the breakdown of the nuclear family in America.

CHAPTER 3

IS THE GENIE OUT OF THE BOTTLE?

A significant number of modern Americans lack certain core values in their current culture. This does not mean that the entire current culture in America is poor and in need of change. Rather, the current culture in America is declining in some core areas: fundamental family values and sexual morality. Modern Americans must change this current way of family life and sexual immorality. Failure to change these will precipitate the decline of the entire nation.

There is agreement among members of the general public, economists, and sociologists of an impending "family catastrophe." However, these same individuals believe they are powerless in their ability to successfully effectuate changes to avoid the family catastrophe. In other words, they abandon themselves to defeat by telling themselves that constructive cooperative changes to improve nuclear family life in America is impossible. To my disappointment, I find that very few people are willing to take effort to restore and resolve this impending family catastrophe because of the perceived zero probability of achieving success. Even very well-intentioned Americans expend zero effort to improve nuclear family life in America because they believe—incorrectly—that they cannot obtain or achieve a stable and strong family in America.

These same individuals who believe there is zero probability of improving nuclear family life in America are enthusiastic to prioritize steps to grow the economy for a higher standard of living, invest in scientific and technological advancements, and improve military defense strategies against potential threats. Investment of time and energy towards the economy, science, technology, and defense will not bring the necessary changes in the most important area: the nuclear family. No nation can claim itself to be wealthy when family life is unhealthy. In the area of nuclear family relationships, America grows poorer and poorer.

Some of my students have told me that bringing about change in the American nuclear family is not possible. "The genie is out of the bottle," they explain, "and that genie cannot be put back into its bottle." These students 'solve' the impending crisis by thinking that the rehabilitation of the nuclear family will correct itself—somehow. I do not subscribe to this solution of automatic re-stabilization. The current crisis is man-made; therefore, man is capable of enacting solutions to solve the crisis. Human intervention is needed. We create the cultures and institutions we live in; therefore, we all must work together to solve this man-made family catastrophe.

I predict that if the current culture regarding family life is not changed, the fundamental fabric that binds all people will unravel and individuals will be lost and without purpose—like animals. There will be lack of order and lack of discipline because individuals will lack their mother, their father, their family lineage, and their family bonds and relationships. Blended families will become the norm, while nuclear family life will be the exception.

CHAPTER 4

WHY DOES AMERICA NEED STRONG NUCLEAR FAMILIES?

A strong nuclear family is vital because the family is the most basic institution that affects everyone else in every other aspect of their life. Above all, the "family is a living cell of the great and universal family of mankind."[1] The family is the foundation for all social and political institutions: all governments, economies and cultures begin with and stand upon the family. All cultural and economic organizations and systems are maintained and grown by the investment of time and effort from families. No artist, lawmaker, doctor, banker, or farmer in America would be able to function in their daily life without the encouragement, support, and help of their own family and the families around them. The family is the beginning and the end of a nation, its government, its economy, and its culture.

If the nuclear family fails, then governments fail, economies fail, cultures fail, and nations fail. All institutions and organizations that involve people will fail. When an individual has no family, that person develops an anguished sense of pain and loss that will subsequently burden his whole life; he or she will always feel that something is missing.[2] Thus, there is

---

[1] John Paul II, Letter to Families, 1994
[2] ibid

an urgent need to cultivate and support strong nuclear families like never before.

In today's world, what happens in America quickly becomes a global problem. When America goes to war, when America's economy is unhealthy, or when America makes decisions, the repercussions have effects on a global scale. Thus, the whole world has a stake in the health of the American nuclear family. As the American nuclear family declines, the subsequent decline in its culture, economy, and government will become a global problem.

There are seven reasons why the nuclear family is important. First, the nuclear family provides support and security to its members in good and bad times. Second, the family gives unconditional love and affection from the parents to the children. Unconditional love from parents satisfies emotional needs, which is essential for mental and physical happiness. Third, the nuclear family protects children, who are vulnerable, from external forces such as peer pressure, media pressure, and outside negative influences.

Fourth, the nuclear family is a center of gravity; no matter where its members roam or travel, they will always have a place to return to no matter what happens. Fifth, in the nuclear family, children learn obligations and responsibilities to other family members such as their siblings, cousins and extended relatives. This makes them more responsible and teaches them that they are part of an interdependent community and society. Sixth, the nuclear family helps its members make decisions. In active nuclear families, members directly participate in the analysis of a situation to help each other make decisions. At a minimum, individuals make decisions under the indirect influence of the core values of their nuclear family; usually, though, there are multiple members involved in giving feedback and advice.

Seventh, the nuclear family helps form each member's identity. Each person grows to appreciate their identity as male or female, son or daughter, wife or husband, old or young, through the nuclear family in which they live. Without nuclear families, these benefits are greatly lessened or nonexistent. It is no surprise that when sociologists and economists find broken cultural or social areas of life in the nation, the underlying factor is an absence of strong nuclear families.

PART II

FIGHTING THE DRAGON

Causes of Nuclear Family Breakdown in
America and Solutions

CHAPTER 1
RETHINKING LOVE

I find that "love" is the most misunderstood word in modern American life. Many people have not seen good examples of true love, so they do not know what it means. In fact, I find that there is a fallacy in the American perception of "love."

Americans confuse love with satisfaction. Consider a person who has bought their 'dream car.' Initially, they are perfectly satisfied with the car; it contains and provides everything they want it to. After a while, however, it loses its appeal. It may take ten minutes, ten days, ten weeks, ten months, or ten years, but, eventually, the dream car will no longer be completely satisfying. It will not provide as gratifying an experience; it will not be as pleasing or satisfying to the owner as it was when it was new. Perhaps the car will have dents; perhaps the color will no longer be the hottest fashion; perhaps the electronics will be outdated. Eventually, the person will find a new car which is cleaner, more fashionable, and more technologically advanced, and they will completely abandon the old car for the new car. Once again, they will be satisfied with the new car for a little while, and then they will begin losing satisfaction with it also.

Similarly, modern American dating and courtship seems to be more concerned with satisfaction than with love. Consider a boy (Tim) and girl (Sally) who have found their "dream relationship." At first, the relationship will be all they think about and want. They may kiss each other and tell each other, "I love you," but what they may really mean is, "I am satisfied with you" or "you are appealing to me." In a relationship like this, Tim may only really care about how much self-satisfaction and self-gratification Sally gives him. Likewise, Sally may only really be concerned with how much self-satisfaction Tim provides her. When Tim and Sally sleep together, they may say, "I love you," but they could just as easily be saying, "you taste good, and I am enjoying it!"

Despite the level of ecstasy Tim and Sally experience for 10 minutes or 10 hours or 10 days or 10 weeks or 10 months or 10 years, they will not always be able to provide each other the same level of satisfaction, sexual gratification, and emotional pleasure as they once did. Whether they become wedded or not, the relationship will lose its luster and lose some of its glamorous appeal. Undoubtedly, Tim and Sally will eventually find someone else who is more satisfying. This person will look better than the old partner, perhaps be richer than the old partner, or have a more gratifying personality than the old partner. Before long, Tim and Sally may feel like they want to completely abandon the old dream relationship because it no longer provides the same level of satisfaction that it once did. Instead, they will break up with the old partner and start a new relationship with the new partner, hoping to regain the sense of self-satisfaction which the old relationship no longer provides. The old partner tasted good (was satisfying), but the new partner tastes better (is even more satisfying).

Satisfaction cannot provide a firm foundation on which to build a relationship. Why? Because the satisfaction of partners with each other is easily manipulated and fluctuates wildly over time. One day, Tim and Sally may be perfectly satisfied with each other; however, on another day may want to be apart from each other. Satisfaction is a form of selfishness, of only looking out for yourself. If you approach a relationship with the goal of making yourself satisfied, you are bringing selfishness to the relationship. Trying to build a relationship on self-satisfaction alone is like trying to build a house on a fault line. Selfishness harms a relationship. Eventually, the relationship will experience an earthquake and be torn in two opposing directions. Many people believe that money or jealousy or infidelity breaks marriages, but the truth is that selfishness is at the root of all of these hallmarks.

To examine true love, one must first find some good examples. Fortunately, there are many good examples of true love. Consider the love between a mother and child (maternal love), a father and child (paternal love), siblings and friends (fraternal love), husband and wife (marital love), and God and humanity (divine love). What is it about these loves that makes them true love as opposed to simply self-satisfaction? There is one common element in all of these types of love: *agape*, or self-sacrifice. In each of these kinds of love, both partners sacrifice something for the sake of the other.

Agape love, or self-sacrificial love, is when each partner sacrifices their own self-interests (things that satisfy them) for the good of the other. *Agape* love replaces self-satisfying with building-the-other-up. *Agape* love is true love. In true love, the two partners want nothing but the absolute best for the other partner, and they will sacrifice their own self-satisfaction or self-gratification to obtain it.

In the typical American dating relationship described earlier in this chapter, Tim and Sally were only concerned about satisfying their own interests and wants. When their relationship no longer satisfied them, they broke it off. In a relationship built on mutual self-sacrificial love, the arrangement of interests is different. For example, a mother-and-child relationship is full of mutual self-sacrifice. A mother gives up her time and energy for the benefit of her child while the child gives up independence and autonomy for the benefit of the mother. In marriage, mutual self-sacrifice should play the main role. The husband (male) and wife (female) each give up several of their own self-interests such as financial independence, time, and energy, for love of the other.

Perhaps the idea of self-sacrifice sounds scary. Perhaps you do not want to have anything to do with something that would require you to sacrifice something. However, self-sacrifice is actually a perfectly reasonable and necessary condition for true love. Skeptical? Consider how self-sacrifice is a perfectly reasonable and necessary condition for something else: sports.

Consider two professional ice hockey players. Both claim to absolutely love ice hockey; they love the feeling of skating on the ice, they love the elation of scoring points, they like the feel of the stick in their hands. The first athlete, however, only cares about ice hockey because he finds it satisfying, because it gratifies his desires. He was born with some natural talent; such as he can skate fast and score goals and hold the stick without much work, so he plays ice hockey for a few years. But then things change. He's no longer the sole star on the team; now he has to work with the other players on the ice. He has to put in more time than before. The competition is tougher. The goalies are bigger and faster; he's not scoring like he did before. What will the first athlete do? If conditions don't become more favorable to what he wants, he'll probably quit ice hockey.

The second athlete starts out like the first athlete; he finds ice hockey to be entertaining and 'fun.' He was also born with some natural talent; he can skate fast, score goals, and hold the stick without much work. But unlike the first athlete, the second athlete doesn't give up when playing hockey become harder. Instead, he starts making small sacrifices. First, he changes his diet. No more candy bars; no sodas; no cereal in the morning. He eats more lean protein and tightens his belt. He spends less time playing video games and more time practicing on his skating and shooting techniques. And he starts building chemistry with his teammates. He still isn't scoring as many goals as before, but he hasn't given up completely like the first athlete. He doesn't quit; he perseveres and finishes the season. Both athletes claimed to "love" the sport, but why did their hockey careers turn out so differently? It was because the second athlete was willing to sacrifice things that satisfied him (soda, cereal, video games) for the sake of his love for the sport. *The second athlete has shown that he truly loves ice hockey.*

If you ask a random person on the street which athlete is the better athlete, they will say the second one is better. If self-sacrifice is required to become truly better at sports, then is it really so surprising that self-sacrifice is required for true love in marriage? In the same way that the second athlete had a better outcome than the first athlete, it is understandable that marital relationships founded on self-sacrifice are stronger than relationships rooted on self-satisfaction. Consider a relationship where Tim and Sally give up their own self-interests for love of the other. If you thought the second athlete was doing something good, wouldn't you consider this kind of relationship even better? You must invest yourself if you want to see a large payoff, and marriage is no different.

CHAPTER 2
RETHINKING COMMITMENT

Another word Americans largely misunderstand is commitment. This is because there are very few role models of commitment, especially committed love, in modern culture. To begin with, commitment cannot exist if there is no love. Enduring commitment and enduring love are two sides of the same coin.

A person will not commit totally to anything he does not truly love. A man who does not love watching football will not commit to buying season tickets to cheer his local football team. He may go to a game or two because he is afraid of being left out or because his friends want him to, but he will not be committed to watching football the entire season. Similarly, a man who does not truly love a girlfriend will not commit to her. As soon as hardship strikes in the form of an unplanned pregnancy or financial difficulty, he will leave. In fact, lack of commitment is the number-one cited reason by spouses who divorce (Beiber and Ramirez, 2023, Forbes).

Americans tend to believe that commitment in relationships should be proportional to the level of satisfaction the relationship gives them. If you are in a relationship with someone who satisfies you emotionally and physically, you should be committed to them. If, however, the relationship has become draining and dragging, you should commit as little to it as possible and get out of it as soon as you can. This is good advice for things that you own, like a new shirt. Your level of commitment to the things you own changes depending on your current level of satisfaction. You can buy the new shirt, own it 10 days, 10 weeks, or 10 years, and when it gets too old or you grow tired of it, you can throw it out and replace it.   However, this is not good advice for marriage.

Let us consider one of these marriages founded on the convenience of satisfaction. We will start with a young man named Mike. Mike is dating a girl his age, Myra. She is young, healthy, skinny, and makes him laugh. When Mike is dating Myra, he feels a rush of good feelings when he sees her and talks to her and spends time with her. He declares that he is 100% satisfied with her, that she was meant for him, that she is "the one." After he weds Myra, he still feels strongly for Myra for a while.

But, after ten years, things change. Relationships are dynamic and evolving; daily household chores, work responsibilities, and young children influence and change Mike's relationship with Myra. They have heated discussions about in-laws and finances; their relationship may not feel as 'steamy' as it was initially. As Mike's good feelings or satisfaction for Myra begin to drop off, he begins to wonder, "Is something wrong? What happened to the old spark? Maybe I should leave?" Mike has decided that since he is no longer 100% satisfied with his marriage, perhaps he should end his marriage to Myra.

This change in Mike's level of satisfaction will eat away at him inside and cause him to be short-tempered, inconsiderate, and rude towards Myra. It may also cause him to look at other women with interest—if there is a young, attractive coworker at his office who appears more satisfying than Myra, Mike may feel like he should have been with her. However, this is an illusion. If Mike divorces Myra and marries his coworker, he will eventually arrive at a point where he is no longer satisfied with his coworker—perhaps with her looks, or her attitude towards money, or how she wants to divide household chores, or how well she cooks, or something else. His level of satisfaction with his wife will always decline over time.

Mike's experience reflects the great contemporary gap in society's logic: the idea that one's level of commitment to a marriage should be proportional to how satisfying it is for them. As long as Myra continues to be pleasing to Mike, he should be committed to her; once she is not, he can throw her away like a piece of clothing.

So, if Mike is a bad example of commitment to a marriage, what would be a good example? Specifically, what is commitment and how does it work? Enduring commitment and true love are two sides of the same coin. If a man has true love for his spouse (he desires her well-being and is willing to give up personal desires to ensure her well-being), then he will take responsibility to do what is best for her. In other words, he makes doing what is best for her a personal obligation. This obligation is not written down like a legal document; he may not even be conscious that he has made this obligation. However, conscious or unconscious, written or unwritten, he has taken responsibility because of his true love for her. This is tru commitment.

A person can commit to anything if he loves it. A man who loves his children will commit himself to driving them to school every day and feeding them and clothing them because of his love for them. A person who loves playing bridge will commit to starting a bridge club. A soldier who loves his country will commit to defending it.

There are many levels of commitment. Some commitments are low level, meaning they are weak or temporary. Some commitments are medium level, meaning they are binding or obligatory. Some commitments are high level, meaning they are permanent. The appropriate level of commitment you should make to something changes depending on what you are committing to.

A low level of commitment is made when you buy a commodity, like a new shirt. That low level of commitment changes depending on your current level of satisfaction. You can buy the shirt, own it 10 days, 10 weeks, or 10 years, and when it gets old or you grow tired of it, you can throw it out and replace it. A medium level of commitment is a formal course of action or a legal responsibility. Such a level of commitment is more binding, usually until the obligation is satisfied. If you borrow money from a bank to buy a house and commit to paying a 30-year mortgage, you must continue to make payments until it is paid in full. If you have the money to repay the loan balance, you are obligated to repay the entire loan balance. No matter how much you wish to say, "I am going to stop paying this mortgage," you cannot end your payments until you are finished repaying the full amount due under the entire loan.

Even higher than a mortgage or loan repayment are high level commitments. Marriage vows are a high level of commitment which you are obligated to fulfill. This is also known as a promise. The highest level of commitment is commitment to true love. If you make the commitment that you are going to truly love someone (do what is best for them even against your own self-interest), this high level of commitment is lasting and lifelong.

So, can you let your level of satisfaction with a commitment influence the level of the commitment made? It depends. In the case of a low-level commitment to a commodity, such as a shirt, yes, you can let your level of satisfaction with the commodity influence the level of your commitment. If you are no longer satisfied with your shirt, you can break your commitment to it and buy a new shirt. If you are no longer satisfied with the color red, you can break your commitment to your red shirt and replace it with a new one in your new favorite color.

However, as the level of commitment increases, the role that satisfaction plays decreases. If you enter into a medium commitment to a course of action or a responsibility, even if you are dissatisfied with it, you cannot reduce your level of commitment. If you have committed to paying a 30-year mortgage on your house, you cannot stop paying the mortgage even if you are dissatisfied with your house or because you want to use the money to travel instead. Although you may be dissatisfied, you must invest your willpower to make yourself continue paying off the mortgage or loan balance and fulfill your commitment. Similarly, when you make a high-level commitment to a person, you must fulfill that commitment regardless of whether you are satisfied with it. Hence, it is no surprise that when you commit to truly love someone in marriage, you agree to put their well-being ahead of your own self-interests and the amount of satisfaction that you feel with the relationship at any given time should have zero impact on the high level of that marriage commitment.

For example, if a father loves his son and his son makes bad decisions, the father may feel dissatisfied or disappointed with his son's behavior, but he cannot reduce his level of commitment to the son. The father is still his father and must still feed, clothe, and educate his son. Similarly, in marriage, if a husband truly loves his bride, he must understand that while his level of satisfaction may fluctuate from being very satisfied to no satisfaction at all, he must invest his willpower to maintain the high level of commitment—that is, total commitment—to his bride. She also must follow this same high level of commitment. The couple may argue and disagree occasionally or even frequently, but even if the disagreements affect their levels of satisfaction, it has no bearing whatsoever on the nature of their high level of commitment. They must still invest both of their willpower to adhere to their marriage vows with a high level of commitment.

High levels of commitment, such as marriage vows, are serious. This is why there is a special ceremony where the bride and groom make the vow of total commitment to each other in the presence of others. When they 'tie the knot' in a wedding ceremony, they have just established the highest level of commitment to each other, regardless of how satisfied they may feel further on down the road. They have promised that even if their satisfaction with each other declines or even drops to zero, they will muster their willpower to maintain the high level of commitment they have made to one another. The high level of a marriage commitment is permanent.

If satisfaction is not supposed to drive one's level of commitment to a high-level relationship, then what should? After all, nobody wants to feel 'stuck' in a relationship that no longer satisfies them. The key here is to recognize that there are more measures of wellbeing than satisfaction. There is something much more important than satisfaction that should determine how much you commit to a high-level relationship, and that something is a different virtue: contentment.

What is contentment? Let us learn about contentment by looking at three siblings who are eating dessert. The eldest child, Tess, is ten years old and gets five marshmallows. The other two children, Thomas and Steve, are twins and are both four years old. They each get two marshmallows. When Thomas and Steve receive their marshmallows, they are 100% satisfied. Then, Thomas notices that Tess has received five marshmallows. Suddenly, he is no longer 100% satisfied with what he has. Thomas starts crying.

Steve also notices that Tess received more marshmallows than him and is no longer 100% satisfied. Rather than crying, he instead thinks to himself, "I have enough marshmallows as are good for my age." When Steve realizes this, although he is not 100% satisfied, he becomes 100% content with his situation and happily eats his marshmallows. A person can be 100% content with their situation even if they are not 100% satisfied with it. They can be accepting of what they have even if they do not want what they have or want what they do not have.

Remember what happened to Mike? He grew up and married a charming young girl named Myra. After 10 years of marriage with her, however, his level of satisfaction with his relationship declined. There were more responsibilities and less time for steamy, romantic outings. Mike decided that the problem was with his marriage and left Myra for another younger woman. He believed that his level of commitment to his marriage should have been based on his level of satisfaction with his wife. But is Mike right? No.

Satisfaction is an empty metric. Mike can chase personal satisfaction for his entire life, but he will NEVER find anything that satisfies him 100% of the time, whether it is a new flashy car, a million dollars, or a relationship with an attractive coworker. No matter who or what Mike chases, he will not be able to stay 100% satisfied with anything permanently. This is exactly why satisfaction cannot be tied to commitment.

Contentment is a completely different gauge from satisfaction. Your level of satisfaction with something can bounce up and down based on how you are feeling; hormones, novelty, excitement, and other factors can make you feel more or less satisfied. But your level of contentment is controlled by an act of your will; it is only dependent on how accepting you are of your situation. Because contentment can be controlled by your own willpower, it is the only metric that should matter for your level of commitment.

Let's return to our marshmallow analogy. Thomas' brother (Steve) also grows up and moves on in life. Steve marries Sarah. They are together for a few years, and their hormones and good feelings make them very satisfied and content with each other. Eventually, however, Steve senses that some 'spark' or sexual energy is beginning to fade from his relationship with Sarah. Steve realizes that chasing new relationships for the sake of his personal satisfaction will be like chasing the wind: it will never make him 100% satisfied forever. Instead, Steve decides to stay faithful to Sarah and his children, stay at his house and his job, and live his life forward. Steve accepts what he has—he is content—even though he is not having all that he wants—he is unsatisfied. Steve applies his will to remain committed to his marriage with Sarah. Because of this, Steve's level of commitment to Sarah does not waver even as his satisfaction with his marriage fluctuates up and down.

For a marriage to endure for life, total commitment is required. Once the knot is tied, it is unbreakable; the spouses have no choice but to work towards the successful operation of the family. Because of this, the marriage cannot be built on such wildly variable metrics as satisfaction. Instead, the couple should build their marriage on the stable metric that is tied to their willpower: contentment.

CHAPTER 3
THE SUPREMACY
OF PRIVACY

Among Americans, the prevailing attitude towards decisions related to marriage, divorce, premarital sex, and illegitimacy is one of noninterference. Most people believe that such decisions are private matters and that only those individuals whom they directly concern need to address them. However, this is a misguided view.

To understand why this is a misperception, let's take a step back. In our world, there are three kinds of matters: public, private, and quasi-public. A public matter involves an act or series of acts that will directly or indirectly affect the general order or wellbeing of the general public. An example of a public matter is a presidential election, since the choice of a national leader has profound effects on the entire society. On the other hand, if the consequences or benefits of an action affect only an individual or a group of similar individuals, the action involved is a private matter. An example of a private matter is what color clothes you wear today, since whether you wear red or green today has no effects on the other individuals in society. You can choose to wear whatever color you wish, and the intervention or involvement of the general public is not necessary.

Some matters are quasi-public; these acts fall not just on individual(s) but also on the society or general public. An example of a quasi-public matter is an education at a local public school. A given student has a certain degree of individual autonomy to adopt or ignore certain aspects of school education. Hence, their education is to some extent a private matter. However, the student is not totally independent either, since society is paying for their education through the form of taxes. Society has a claim on the student, namely, that the student should take advantage of their educational opportunities and do well academically because a successful student contributes to the national wellbeing and productivity. Thus, society has the right to decide what kinds of subjects the student must study and how long they must attend school each day.

There is a general notion that marital and sexual acts (that is, marriage, divorce, premarital sex, and illegitimacy) are simply private matters. The prevailing attitude claims that since such acts are performed by consenting adults, nobody else has any business to interfere. These are personal choices, many claim, and therefore they are private matters. It is claimed that such acts fall into the category of personal autonomy. However, remember that if a person's act has consequences for the general public or the society at large, then it is no longer a purely private matter but a quasi-public matter.

How do these things affect the general public? A quick examination of the evidence shows that they have significant financial consequences, educational consequences, and societal consequences for the general public. For example, consider the decision to divorce. Divorce always involves a financial cost as parents negotiate a financial settlement for the distribution of marital assets. However, it involves significant costs for society as well. Children of divorced parents have markedly worse educational outcomes, dedication to social institutions, crime and drug addiction problems, and health issues than peers from unbroken families (exact statistics and citations on this will be provided later in the book). None of these are consequences which affect only the 'consenting, grown-up adults.' Rather, the general public must shell out tax dollars to pay for the extra learning support, citizen welfare support, drug addiction treatment, and healthcare. The general public will also be the victims of the increase in crime. Thus, if the society must bear such significant financial and social costs from divorce, then divorce is not a private matter but a quasi-public matter.

It is certainly appealing to claim that sexuality is a purely private and personal matter; if it is, then one can claim, "I am well within my own bounds and rights to determine what sort of sexuality I desire and express. I can control my sexuality and choose what I do with it. Nobody else can interfere and say no. If I think it's OK for me, then it's OK for me to do it." Leaving aside that this is a self-centered outlook with a narrow vision, this is all true if sexuality is a private matter. But, sexuality is not. When a man and a woman have sex, they are not simply beholden to themselves or to each other; they are beholden to the children that may come from that union. Once children have come from their sexual union, the man and woman cannot simply break off from one another with a declaration that they made a private decision to unite and are making a private decision to split. The child also must have some voice in the decision. In addition to the child, society also should get a voice in the decision.

Why? Realize that the decision to divorce after a child is conceived results in large social costs for the society. For one thing, children from divorced families are more likely to become involved in crime or drugs and are more likely to fail in school. This means not only that these children are not able to help contribute to the culture and wellbeing of society; they are also more likely to require more of society's resources to address their situation. When crime increases, more policemen and larger police departments are needed; policemen wages and police department costs are the financial burdens of the community they service. The damages from the crimes are costs society must bear; the costs of prisons are borne by society; the victims of the crimes are other members of society. When drug use increases, more rehabilitation centers, medical care, and therapies are needed. These services are often directly or indirectly subsidized with funds from Medicaid or state governments, meaning the larger community is paying for it. When children fail in school, more counselors and special education teachers are needed. In public school systems, these additional personnel are paid with funds from the communities in which they work.

In addition, welfare payments to care for single mothers and their children are shouldered not by the individual man and woman but by the society. It is society's tax dollars, society's hard work, and society's effort which is required to manage the fallout of the divorce. Society wishes to give each child a quality education and instill in each child correct moral values. Insofar as the decisions of a man and a woman run parallel or contrary to these wishes, they are affecting society. Once again, the obvious realization is that the decisions of the man and woman regarding wedlock and divorce are not isolated or just private, but quasi-public. Clearly, wedlock and divorce both have profound and far-reaching effects on a society.

Consider, for example, how agitated you feel when analyzing the next four examples. The first is Bill Clinton, the former President of the United States. When his daughter, Chelsea Clinton, campaigned for his wife, Hillary Clinton, she was asked about her father's relationship with Monica Lewinsky. Chelsea retorted, "It's none of your business." The second is Donald Trump, another former President of the United States. Trump has had 3 wives and innumerable girlfriends over the course of his tumultuous political and economic history. The third is Eliot Spitzer, the former governor of New York, who was ousted in disgrace after it was revealed that he was involved with a prostitution ring. The fourth and final example is Newt Gingrich, the 50th speaker of the House of Representatives, who also had three wives and other dubious relationships with women.

Today, no American would dare suggest that these men's treatment of their marriage and sexuality was a purely personal matter that had no effect on anyone else. Their decisions regarding their marriages, divorces, and sexuality resulted in significant political and cultural effects. Their decisions affected society, whether from the poor role models they cast for young Americans to the wake of destruction they left in their political lives. They created a domino effect. While the deeds of former presidents like Clinton and Trump have very well-publicized and ostracized effects, the deeds of every American couple have similar effects even if they do not cause such a media storm.

When it comes to other public matters, society does not hesitate to act. In the 1970s, a man robbed the ice cream store my wife and I started and operated. However, we did not have to bring the case to court; instead, the police brought the case to court. Why? The state considered this a public matter, not a private one. Even though my wife and I were the ones who suffered directly from the robbery, robbery in general affects the public's safety and wellbeing. When the government prosecuted the case, it proceeded on the grounds that society was bringing the case against this man. Although it was my store which was robbed, it was understood that it is society which inevitably bears the social cost of robbery and theft. Thus, the matter was treated like a public matter, not a private matter. Notice that to prevent crime in general, the government took the necessary steps to prevent this individual crime. Even though the one robbery in my store does not directly mean that all stores are being robbed, the government understood that it had to address my individual case to preserve the wellbeing of the society at large.

So, why have we as citizens, the government, and the courts refused to take any action to stem the breakup of the nuclear family? We have simply written it off as a personal and private matter, one that does not deserve our attention or require our intervention. In the same way that one crime unchecked becomes ten crimes, and one murder uninvestigated and unprosecuted becomes ten murders, one implosion of a nuclear family unaddressed becomes ten implosions. And just as any society will suffer from unchecked crime and unchecked murder, so our society is suffering from the implosion of the nuclear family. Today, we attempt to restrict texting while driving in the hope that we can prevent car accidents and their adverse effects on society; however, while nuclear families break up and children are left with heartache and instability and chaos, we do nothing but stand by. We should not stand by. We must fight the unquestioned supremacy of privacy and bring our nuclear family lives into the public spotlight where they belong.

CHAPTER 4

JUST MARRIED!
(AGAIN)

Most people use the words marriage and wedding interchangeably. This common misperception, in my opinion, does not properly explain what is a marriage.

What is a marriage? For most people, the word 'marriage' means a man and a woman taking an oath in a religious setting or civil setting to be husband and wife. It does not matter, for most people, whether the oath-taking ceremony takes place in a church, in a temple, near a seashore, or in a garden. By and large, being in a state of 'marriage' simply requires the taking of the promise by the man and woman, regardless of the number of guests or family members present when the promises are made. However, I disagree that the vows ceremony is when the marriage occurs. I define the taking of the oath or proclamation of vows as the mere "wedding." It is a celebration or occasion on which a man and a woman declare that they promise to be husband and wife.

In truth, a 'marriage' begins when there is a physical consummation between a man and a woman. Under this specific definition, two men cannot be married, nor can two women be married, because the biology of two men or two women does not permit the physical consummation. In addition, this means that any man and woman who have physically consummated a relationship are married, regardless of whether they have had a wedding or oath-taking ceremony. Thus, a man who consummates a physical relationship with multiple women is married to all of them. Similarly, a woman who consummates a physical relationship with multiple men is married to all of them.

With this definition, is pre-marital sex a marriage? Yes. Is cohabitation of a man and woman marriage? Yes. Is prostitution a marriage? Yes, as long as there is a physical union between a man and a woman. Is casual sex marriage? Yes. Can homosexual relations produce a marriage? No. It is not some abstract moral or philosophical or religious ideal which prevents this; biology does not permit it. You cannot call something a marriage if it is not a marriage.

What is important to realize here is that a marriage is completely separate from a wedding. A person can be wedded but not married (they have taken the formal vows in a church or in front of a notary but have not yet had a physical consummation) or a person can be married yet unwedded (by engaging in physical consummation). In modern language usage, we interchange the terms, and this distorts and confuses the significance of the oath-taking ceremony versus the physical consummation. As a society, we must be clear that these are distinct and separate events. I submit that a marriage and a wedding are two separate and distinct state of affairs. In particular, I submit that every adult in America should not just have one wedding, they should only have one marriage, with exception if a spouse dies.

At a wedding ceremony, a man and a woman promise to be husband and wife. This is why the wedding should precede the marriage—the wedding is where the man and woman commit to becoming husband and wife until death. Then, after the wedding, the husband and wife should be married; that is, have a physical consummation. The physical union can proceed securely after the wedding in the assurance that the man and woman have committed themselves to loving each other exclusively.

It is wrong to have the marriage before the wedding, even if the wedding is planned for later. Why? True love is patient. It waits until a relationship has reached the right stage before exposing each person to the profound intimacy and vulnerability that a physical union causes. Similarly, it is wrong to have multiple marriages with other people before being wedded. Why? Having multiple pre-wedding physical consummations means that you are already married! In other words, you are a polygamist who is cheating on your previous marriages.

Not only that, but when you tell the person you "they are the one" and "you love them" at a later wedding, you are lying. Part of you has been irrevocably committed to somebody elsewhere by a physical consummation. It is incorrect to think that cheating can only occur after a wedding; it occurs with every physical union that happens prior to a wedding. People should be horrified at the idea. You cannot build a marriage on lies. It is impossible to wed someone who has had previous marriages and expect your unique relationship to be so much stronger than any of the other married relationships they had before. You cannot have a wedding and expect life afterwards to be faithful and monogamous when you have already had previous marriages. You will be living in polygamy.

Why are polygamous unions so evil? Let us see why with an analogy. Pretend that today, the Supreme Court, President, and Congress came out and announced that having one Constitution was outdated. They instead give America dozens of Constitutions, each of which has competing values and declarations. Some say that there are no God-given rights, that not all men are created equal, that the government does not have to protect the citizens, or that some states are less important than others. Can you imagine how you would feel? Maybe not, but you can certainly imagine what would happen. Everything which has been built on the one true America Constitution (democracy, the United States, governments, currencies, human rights) would come crashing down. It would be laid to waste.

In the same way, multiple marriages will rip apart an individual and a couple. Pre-marital sex causes two people to become married. There is no way out of that or around that. Thus, if the partners go and wed someone else, they have brought an existing marriage into their new marriage. Just as the United States cannot have two different Constitutions, your wedding cannot have two different marriages. If the United States had two different Constitutions, it would fall apart. Today, we see nuclear families falling apart all across the United States and the primary cause of this is that the spouses already have two, ten, or even more different marriages before their wedding. A house divided against itself cannot stand; no wedding should have to compete with prior existing marriages.

CHAPTER 5

THE ISSUE OF INFIDELITY

Infidelity involves having more than one marriage at one time. Prostitution, adultery, extramarital affairs, cohabitation, and "hooking up" all result in a person having more than one marriage (physical consummation) at a time; hence, they qualify as infidelity. In today's culture, we have incorrectly restricted the meaning of infidelity as to having an extramarital affair while being wedded. If a man has taken marriage vows at a wedding and then has a physical consummation or union with a woman other than his wife, we accuse him of infidelity. However, if that man has not made vows at a wedding ceremony and is sleeping with two different girlfriends, that is not considered infidelity. I define infidelity broader. In my definition, once you have entered into a physical consummation with a person of the opposite sex, you commit infidelity against them if you have a subsequent physical consummation with another person.

Under my better definition, you can enter into physical consummation with only one person of the opposite sex after the wedding ceremony. You must choose your spouse very carefully and exercise discipline to have a physical consummation only after you and your spouse make a commitment to one another at a wedding ceremony. Once you have a physical consummation with your spouse, you cannot replace them with someone else (exception exists where the spouse dies). It is a Hollywood illusion to think that you can have physical unions with multiple persons, marry just one of them, and then be completely satisfied with the one you married (in comparison with your previous ones) to remain faithful until death.

Infidelity has been a cause of divorce for millennia, even outside America. Today, however, it has become less stigmatized and is dealt with less severely, allowing it to continue unfettered. Data on cheating have varied significantly. Some surveys estimate cheating and infidelity rates to be around 15-20% for women and 20-25% for men; others estimate infidelity rates to be higher, closer to 50%. Although the data for how much infidelity occurs is indeterminate, one thing is clear about infidelity: it wounds marriages. Infidelity is the number one cause cited for divorce (Dr. Scott Stanley, PhD, Psychology Today, 2017). Infidelity destroys the nuclear family!

Extramarital affairs do not succeed. Only 3% of extramarital affairs grow into a marriage. When a spouse commits an extramarital affair, a mere 3% of those spouses then proceed to wed the person with whom they were committing the affair. If they do, these extramarital marriages result in divorce 75% of the time (Frank Pittman, Dr. Jan Harpers). Hence, it is ludicrous to claim that extramarital affairs will provide lasting fulfillment or satisfaction. They simply do not.

Enough has been written about why people commit infidelity and about how infidelity has painful consequences, including often leading to divorce. What should be expounded is why infidelity is an empty choice and what it cannot do. People commit infidelity because they are no longer 100% satisfied with their current spouse and they believe that engaging in another physical union with someone other than their spouse will restore them to 100% satisfaction. They engage in the extramarital affair as a method of regaining 100% satisfaction with their married life.

In an extramarital affair, for a short time, the thrill and excitement return. However, the reality is that no person can keep you 100% satisfied forever, whether you are wedded to them or not. The secret to fidelity lies in your own willpower to remain 100% content with your situation even if you are not 100% satisfied all the time. The secret is to rely on love and sacrificing your own self-interests for the good of the other rather than to rely on pleasure or self-gratification.

If infidelity causes divorce, what causes infidelity? I submit that the causes are unrealistic views and moral decay. A person who believes that the secret to happiness is 100% satisfaction with their spouse will never find fulfillment outside of the marriage, in either a wedding or in an extramarital affair. This is an unrealistic view. A person who understands that the secret to happiness lies in your own attitude and that you can be 100% content with your situation regardless of your spouse will find great fulfillment and lasting unity in their marriage. Even if a person does not understand this, however, strong moral values are the last line of defense. A person with strong moral values will stick to their promises no matter how tough it becomes. Even if they do not understand the difference between satisfaction and contentment, they will remain loyal to their marriage to fulfill their marital promise. A person with weak moral values, on the other hand, must be taught the difference between satisfaction and contentment. If they do not understand the difference, they will have no reason to remain loyal to their marriage when they become unsatisfied.

CHAPTER 6

CALLING OUT COHABITATION

There is still general agreement among Americans that infidelity is bad, even if they are hesitant to publicly condemn it. However, there is a much more insidious cause of divorce that has become commonly accepted: cohabitation.

There is no legal definition for cohabitation. The Census Bureau defines cohabitation "as a person age 15 years and over who is not related to the householder, who shares living quarters with the householder, and who has a close personal relationship with the householder." Many couples choose to cohabit because it brings social and physical union without legal or social responsibility for the long-term health or wellbeing of the relationship. Cohabitation is essentially uncommitted marriage. Cohabitating couples are living under one roof, sharing personal resources, having sexual relations, and even raising children.

Cohabitation is marriage because it involves a physical union. However, cohabitation only lasts for as long as the couple "feels" loving to each other, which is not necessarily as long as they live. Instead of "I do," it is *Maybe I do.*" Cohabitation is a substitute for a wedding, not just a test-drive of a marriage.

Before the 1960s, cohabitation was not socially acceptable in America. "Shacking up" with your boyfriend or girlfriend was frowned upon. Today, a dramatic shift exists to the point where cohabitation is not only socially acceptable but common. The Census Bureau estimates that 7% of adults today are cohabiting and that it has increased ten-fold between 1960 and 2000 (Gurrentz, 2019). Serial cohabitation, that is, cohabiting several times throughout the lifetime, is also on the rise in America.

Cohabitation fosters a completely different mindset from a wedding. Dr. Scott Stanley explains (Psychology Today, 2018), that people who cohabit have a different mindset compared to people who wed. Couples who cohabit come with the mindset of a "bail button," in other words, they implicitly assume that if things do not work out, they can hit the button and bail/exit out of the relationship. Couples who wed come with a mindset of complete and total commitment. They do not give themselves to each other with reservations or with their fingers crossed behind their back; rather, they give themselves to each other completely and totally. There is no holding back in the wedding, but there is plenty of holding back in cohabitation.

Those who support cohabitation claim that it provides an opportunity for couples to practice living together and experimenting with the relationship. If things do not work out, these people claim, it is better for them to split rather than work out their differences. Since they were never wedded, divorce is not involved. And if things do work out, then they can get wedded—maybe. However, the data shows that cohabitation does not improve how long marriages stay together or how couples feel about their marriage. In fact, cohabitation makes things worse. Cohabiting couples are significantly more likely to undergo a divorce once they have become wedded. Some experts have simply written it off as an irony that cohabitation increases divorce rather than prevents it (Scott Stanley, Psychology Today, 2018). However, after a careful assessment, it is easy to understand why.

The decisions to cohabitate or wed approach dedication and commitment completely differently. The difference is best illustrated using an analogy. Consider two athletes who are joining a baseball team. The first athlete joins the team, but with reservations. He is not interested in committing to the team or giving his all for the team; he is not interested in putting his best foot forward. He just wants to 'try it out' and see what happens. He has a "bail button" in his mind; the good of the team is not his highest priority, only his own comfort and feelings. When the team does well for the first couple of games, he is pleased and satisfied with his choice. When the team begins to do poorly, however, he decides it is time to cut his losses. He hits the bail button and quits the team. What will happen to the team? It will suffer. Each of the individual players on the team will suffer. The team suffers because it loses the expected talent of that player and the role (or position) that he played. In short, the team is abandoned by a player which they thought was solid, but in reality was not. The league will also suffer, too, perhaps not in a direct way, but in an indirect way because it has lost something good.

Contrast this athlete with a second athlete who joins the team without reservations; he decides that he is going to be part of the team and gives the best he can. There is no bail button in his mindset; he is there for the team. When the team does well, he is satisfied and pleased; when the team does poorly, he is not pleased or satisfied, but he does not bail and quit. Rather, he works with the team to improve his individual performance and their collective performance to iron out their mistakes. In the short term, the team may suffer from longer practices or more losses, but in the long term, the team will benefit because they stuck it out. Some benefits include a growth in confidence by each player and overall team confidence in their collective ability. The team also witnesses to each other the virtue of reliability, commitment and hard work. Moreover, the league also benefits by the development of these positive virtues.

The athletes' incoming level of dedication and commitment is what shaped their response to adversity and their relationship to the rest of the team. A dedicated and committed mindset (the wedded mindset) leads to resilience and unity. An undedicated and uncommitted mindset (the cohabitation mindset) leads to laziness and separation. Without the mental makeup of unshakeable commitment, small problems can quickly drive the cohabitating couple to split.

When it comes to sports, we expect a high level of dedication and commitment from the team members. If it was your baseball team, which athlete would you want? You would want the second athlete. So, if it is undesirable or even wrong for an athlete to join a team with a bail-button mentality, it is also undesirable and wrong to have anything less than a complete level of dedication to a person when you establish a wedded relationship with them.

You can test-drive a car because you do not need to have any level of dedication to the car. You can hit the bail button and get rid of the car anytime you want. You cannot carry this attitude over to relationships. It is simply wrong to think that you can test-drive a wedded relationship and not match that with any level of commitment or dedication. You cannot just hit the bail button on a human relationship because there is another human person on the other side with their own feelings and values, there are possibly children with their own feelings and worth, and there is a society which will be severely impacted by your actions.

Cohabitation is an insult to the unity and vulnerability of a marriage. In a wedding, you give someone all of you, regardless of what circumstances you may find yourself in the future. In cohabitation, you are not there for good times and bad, sickness and health, until death. You are only giving some of yourself, your genitals and your finances and your kitchen, with the condition that you can snatch it all back and walk away when you are unsatisfied with the performance of the relationship. This is a horrible mentality to introduce into the core of a wedded union; it will poison the relationship and rot away at the attachments between the partners.

It is not enough to simply look at cohabitation rates and divorce rates; the cohabitation mentality must also be examined and rejected within our society. This mentality of the "bail button" is a cause of the skyrocketing rate of divorce in America and around the world.

CHAPTER 7

DESPERATE DATING

The next cause of divorce is a tricky topic to tackle: dating. The reason that dating is difficult to discuss is because there are many methods of dating and they are not equal. I will point out that some of these methods of dating have been primary causes of divorce.

The first thing we must ask ourselves is, what is the purpose of dating? Simply put, the purpose of dating is to find a suitable life partner. Through the dating process, individuals seek out prospective life partners, evaluate them for compatibility and temperament, and hopefully grow in maturity to the point where they are able and willing to make a lifelong commitment. Dating itself is, I think, a very good system for finding such a partner, given that it is carried out in a morally sound and intellectually rigorous manner.

Why am I addressing dating in this book? Dating must be addressed because it is a cornerstone of Western cultural companionship and courtship. Undoubtedly, then, dating carries great power and bears great responsibility. If done correctly, it will help an individual find their right lifelong partner. If done incorrectly, however, it can be disastrous. I have observed many dating couples between the 1960s, when I came to America, and now in 2023. I find that American dating has changed significantly in this time.

In the 1960s, the couples I knew used dating as a method of finding the best possible spouse. Couples sincerely wished to learn more about each other. They would 'go out' together, take walks, meet in restaurants, and do a lot of verbal communication (talking). Couples would try to learn about the other person (hobbies, interests, strengths, flaws, character, religion, political views, social engagement). Then, they would (try to) objectively evaluate whether the person they were dating was a good lifelong match; if he/she was, they moved on to engagement and a wedding; if not, they moved on to dating another person. This method of dating allowed couples to find the right partner to marry. I will not pretend that this method of dating produced 100% satisfaction, because nothing does, but I would contend that it could produce strong marriages and 100% contentment.

Today, however, dating has taken a dramatic shift. The purpose of dating has changed from finding a lifelong partner to having fun and getting pleasure. People do not try to get a spouse out of dating as much as they try to 'get a kick,' that is, a thrill. Rather than 'going out,' couples are 'making out' on their first or second date and having sex right at the start of the relationship; in other words, they 'date-to-mate.' In fact, in 2004, ABC News reported that 29% of dating couples were having sex on their first date (Langer et al., 2004)!

Today, date-to-mate couples stick together only 'as long as there is love'—though this is usually a euphemism for sexual desire. Once the desire is lost, the couples separate. If the woman conceives a child, it is often aborted or becomes a dependent of the mother. While the government often steps in financially to help support the unwed mother and child, it does not (and cannot) replace the role of the father. This contemporary behavior would have been unacceptable in America in the 1960s. The date-to-mate method has several adverse effects on couples. Areas of incompatibility are ignored, the relationship lacks mutual respect, and they hide their feelings. We shall examine each effect next.

Introducing sexual relations early into a relationship often crowds out other items which need to be addressed, like verbal communication and deep personal knowledge of each other. Modern dating does not allow couples the space and time they need to truly get to know the other person, and the sexual pleasure obtained from the relationship often blurs out incompatibilities in attitudes or personalities between the couple. Areas of incompatibility will break to the surface later and, whether the couple is cohabiting, dating, or wedded, rupture the relationship.

An excellent example of this lies in the best-selling romance novel of all time, *Fifty Shades of Grey.* In this book, the two lovers (Christian and Ana) have wildly incompatible ideologies and personalities. Ana is insecure and is easily dominated by the controlling Christian, yet the physical pleasure of their many sexual escapades clouds her judgement and prevents her from backing out of the relationship when her mother and friends urge her to do so. Once the sexual pleasure can no longer obscure their incompatibilities, however, she must break off the relationship and both of them withdraw with a broken heart. And so, we find that the first effect of the 'date-to-mate' type of dating is to cover up incompatibilities between the couple and stunt the healthy growth of the relationship.

In addition, when couples have sex while dating, it often becomes the focal point of the relationship. The couple does not get the opportunity to learn about their partner's personality, desires, hopes, dreams, wishes, and plans for the future. All of these take a backseat to the sex. If a girl is dating a boy and they begin having sex on the first or second or third date, they often do not build up any significant level of respect for each other. They may not have known each other's full names before sleeping, so how will they know about each other's aspirations, plans, hopes, or dreams? And without knowing any of this, how will they gain any level of respect for the other person? If you do not know anything about something, you cannot truly appreciate, understand, or respect it.

Consider a man who loves baseball. He may go to work and find that his boss does not like baseball. He is shocked and wonders how anybody cannot love baseball. After inquiring a little bit, he finds that his boss does not know the difference between a strike and a home run. It then makes sense to him: since the boss does not know much about baseball, of course he doesn't appreciate, understand, or respect it! The same challenges apply to dating and relationships. Not taking time to get to know someone will prevent you from learning how to love them. And so, we find that the second effect of dating-to-mate is that it engenders a relationship without mutual appreciation, understanding, or respect.

I have found many other problems with the date-to-mate method but let me focus on just one more here. In these relationships, the partners often hide their feelings from each other, particularly feelings of insecurity or want, so as not to 'rock the boat' and scare away the other partner. Contrast this with marriage, where the spouses provide emotional support to each other. In 30 years of teaching college level students, I have had many experiences, good and bad, with my colleagues and students, but I did not talk about them while at work. I came home and told my wife. Similarly, when she has something good (or bad) to say about somebody (especially politicians), she vents to me.

When I taught at the university, I provided academic counseling for my students. Although it was officially academic counseling, really any topic could come up. When I met with poorly-performing students, at least five times out of ten, they were having sex with somebody and they were having second thoughts, doubts, or inner turmoil as a result of the relationship. The more closely they knew me, the more willing they were to reveal their inner concerns, but they often ended with the admonition, 'please don't tell anybody.' This is a flashing warning sign that something is wrong in a relationship. The marital relationship is the most intimate relationship on earth; if you are afraid of talking to the person you are having sex with, then something is seriously wrong!

The new form of dating-to-mate often prevents couples from truly getting to know each other before they are physically and emotionally entangled. Because of this, it leads to emotionally risky relationships where the couple hardly knows or likes each other but are too scared to leave. The increase in these types of relationships has caused great emotional and physical damage to men and women across America, and as a result has been a significant contributor to the breakdown of the nuclear family.

Now I would like to point out that dating is a very Western concept of courtship. In my Indian culture back home, things were different. I have lived in the United States since the 1960s, yet I have never dated. Why? I chose to stick with the Eastern cultural convention for companionship and courtship, that is, an arranged marriage. I will not say that one is better than the other; I have seen both result in strong marriages.

I mentioned earlier that there are many different approaches to dating. Similarly, there are many different approaches to arranged marriages. For the average Westerner, the words 'arranged marriage' may conjure images of stern parents forcing a weeping bride to marry a faceless groom. Some of my students, upon hearing I had an arranged marriage, accused me of being a barbarian. While there certainly have been (and, unfortunately, still are) arranged marriages which occur like this, the ones I know of (as well as the ones which I participated in) are very different.

My arranged marriage proceeded as thus: first, I told my mother (my father had already passed away) I wanted to get married. I was 27 at the time and had just completed my MBA at Duquesne University in Pittsburgh, Pennsylvania. Second, my mother proceeded to meet with the parents of eligible young women in the community. She was explicitly searching for a girl with strong moral values, a reputable character, a supportive family, and the same religious faith as my own (Catholicism). These elements are probably common elements to seek in a life partner in the Western cultures, as they are also sought elements in my Indian-Eastern culture. In addition, my mother sought a bride with a good dowry and who also came from the same caste. (Some families in India will also look at Zodiak signs, wealth, status, job security, etc.) In India, if the seeking parents meet with a family and learn that the potential bride does not have one of their sought-after elements, they chose not to pursue any further.

In my case, I agreed to have an arranged marriage and gave my mother the final authority on any prospective bride because she knew me (both my strengths and my faults) better than anybody in the world and was more honest about it than anybody else (including myself). Therefore, when it came to objectively finding someone who would complement me, she was, in my opinion, the best-qualified 'expert' in the world. Within four weeks, she had found several potential matches for me. This may sound quick, but realize that the parents of many marriage-aged girls were also looking for potential grooms, so finding potential brides was not a problem. Once my mother had a list of potential matches, she began inquiring deeper about the prospective brides and their families. As my mother learned more and more about each prospective match, she considered who she thought would be best for me and narrowed down the list. I did not go and personally meet every girl—not yet. Why? Meeting with the girl indicates a strong interest, and my mother and I were not at that stage with anyone yet.

After several weeks, however, my mother had found a girl that she liked, Justice Thangam. My aunt knew the girl and her family well and vouched for her strong morals and faith, and my mother liked the things she heard. Besides, my mother had seen her before in church and already knew a few things about her. She came from a large and supportive family and had many siblings: seven brothers and one sister. This girl was not the richest or most advantageous match; other prospective brides came from wealthier families and one already had a medical degree. However, my mother analyzed and considered and made her decision. I asked my mother who she thought I should marry. She told me that she liked Justice Thangam the best. At this point, I asked to meet Justice Thangam and her family at her house and we arranged to do so. I liked her and I liked the family. When we came home, I told my mother, "Yes." She communicated this to Justice's parents. At this point, Justice could have either accepted or rejected the proposal. She said yes.

We were engaged one week later, exchanging engagement rings at her house. We were married on August 17, 1966 in Kotavillai, India, at Justice's parish church. (Just like here, it is custom to be wedded in the bride's church).

So why do I go into such detail about my arranged marriage? First, to show that it is an equally viable method of finding a lifelong partner as dating. But second, I want to point out something about arranged marriages and how they differ from dating marriages. In an arranged marriage, the couple may not be 'in love' before the marriage, meaning that they may not have a "crush" on each other before they get married. Conversely, in American marriages, this is a common prerequisite; American couples think it would be ludicrous to get married to someone you do not have strong feelings of attraction for before the marriage.

However, arranged marriages still become happy and strong marriages. How? Because even if the couple was not 'in love' before the marriage, they learn to love each other with *agape* love after the marriage. In other words, 'being in love' is not required to create a solid, happy marriage. Feelings are like flattery: they are nice, but they are fleeting. They may be icing on the cake, but they are not the cake. The cake in a marriage is the *agape* love the spouses have for each other, that is, the dedicated commitment they make to do what is best for the other person (even against their own self-interest). Hence, 100% contentment can be found in an arranged marriage, just like it can in a marriage the results after dating.

In the Indian culture, it is assumed that the "crush"—the romantic, attractive feelings—will develop after the wedding has taken place. It may seem odd to Americans to assume that romantic feelings will naturally develop, but remember that the parents of the bride and groom have selected partners who they believe will be a good fit for each other. For this reason, after a wedding, arranged marriage couples are just as likely to report satisfaction with each other than couples who have met through dating (see research in *Psychological Reports*, Regan, 2012). Even though the two systems have relatively equal levels of satisfaction, arranged marriages are much less likely to result in divorce. In fact, NBC News reports that arranged marriages have a divorce rate around 4%, compared to the 40% divorce rate of dating marriages (Page, 2017).

Today, when I return home to India, I find that this cultural tradition is slowly being replaced with the Western culture of dating. Even though this is the case, parents still continue to play a primary role in helping their child select a spouse. Modern dating in India most closely resembles a blend between arranged marriage and 1960s-era American dating—the purpose of the dating is to find a spouse, and the parents continue to vet the potential spouse and help the child find them. In many cases, the parents will use the traditional methods of finding the potential spouse, after which their child and the potential spouse will go on a few dates. If they feel a romance blooming, the two then agree to be wedded.

So, what do I advocate? I do not suggest that Americans should stop dating and begin having arranged marriages. Although this is a possibility, I do not think that American culture has the ability or experience to do this properly in any short amount of time. I advocate a return to the traditional aim of dating, that is, to find a lifelong partner. I strongly urge Americans to move towards methods of dating that resemble either modern Indian dating or 1960s American dating. This will go a long way towards restoring the stability of the nuclear family. I also advocate the abandonment of the modern form of dating, dating-to-mate, and the mentality which accompanies it.

Now I am not looking at dating with rose-tinted glasses. It will not always yield 100% satisfactory results. I know a woman who dated several different men but, for whatever reason, she was never married until after several years. One day, upon seeing one of the fellows she used to date, she started crying. After all, it is human nature to get attached to someone when dating them. In dating, you may have to say 'no' to one or two or more people before you say 'yes.' However, saying 'no' can still be painful. It is hard to set your feelings aside and make an objective, rational decision. But even though dating has this flaw, it can be a worthy, serviceable method to creating lifelong companionship and courtship.

CHAPTER 8

WHAT'S MY ROLE AND RESPONSIBILITY?

Americans have spent much of the past few decades questioning the roles and responsibilities of a husband and a wife (parents). Many recent fads have confused rather than clarified the expectations, roles and responsibilities for a husband and wife in a strong marriage. Specifically, traditional roles and responsibilities have been rejected and replaced with poorly defined new roles that leave families confused. In this chapter, I correct the misconceptions surrounding these two most vital roles in a marriage, a husband and a wife.

A husband and wife must know what is expected of each of them to make a marriage strong. Are the husband and wife equal? Absolutely, yes. This is not questionable. However, it is important to note that equal rights does not mean equal roles. The husband and wife each have equal rights, equal importance, and equal worth. Rights, importance, and worth are God-given. They are absolute, unchangeable, and immutable. All people possess equal rights, importance and worth because they are human. However, a husband and a wife do not have equal roles, equal talents, and equal abilities.

In general, roles, talents, and abilities, are not equal among all people. For example, if I learn tomorrow how to ice skate, I will gain a new talent. I can thereafter buy a pair of ice skates and then I have a new responsibility (to care for the skates); I can join an ice hockey team and then I have a new role (perhaps as a goalie). Alternatively, I can quit ice skating and then I will lose those responsibilities and roles. The talent to ice skate remains with me over time until I cannot ice skate or forget how to ice skate.

Next, let us examine the relationship between a man named Tom and a lady named Marla. Tom and Marla meet and become acquaintances. They spend time together and grow to become friends. After sometime, they decide to date for the purpose of considering marriage. After dating for some time, they decide to get married. Tom and Marla possess equal rights, importance and worth because they are human irrespective of whether they are acquaintances, friends, dating or married. However, Tom and Marla's roles and responsibilities change as the nature of their relationship changes. Tom and Marla do not carry the same roles and responsibilities throughout their relationship as acquaintances first, then as friends, next as a dating couple and then as a married couple.

The need to understand how roles and responsibilities change when Tom and Marla become married as husband and wife is very important. Why? Because after the wedding, they establish a new institution as husband and wife. The new institution is a new family. Like any institution, a new family must create policies and procedures on who will manage what and how (finances--taxes, bills, investments; foreign relations--neighbors, friends, family; sustenance--shopping, laundry, meals; etc.). In most cases, a wedded couple will be able to quickly agree on a policy or procedure for their family (e.g. we are going to be friends with our neighbors) and they are able to quickly assign new roles (e.g. I'll handle buying groceries and cooking meals).

However, every institution must have a leader. For example, Costco, a multi-billion-dollar global retailer, has a Chief Executive Officer or CEO. The CEO's role is to craft the company's decisions on matters of great importance which arise through the course of doing business, like what amount of profits Costco shall reinvest in its stores or what sort of expansion plans Costco ought to pursue. Naturally, the family, as an institution, must also have a head person, one who crafts the decisions on matters of importance. In the case of Costco, the CEO can be a man or a woman; as long as they have the necessary abilities and talents to take the lead in crafting competent decisions for the good of the company. Just as Costco needs a CEO, so, too, does the family need a leader.

In the case of Tom and Marla, the new wedded couple, who should the head of the family be? Many say that it does not matter whether the wife or the husband leads the family. My opinion is that the head of the family is the husband. The husband has the role of serving as the head of the family. There are several reasons why I believe the head of the family is the husband (male). First, the husband is more adept to discipline children (especially male children) when necessary, more so than the wife (woman). Second, in general, the husband has a more dominant physical and mental presence; men are, on average, taller, stronger, and more intimidating than women. Third, there is evolutionary or natural precedent favoring the husband (male) as head of the family. In most cultures and religions, since the dawn of human history, the husband (male) has been the head of the family.

In the three largest religions in the world, the husband's role as head of the family is recognized. Let us briefly examine the role of the husband as leader of the family in Hinduism, Islam, and Christianity. The Hindu model of manhood is what is most prevalent in my home country of India. In Hinduism, all children are told that they have four gods: *matha* (mother), *pidtha* (father), *guru* (teacher), and *deva* (God the creator) in that order. However, when a woman is wedded, the four previous gods are replaced. After marriage, the wife is told that her only god is her husband (this may be absurd to you). This kind of teaching puts family members in specific roles in relation to one another. For the children, the mother is a god. For the wife, her husband is the only god. For the husband, his wife is not a god and he is god.

Islam has a favorable perspective towards woman in the Qu'ran, the holy book of Islam. The Qu'ran teaches that the man and woman are equal (Dr. Asma Lamrabet, 2019). It also states that the man is the head of the household by right of what Allah, God, has given him. In short, there is a precedent for male leadership of the family in Islam.

The Christian position is found in the Bible. In the epistle of St. Paul to the Ephesians, it states, "Wives should be submissive to their husbands as if to the Lord because the husband is the head of his wife just as Christ is head of his body the church….As the church submits to Christ, so wives should submit to their husbands in everything. Husbands, love your wives, as Christ love the church. Ephesians 5:22-25.

While the Christian teaching considers the husband is the head of the household, that does not mean that the husband is superior. He is not. Jeff Bezos may be the head of Amazon, but he is not superior to the security guard, janitor, or anyone else at Amazon. Christianity teaches that the husband should be like a good President: a servant leader who is one of the people, not above them. The husband is not superior to the wife even if he is the head of her and his family.

It is important to note that the head of the nuclear family will not look identical in all families. I remember the story of an interviewer who asked a man whether he was the head of his household. The man said, "Yup! I am." The interviewer asked, "What does that mean?" The man said, "Well, I have the final word on the major decisions." The interviewer asked, "Who handles the minor decisions?" The man said, "Oh, my wife does that." The interviewer asked, "What are the minor decisions?" The man responded, "Oh, deciding where the kids are going to school and whether we eat organic food or fast food and who the kids are going to marry and what time dinner is." The interviewer stared at him and then asked, "Hey, if those are the 'minor' decisions, then what on earth does a major decision look like?!" The man responded, "I don't know, we haven't come across one yet."

My point with this anecdote is to illustrate that I am not advocating for husbands to micromanage every aspect of their wives' lives. I am not advocating for them to be given absolute power over what is and is not allowed in their house. I am not even advocating that the man have more 'power' in making decisions than the wife. I am advocating that men lead their households by the example of their service to their families. In short, that is the role and responsibility of the husband in his family.

CHAPTER 9
MILITARY COMBAT

Prolonged periods of military combat have negative effects on family life. I identify three negative effects of miliary combat on nuclear families. First, wars result in the deaths of young men and women. Second, combat veterans have trouble forming committed marital relationships. Third, wars separate nuclear family members.

The United States has fought many long wars. World War I, World War II, The Korean War, The Vietnam War, and The Gulf War are all examples of long wars the United States has fought in the last 150 years. The soldiers we sent to these wars are away from their homes for years. During World War II and The Vietnam War, combat soldiers went overseas to fight for two, three, four, or even more years without seeing or being with their nuclear families. Some Prisoners Of Wars (POW) spent nearly the entire war away from home. When these men and women returned, some had mental illnesses like post-traumatic stress disorder (PTSD), some had horrific war injuries, and nearly all felt uncomfortable in their hometowns, cities, and families because they had changed a great deal since they left for war. In other words, the problems of war do not end when the war is over; actually, the long-term problems are just beginning when the troops come home.

Let's consider PTSD ('shell-shock' in World War II). Many men get engaged or married before going to war. In war, they see horrible sights, kill others, witness their comrades being killed and are knocked around by explosions. Then, they come home. They are not the same as when they left; they have become a different person. Their wives, girlfriends, even their own families may not recognize them anymore because they behave differently. Long absences in a vicious, stressful environment like war harm mental health, marriages and families. Following every major war, the divorce rate in the United States spikes. Why? Because veterans are coming home changed. Brigham Young University found that combat veteran's marital dissolution rates (divorce rates + separation rates) were 62% higher than among civilian men who did not go to war (Veteran's View). Sven Wilson, the lead professor in the study, notes that although marital dissolution rates increased for civilian men from the 1960s to the 1980s, they began even earlier for combat veterans from World War II and The Korean War, not to mention World War I.

Many married U.S. servicemen and servicewomen fought in World War II, The Vietnam War and The Korean War. From these combat situations, many marriages were ended by the death of the husband or wife. As both military and civilian casualties increased, it was inevitable that their deaths would result in a large increase in single parents and single parenthood; thus, a loss of many marriages.

No victory comes without costs. Even though World War II was a resounding victory for the United States, the harm and costs to the nuclear family, such as marital dissolution, needs to be examined, acknowledged and prevented. Military combat is not recognized as a cause for destruction of the nuclear family. Wars contribute to the breakup of the nuclear family which is a high cost to endure for military victory. This high cost must be taken into account in calculating the burden of going to war.

CHAPTER 10

ALL WORK AND NO PLAY

Americans have a strong work ethic. Regardless of socioeconomic status, occupation, or age, American culture emphasizes working hard and working long. This has led some to say, "Americans live to work, not work to live."

Consider a typical working American couple, Tom and Jane. Tom and Jane have two children and live in northwestern New Jersey. They are accountants working for large accounting firms in Manhattan. Their salary is good. Every day, they must report for work by 8am, requiring them to travel between New Jersey and New York during rush hour in the morning and evening. To get to work on time, they have to wake up at 6am, get the kids ready for school (or a daycare), make coffee, get in the car, and leave. They each get a 1-hour lunch break at 12 and finish working at 5pm (they will have to stay longer sometimes). Since they are tired after work, Jane tells Tom to pick up something to eat for dinner on the way home. They reach home at 7pm and eat. By now, the Tom and Jane are more tired. How will they have any energy to spend with each other or with their children? What if they have to work during the weekend or late on a weeknight? If they have two cars, two car payments, a mortgage, utility bills, taxes, babysitter fees, parking fees, and other household expenses. Clearly, this daily schedule could become a vicious cycle of hustle and bustle where Tom and Jane struggle to stay ahead of the game.

Fatigue, stress and pressure—all these would grow and thrive in a family environment like Tom and Jane's. One small difference of opinion among family members could set off a volcano. One of the children might be upset with one of the parents for taking away TV privileges. Tom and Jane do not have the time or energy to address the matter with a cool head, so they start yelling. Then maybe they yell at each other, too. I can hardly see how this is a healthy way for the family to live. And if this is all that Tom and Jane can do to stay individually sane and survive, how can they have more time to make sure their marriage remains strong and survives? Family life not only becomes unpleasant, it becomes unbearable. Tom and Jane may reflect upon their past longingly, back to when they were dating. "Tom used to be nice and understanding," thinks Jane. "Now, he's a different man!" "Jane used to be so soft-spoken, patient, and understanding," recalls Tom. "Why is she so different now?"

Perhaps Tom and Jane try to cover up their family pressures and keep going, but the tension keeps building at home. Meanwhile, at work, everyone is just so nice, friendly, and understanding. At lunch, Jane can talk to her friends. They chat politely and laugh and share their opinion on everything. Similarly, Tom's friends at work seem to understand. One of Tom's work colleagues is Judy. Tom thinks Judy is so nice. And Jane finds that her work colleage, Harry, is so understanding. Errant thoughts begin to fly—"Should I really have wedded my spouse? Would my coworker have been better? What if…….?" Tensions at home lead to instability, and nn enticing way to change it all emerges. Suddenly, divorce looks like a neat way to hit the reset button and start again from fresh. Let the children live with Jane (their mother) and stepfather or Tom (their father) and stepmother. Let some lawyers get Tom and Jane a divorce settlement.

Will Tom and Jane getting a divorce fix everything? No! The underlying problems have not been addressed. The problem was not the marriage or the people in the marriage. The problem was the living to work rather than working to live. If someone lives to work, eventually, they will not live. Work is not the objective for human fulfillment. Although work is necessary and can seem very satisfying, it not the end goal of life. When Tom's boss praises him, Tom feels satisfied. Tom likes looking at something he built or created with his own hands and feels satisfied knowing that he did a good job. However, no matter how satisfying his work is, that work has a limited role and place in a family's life.

I think that in America today, people have trouble figuring out what should take the greatest role in their married life. What is the highest priority? I think that for many, work takes the greatest priority. Their job calls the shots of how they spend their time and energy. But work should not be the highest priority. If it is, it will lead to bitterness. It can—and has—led to divorce. The two highest priorities in a marriage are the wellbeing of your spouse and your children. Period. Anything which dares to interfere—whether it is your boss or your work or your sports or something else—should be controlled and limited. The worship of work has become a cause for the breakup of the American nuclear family. It cannot stay this way.

There is a misperception that American businesses, such as corporations, should just focus on creating products or on making money. None of this means anything if their own employees are getting burned out at home. In the long run, employees whose nuclear families are hurt by the demands of the corporate employer will injure the corporation itself. Thus, I would contend that every corporation and company has an obligation to support and ensure the wellbeing of its employees and their family lives. The workplace must respect the marriages and families in their employee ranks. This attitude will both benefit the employee, his family and the corporate bottom line.

When an employee's family life is healthy, he is a happy employee. Happy employees work harder with less fatigue because family tensions are absent. When an employee works harder with enthusiasm, then he is more productive. More productive employees increase the overall productivity of the corporate employer thus increasing the corporation's bottom line. In sum, strong nuclear families benefit corporate employers. America needs strong nuclear families to have more profitable corporations.

CHAPTER 11

THE
EMPTY NEST

In 1976, the French feminist Simone de Beauvoir declared, "No woman should be authorized to stay home to raise her children. Women should not have that choice, because if there is such a choice, too many women will make that one" (Venker, Fox News, 2017).

In America, there are many women who work. Some are single mothers who must work one or two or even three jobs to sustain their families. Others are professionals and corporate executives, many of whom must work long hours and cannot spend much time with their families. In other families, the husband and wife must both work full-time to financially make ends meet.

I am not against women in the workplace. It is a positive improvement to see women contributing to the society and the country in more ways than they historically could before. It is good that women can have the same sense of pride in a job well done at work. It is a sign of progress in America that women have equal rights and opportunities like men. It is good that women now have the power to keep their families out of poverty even if their husbands die, become incapacitated, or leave. It is a change for the better that wives can help their husbands by bringing in enough money to meet their family's needs (although one must wonder why it is now necessary for both parents to work to make ends meet. Are Americans getting poorer?). Today, in America women can exercise their educational qualifications and put in practice their talents for the benefit of society as nurses, doctors, teachers, lawyers, and leaders; this is a boost to the society. Work can be a useful, fruitful, and ideal way for women to spend their single years (and their married years).

However, I see three dilemmas with the current cultural shift of women to the workplace which contribute to divorce and the breakdown of the nuclear family. First, someone must still spend time with the children. Second, two full-time working spouses have less time to develop their marital relationship. Third, professional women are given higher prestige and respect in society compared to women who do not work outside of the home.

The first dilemma involves children. In a working family, the parents must answer two questions: "Who is staying with our children?" —and— "How much time are we spending with the children?"

Perhaps the parents decide that neither of them is staying with the children. What will necessarily result is some arrangement like the following: the children will see their parents for a short period of time in the morning before they go to school, they will spend seven hours at school (more if they have sports or extracurricular activities), then they will go to day care or a baby sitter for another two hours until one of the parents comes home. The parents will be exhausted from a long day at work; dinner will be quickly put together, everyone watches some TV, and then the children go to bed. I consider this situation most undesirable for several reasons. First, children *need* time with their mother and father, whether the children are five months, five years, or fifteen. No institution or babysitter can replace the love, affection, attention, and involvement of the parents.

This situation also prevents parents from giving their best hours of the day to their children; rather, the kids get the leftovers, after the employer and the errands have taken their share. I think it is reasonable to say that this arrangement is unfair to the children and unhealthy for fostering strong relationships. Since humanity's inception, children have needed their parents. That has not changed even now. Now, I understand that harsh economic conditions or employers can sometimes force the parents into this arrangement, but we, as a society, should then put a stop to it as quickly as possible, not let it slide and continue. We have already let it get too far out of hand; we have let it become normal, and that is ludicrous.

It is better for one of the parents to stay home, either the mother or the father. It may be that for social or cultural or psychological reasons, one is more preferable than the other, but the children should have at least one parent who spends at least half of each day with them. I think that this is not impossible to achieve and that it will help the children grow while helping the adults pursue their professional objectives.

The second dilemma involves the marital relationship. All relationships require time and active attention towards one another. You can try building a relationship on things, but things cannot replace time and active attention. Spending time with someone is the best (and perhaps the only) way to truly strengthen your relationship as husband and wife.

In the years before Christ (BC), there were 24 hours a day and traditionally only men went to work. In the 1400s, there were still 24 hours a day and only men went to work. Now, in 2024, both parents can and often do go to work, yet there are still 24 hours a day. We do not have any more time than before, even if we have more things to do. It is good that women and men have equal rights in today's society, but just as they have more and more opportunities, they must say no to more and more things if they are going to have vital time to spend with each other.

Currently, I find that if both parents are working, they often do not have enough time to establish a good relationship with each other. They may lose their understanding of one another, they may be unable to communicate with each other, and they are so busy they cannot address challenges until those challenges are too large to ignore. Thus, if both parents are working full-time, I suggest that they, their employers, and society have an obligation to ensure that husbands and wives are able to spend quality time together.

The third dilemma is that women in a professional career are more highly regarded compared to housewives, whether in the media, among friends and family, or among neighbors. I find that Americans respect more a woman with two children who works full-time as a doctor or lawyer compared to a woman who stays at home to rear her two children. This is a problem because it undermines the value of child-rearing, motherhood, and staying at home. If society frowns upon staying at home, neither the wife nor the husband will wish to be associated with it. They will be caught in a dilemma between staying home with the kids or going to work full time. If society's influence controls, then the parents will say, "Let us hire a babysitter or pay a day care center. Let us send the kids to school; let the teachers work with them." I find that American society even regards teachers in the school with greater deference than the stay-at-home mothers of those children who go to the school. I am not saying that teachers are bad (I was a teacher myself), but I am asking us to remember who the real primary educators of children are. The primary educators of the children are the parents.

I find that when society values work more than the family, the parents will also begin to value work more than their family. When people love their work more than they love their family, they find it easier to divorce (this is true of both men and women). Thus, I say that status is a subtle but nevertheless important factor which can turn something good (women in the workplace) into something bad (family breakup). This does not mean women should not work; it means that the society needs to re-identify priorities and then support those priorities to maintain those priorities.

American society does not just have less respect for childbearing women in the cultural media—it even considers the work of married women outside the home to be less valuable in comparison to unmarried women and married men! It has been often cited as an example of sexism that the median salary of a working woman (married) in America is 82% of the median salary of an American working man, meaning a median woman (married) makes 82 cents for every dollar a median man makes (Bleiweis, 2020). However, it is important to note that the wage gap *only exists for married women.*

According to 2017 data from the US Department of Labor, single women (unmarried) earn a median of $11.87 per hour of work. Single men earn an almost identical $11.97 per hour of work; the 10-cent difference is not statistically significant. However, what is significant is that married women without children earn a median of $15.53 per hour of work. In comparison, married men without children earn a median of $21.07 per hour of work; this difference is statistically significant- married men without children make 35% more compared to married women without children.   This difference reflects the prejudice against working married women.

The wage gap persists for married women with children: they earn a median of $18.20 per hour of work, while the median hourly wage for married men with children is $24.56. In other words, married women who have children are penalized roughly 35% relative to their male peers, while unmarried women face no penalty. The difference led researchers to conclude that the wage gap in America does indeed exist. The discriminating factor, however, is not   whether the wage earner is a man or woman; it is whether she is married! (Taei, 2019) This unequal treatment of married American women (especially married women with children) is shameful; their work is just as valuable as a married man's work and it should be treated as such.

In sum, there are three dilemmas associated with women working and these dilemmas are contributing to the breakdown of the nuclear family.

The three dilemmas (who is spending time with the children, lack of vital time for the married couple, and a misperception that staying home with the children is inferior to working out of the home) must be addressed to restore the nuclear family in America.

CHAPTER 12

NOBODY
TO BLAME

Laws are the adopted rules which govern a society. They carry enormous power because they dictate what behavior is and is not allowed in a society. Good laws either encourage good behavior or discourage bad behavior. For example, a good law encouraging good behavior is that those who buy a home in a real estate property sale keep the home as their own. A good law that discourages bad behavior is that those who evade their taxes get punished.

However, not all laws are perfect. Some laws are unjust. For example, in Nazi Germany in the early 1940s, it was illegal to help Jews escape persecution. In Ancient Rome in the time of Nero, it was illegal to practice Christianity. In the 1700s and 1800s in the United States, slavery was legal. These are all examples of unjust laws because they discourage good behaviors or encourage bad behaviors. As Thomas Aquinas once put it, they are unjust laws because "they are not rooted in eternal laws or natural laws."

In the case of marriage and divorce in the United States, I find at least two unjust, misguided, or senseless laws. The first is a failure of law to recognize a violation of a marriage when one of the spouses has an affair. The second is a failure of no-fault divorce laws to require responsibility for poor relationship choices.

The first unjust law I take aim at involves polygamy. Consider, that it is illegal for a man who is wedded to one woman to try and wed another woman (polygamy). However, it is not illegal for a man who is wedded to one woman to have a physical marriage to another woman (an affair). This is still polygamy, but it is ignored by the laws and brushed under the rug. The polygamist can get away with the 'mutual consent' clause in the law, which states that if the post-wedding adulterous union was performed with mutual consent, then it is OK. In essence, polygamy is illegal if your first wedding is recorded on paper and you try to record a second wedding, but if a post-wedding affair is unrecorded, then go ahead! This legal policy overlooks the fact that something can still be morally wrong even if the parties involved mutually consent to it.

This also opens the door to polygamists: as long as they do not leave any legal trail, then they have no legal obligation. They have moral obligations, but the law conveniently ignores that. This is absolutely mind-boggling, but cheating on your spouse is not illegal in most states! Even in states where cheating (adultery) is illegal, laws are rarely enforced (Lee, 2014). Considering the horrible social and marital pain that cheating or an affair can cause, one wonders why it is not universally illegal.

Is it appropriate to regulate human sexual behavior by law? Of course!! Consider that if you ride a horse, you probably want it to have reigns so you can control it. Otherwise, the horse can go anywhere it wants and you cannot direct its motion. Similarly, human sexual desires need to be reined in. For most people, an internal moral compass is enough, but for some, external laws are needed to exert enough guidance, like guiderails, to prevent them from doing wrong. When you regulate which direction a horse goes, people do not consider it repression but necessity. Similarly, it is not repression to regulate human sexual behavior, it is a necessity. Affairs should not be tolerated in America and worldwide.

The second unjust law I take aim at involves no-fault divorce, the idea that a married couple can divorce with each spouse assumed to be innocent of wrongdoing—it is nobody's fault. Now even a preschooler can tell you that when people are having a relationship problem, it is usually somebody's fault, but when the idea came to California Governor Ronald Reagan's desk in 1969, he signed it into law. The rest of the nation followed, and no-fault divorce prevails today (Willet, 2019, Washington Examiner).

In India, even today, there must be a ground for a married couple to obtain a divorce. There are five acceptable reasons: adultery, desertion, cruelty, impotency, and chronic disease. Indian courts operate on the principle that there must be actual evidence that a marriage is in danger of being strained or breaking before they intervene. However, in the United States - which is unwilling to regulate human sexual behavior - the courts and lawyers are all too eager to jump into someone's marriage and rip it apart with nothing more than an allegation of incompatibility or 'irreconcilable differences.' Never mind taking efforts to identify the grounds for the divorce; never mind taking efforts to save the marriage; if one spouse wants out, the courts are willing to use their authority to break a marriage apart regardless of the wishes of the other spouse (Willet, 2019, Washington Examiner). This overlooks the hypocrisy that the court requires both partners' consent to create the marriage in the first place but does not ask for both to consent (if there is no fault) to dissolve the marriage.

Later in life, Ronald Reagan told his son Michael that approving no-fault divorce was the "greatest regret" of his public life. Why? Perhaps Reagan finally recognized that it is wrong to empower human rights without equally emphasizing human responsibility. No-fault divorce strips children of their rights and adults of their responsibilities. When a couple is married, they create an obligation to each other to try and make things work. When they have children, they create an obligation to do what is best for the children. No-fault divorce throws these obligations out the window by pretending that it is fulfilling individual rights to freedom.

While no-fault divorce may make the process of separation convenient for the couple, its effects are far less beneficial to the children and society who must deal with the fallout.

Before adopting specific legislative policies, the purpose of a law should be considered. The role of civil law is to provide minimum moral standards for a community. Society should strive to enact civil laws that are consistent with the intuitive moral law, the conscience, of every human being. I do not believe that divorce laws are completely immoral and should be made illegal; rather, I propose five reasonable changes to the current divorce laws and outline each change below.

The first law that should be eliminated is no-fault divorce. No fault divorce allows either partner to easily quit their marriage without a reason, regardless of consideration for the wellbeing of the children from that marriage. It is unreasonable that the law permits married persons to impulsively end their legal commitment in marriage without a reason. This promotes a total lack of responsibility among spouses for the wellbeing of their marriage. The law requires more responsibility from a tenant who rents an apartment; a lease cannot be simply terminated on a whim; a valid reason must be given to the landlord. If apartment leases (contracts) are taken so seriously, then how can legal marriage commitments be taken any less seriously? Marriage is far more serious than any other contract that a person can enter!

The second change I propose is that divorce can only occur because of a valid reason such as adultery, desertion, abuse, impotency, chronic disease and other such serious grounds. Simply feeling that they have "irreconcilable differences" or incompatibility would not qualify as a reason for divorce.

The third change should be that both spouses must agree to divorce for the divorce to occur. The current no fault divorce laws allow either spouse to divorce the other, without mutual consent. According to the law office of Molly Kenny, this means that "if one person wants out of a marriage, he is legally able to do so, whether the other person agrees or not." This is a travesty; why should the spouse who wants the divorce get special privilege over the one who wants to keep their marriage and family together? Except in special circumstances, where a spouse needs to be separated from a manipulative or abusive partner, both spouses should agree to a divorce before it should be allowed.

The fourth change should be that states should implement a waiting period before granting divorces to a couple. In some countries, the waiting period is 2-4 years, to provide time for the spouses to try to repair and improve their relationship to overcome their difficulties and reunite. This strategy has a very high success rate, with many couples emerging from their challenges stronger than before. Once again, there can be an exception in the case of an abusive or manipulative spousal separation.

The fifth change required in divorce law is to give more power to children. For divorce to occur where there are children from the marriage, the children have a right to put their voice in the decision. If a couple with children under age 18 wants a divorce, the children must all consent. If even one child does not consent, then the divorce should not occur. Children are affected even more by a divorce than adults. Putting the power exclusively with the adults without any power with their children is like putting the cart before the horse. It has already been well established that a divorce will dramatically change a child's life, so minors should have a say in their future including their living arrangements and educational arrangements after the divorce. Alimony for divorced or separated partners should be required to be hefty, so that it is financially burdensome to the spouse without the children. This will help prevent divorce because there is no easy way out.

The current no-fault divorce laws and lack of legal punishment for adultery promote the destruction of the nuclear family. Five legal changes-end no-fault divorce, permit divorce only in limited circumstances, require both spouses and the children of that marriage to agree to the divorce and require a 2 to 4 year waiting period- are needed to end the epidemic of broken families in America.

CHAPTER 13
FREE MONEY

The next cause of broken families involves U.S. government programs, specifically tax and welfare policy. Tax and welfare policies have changed dramatically over the last five years, to say nothing of the last fifty years, but there are still lessons which can be drawn from how the United States government has contributed to destruction of the nuclear family.

Let us begin with a trip through history. In 1963, Lyndon B. Johnson became the President of the United States. In the next six years, he sent 200 bills through Congress, which collectively created the "Great Society program." This program was intended to do many things: defend civil rights, protect the environment, and provide avenues for the arts to grow. In addition, the Great Society endeavored to create a safety net for poor Americans who were 'down on their luck.' Some of these programs, including Medicare and Medicaid, are still in existence today. One of the programs was known as Aid to Families with Dependent Children (AFDC). AFDC was a welfare program whose objective "was to provide aid to all children whose mothers lacked the support of a breadwinner, no matter how they got to that position" (Virginia Commonwealth University, 2011).

At the start, AFDC seemed like a good idea. After all, it would help poor women who needed money to support their children. A woman whose husband had left her or a woman whose husband had died would not have to worry about lacking the money to pay the bills or buy food; now, the federal government would help her. Although AFDC had good intentions, it did not conceive of the myriad ways it could be manipulated.

For example, a woman who was single and did not have a job might have a boyfriend. If she wedded the boyfriend and they had children, she would not qualify for any AFDC money from the government. However, if she did not wed the boyfriend but had children with him, she suddenly qualified for payments from the government for those children. In essence, AFDC provided an incentive for single young women to stay unwedded but still have children. In other words, it encouraged mothers to have illegitimate children.

In 1993, after 30 years of AFDC, the Census Bureau analyzed the characteristics of mothers on AFDC. They found that 48% of AFDC-dependent mothers had never been wedded; it found that a given AFDC-dependent mother had (on average) more children than a non-AFDC-dependent mother, and it found that AFDC-dependent mothers had children (on average) three years earlier than non-AFDC-dependent mothers. Thirty years after its passage, AFDC was creating the problem it was trying to address! Rather than helping women and children who had lost their husbands and fathers, it was paying women to be husbandless and raise fatherless children! AFDC was creating more mothers without a husband because it gave financial incentives to be a husbandless mother.

Similarly, AFDC encouraged families to break up. A woman who divorced but retained children qualified for AFDC payments. In addition, a woman who claimed to be separated from the father or who claimed he was 'absent' received AFDC payments. AFDC lacked any effort to encourage familial stability, either by helping women find husbands or by rewarding better relationship decisions. AFDC also made no effort to encourage good moral behavior among its recipients; by treating all recipients as helpless victims, it overlooked the fact that some were willfully leeching or taking advantage of the program. In 1993, the Census Bureau reported that one in ten American mothers was on AFDC. One in ten! Absent fathers had gone from being a rarity to a commonality.

Many users of AFDC switched to Supplemental Security Income (SSI), another welfare program because it did not have the same work requirements as AFDC and gave greater payouts (Wamhoff and Wiseman, The Social Security Administration, 2006). SSI was designed to help disabled individuals pay for necessities. However, it was not long before smart people began taking advantage of SSI's generosity. Single parent families who started on AFDC would qualify for SSI if they could prove that the mother or children were disabled-a small price to pay for more free money.

John O'Donnell and Jim Haner are Pulitzer-Prize nominated reporters who worked for the newspaper Baltimore Sun. In 1995, they uncovered the story of Rosie Watson, a single mother whose family made over $46,000 a year on welfare—over $90,000 in today's money ("America's Most Wanted Welfare Plan"). Ms. Watson began receiving payments from AFDC in eighth grade since she was a single mother with two children. When she realized that she could get more money from SSI if she claimed to have a disability, she jumped at the chance.

Watson had seven children, all of whom she had declared "mentally retarded" or "violent," entitling her to more checks. And her boyfriend (she called him her husband, though they were never married) also received a check for his 'disabilities.' Poorly executed government welfare programs like SSI helped create this situation: a mother who is unwedded but still living with a man, with seven children, being paid by the government to live a broken family life. It would be nice to say that Rosie Watson was one isolated incident, but reporters Rachel Wildavsky and Daniel Levine found several similar cases in their 1995 article, "Two Moms, Too Many Faces" (Seattle Times, originally printed in Reader's Digest).

Apart from the U.S. government's SSI and AFDC welfare programs, the American tax structure also contributes to the divorce epidemic in America. Many couples experience what is known as the "marriage penalty" with their taxes, which is where the couple finds that they pay less taxes if they both stay single and live together than if they get married. The marriage penalty predominantly affects low-income and high-income singles who marry other low-income or high-income singles (El-Sibaie, the Tax Foundation, 2018). In general, the marriage penalty works in two ways. First, it can occur when a single person who used to be taxed on their single income marries someone and their combined income pushes them into a new higher tax bracket. Suddenly, the couple finds that they are paying up to 12% more in taxes per year (Rubenfield and Pandit, 2019, CPA Journal).

The second way a marriage penalty can occur relates to tax incentives. For example, when a poor single person who benefits from the Earned Income Tax Credit (EITC) gets married, they often find that combining their income with their spouse causes them to get reduced benefits or no benefits from the EITC (El-Sibaie, the Tax Foundation, 2018). Research has suggested that the marriage penalty has increased with the transition of women to the workplace and that it will continue to increase as women earn higher incomes (Rubenfield and Pandit, 2019, CPA Journal).

It has been theorized that the current arrangement of the American tax system encourages cohabitation and divorce among couples, particularly among low-income earners (Maag and Acts, 2015, The Urban Institute). In fact, The Urban Institute found that the American tax system most heavily penalizes couples who, when married, have a joint annual income of $40-$50,000. According to the researchers, "Our sample families with incomes of $40,000 and above face marriage penalties as high as about 10 percent of earned income; that is, they would owe higher taxes and receive lower means-tested benefits as a married couple than as an unmarried cohabiting couple." Obviously, to any smart couple, it would make more sense to cohabit than get married in order to preserve government benefits or avoid marriage penalty taxes. I have witnessed this tax outcome not just in theory, but in practice.

While I was an economics professor at St. Francis University, I had a small side job. I would buy properties and rent them to tenants. One of these apartments, I rented to single mothers. These mothers benefited from a federal program known as Section 8, or the Housing Choice Voucher Program. Basically, the Housing Department would pay a single mothers' rent to their landlords (people like me) so they could afford to live in a safe and secure environment while raising their children. However, Section 8 came with a catch: if the single mother got wedded, the Housing Department would stop paying her rent.

When I visited the apartments of these 'single' mothers, I often found men's clothes in the rooms I rented out. Since my female tenants did not wear men's clothes, I asked where the clothes came from. My tenants explained that the clothes were their boyfriend's clothes. The tenants would often let the boyfriend live in the apartment for lengthy periods of time, just like a husband, but they did not get wedded. Why? They knew that if they were wedded to their boyfriends, they would lose many of their welfare benefits—including their rent money. So, they chose to have an 'unofficial' husband who was a 'husband' in everything except on paper.

At a minimum, American tax policies should be neutral, rather than favoring one group over another. With the current tax structure, however, cohabitation is clearly favored over marriage among some economic groups, particularly poorer economic groups (Maag and Acts, 2015, The Urban Institute).

The American tax code also discourages mothers from staying home. For example, under the current tax system, if a mother pays for day care for her children, she is eligible for the Child Care Tax Credit (up to $3,000 for one child or $6,000 for two or more). However, if the mother chooses to be a stay-at-home mom, there is no tax credit to help her pay for taking care of her child. In this way, the tax system punishes mothers who want to stay home with their children rather than going into the workplace and paying for daycare.

In essence, the tax system incentivizes cohabitation, unwedded child-rearing, and parents spending less time at home. Through this combination of push and pull factors, the tax and welfare policies of the American government have contributed to punishing and eliminating stable families and encouraging and creating cohabitation, divorce, and fewer marriages. I recommend government policies that encourage marriage because it brings about greater societal wellbeing and stability. Even if government policies do not expressly favor marriage, then at the very least, they should be neutral between marriage and divorce and cohabitation. However, that is sadly not the case in America today.

I propose several changes to the current tax and financial policies of the federal government to promote pro-stable families. Government policy can be very effective at promoting or changing a person's behavior. For example, the federal government currently offers a $7,500 tax credit to households that purchase an electric vehicle, with the goal of reducing overall carbon emissions from gasoline-powered vehicles. In addition, it is currently investing billions of dollars in creating electric vehicle charging stations across the US. These policies have encouraged and will continue to encourage consumers to buy electric cars.

Two of Elon Musk's companies (SolarCity and Tesla, which make solar panels and electric cars) have received nearly $3 billion combined in state and federal tax credits and subsidies. This is because the government wants to encourage these companies to mass-produce cleaner methods of energy generation. The credits and subsidies have had their intended effect; SolarCity created one of the most efficient solar panels in the market, while Tesla has deployed hundreds of thousands of vehicles in the US. Spending all this money on advanced technology, however, will mean nothing if there are no stable families in the future. Without stable families, there will be no nation to use solar panels and electric vehicles.

If the federal government has this kind of power to change people's behaviors, it would be ludicrous for the federal government to ignore the breakdown of the nuclear family. Currently, many women need to work outside the home in order to support their children, particularly single mothers and rural mothers. As has been demonstrated in this book, it is much more preferable that these same mothers would instead be staying at home to care for their children than leave the home to work.

While parents can currently benefit from a $3,000 tax credit per child, many of them receive no other form of federal assistance for taking care of their own children. Those who do are almost universally divorced or single and receive federal money through welfare. It is time for this to change. It is absurd that the federal government gives a larger tax break to people who want to buy an electric car (many of whom are wealthy anyway) than to parents who want to stay home to take care of their own children. If anything, children should receive a larger tax break; they are more important and they are also more expensive!

Tax policy should not just encourage women to have children. It should also be reformed so women are encouraged to be married. Current tax policies favor unmarried women with children and should instead favor married spouses with children. If a single woman has a child, then she pays little or no taxes. However, if she marries the father of her child, then the couple pays higher taxes, especially if their pre-marriage incomes were similar (TurboTax, 2022). A cohabiting man, woman, and child pay less taxes compared to a married man, woman and their child.[3] A woman should not be penalized by paying higher taxes simply because she married.

----

[3] http://www.americanvalues.org/search/item.php?id=1

There should be tax incentives for marrying and staying married. The government will benefit from this approach because stable families will cause economic growth.

Another tax policy that should be added is a tax break for at-home childcare. Currently, families who send their children to daycare are given a tax break, as they should be. However, stay-at-home parents, who are providing similar care to their own children and who experience the same financial strain as those who place their children in daycare, are not given tax breaks. Instead, I propose that all families with children under the age of 12 should be given a tax break to help fund childcare. Taken together, these policies will help improve the stability of nuclear American families.

CHAPTER 14

WORKING
FOR FREE

Earlier I mentioned that a contributor to family breakup and instability is the way society values a career over a family. I think that this ideology is so engrained that prejudice against stable family structure exists even in certain indicators of economic productivity. Consider, for example, Gross Domestic Product (or GDP). GDP is the most famous measure of economic productivity and performance of a nation and by economists worldwide. GDP is the sum of the value of all the goods and services produced in a national economy. For example, if Country A produces $100 worth of rice, $20 worth of sausage, and $40 worth of plumbing services in a given year, then Country A's GDP is $100 + $20 + $40 = $160.00.

When we calculate GDP in America, we exclude the value of services performed by parents at home including a stay-at-home mother who is caring for her children. What do I mean? Consider any given American family. If a parent pays a housecleaner $500 to clean the house, then this $500 is included in GDP. If a parent pays a restaurant $80 to make a meal for dinner, this $80 is included in GDP. If a parent pays a tutor $190 to teach her child math, then this $190 is included in GDP. However, if the stay-at-home mother cleans the house herself, makes the meals herself, or teaches the children herself, none of this is given any productive value in terms of GDP and it is not included in that country's GDP value.

In fact, if all American homes this year were cleaned by parents instead of housecleaners, GDP for house services would go down, even though the same amount of productive work was done. In this way, I conclude that America's GDP takes for granted and fails to value and recognize the hard work of stay-at-home parents. I think it is cruel for an economic indicator to blatantly ignore the contributions of a group of people, such as stay-at-home mothers, simply because they are "at home." To those who object that such an indicator would simply be an inaccurate estimate, I reply that all economic indicators are inaccurate and mere estimates.

By ignoring the contributions of stay-at-home parents in GDP, American society once again reinforces the idea that greater value should be given to career parents as opposed to stay-at-home parents. Men and women are sensitive to their public perceptions; they are not immune to social pressure. If they believe that their nation places higher value on their working outside of the home and staying away from their family, then they will do so. We should reconfigure GDP estimates to include the contributions of all parents, both stay-at-home and those that work outside of the home. In this way, we will show parents at home that their work and efforts to help their families and their children are appreciated and accounted just like parents who work outside of their home.

CHAPTER 15

MEDIOCRE MEDIA

The next cause of nuclear family break-up is public media. Public media refers to anything which conveys cultural values or information to individuals in a society. America possesses a dizzying array of public media outlets, such as TV (shows and commercials), radio, social media, movies, newspapers, books, music, magazines, and video share sites. Media is a powerful tool to educate, inspire, and persuade—or desensitize, tempt, and deceive. The power media carries can be used either for good or for evil. In this chapter, I focus upon the influence of TV, movies and the internet upon members of society.

Perhaps the greatest power of media lies in its ability to influence what the society believes is wrong and what it believes is right. Essentially, media can help transform an old culture into a new one. Let me give you an example. In the 1800s, smoking became fashionable among certain circles of people. By the early 1900s, the cigarette was developed, and thanks to aggressive marketing, Americans began smoking *en masse* (Surgeon General's Report, 2000). Through the 1920s until the 1960s, almost half of Americans smoked frequently (NBC News, 2014)

American smoking culture was reinforced and glamorized by media sources, especially TV and movies. On TV shows like *I Love Lucy*, both spouses smoked (the actors, Desi Arnaz and Lucille Ball, both died from illnesses due to smoking). Famous movie actors like Humphrey Bogart and Yul Brynner puffed away on screen (smoking also killed them). Singers like Frank Sinatra, Dean Martin, Louis Armstrong, and Nat King Cole also smoked (all dead from smoking) (Clear The Air.org). People smoked in public; my graduate students smoked in the classroom, and I even smoked a pack a day myself. Smoking occurred everywhere and became commonplace.

Then, in 1964, the US Surgeon General announced that smoking caused lung cancer. The U.S. government wished to curb smoking rates. They recognized the role of media in fueling and normalizing smoking. So, in 1969, the US government banned cigarette commercials on TV and radio. By 2014, smoking rates had been cut by more than half; less than 20% of the American population smoked (NBC News).

Today, when my grandkids watch shows from the 1960s, like the comedy *Get Smart*, they are shocked to see the heroes and heroines puffing away on cigarettes. Smoking is no longer promoted or normalized in American media. Rather, it is condemned and kept away from our children's sight. In modern American movies like *The Avengers*, none of the heroes and heroines smoke (sometimes the villains do). Smoking may not be dead, but it is certainly crippled. Through the power of the media, Americans today generally believe that smoking is bad and that it is a vice. As for me, I quit smoking in 2010 and have not touched a cigarette since.

In the same way that I have seen American media stop Americans from smoking, I have seen American media twist and confuse American's views regarding the family. Perhaps the most pervasive and destructive of these have been soap operas. I remember reading a joke in *Reader's Digest* which runs as follows: a young girl and her father got into an elevator on the way down. It was filled with chattering girls. The young girl noticed her father turning paler and paler as the chatters mentioned that someone named Jill was seeing a wedded man, another lady was doping, and a third was pregnant outside of wedlock. The girl whispered to her father, "Don't worry. They're just talking about their favorite soap opera."

Virtually every weekday, when one turns on the TV, a soap opera is running. Programs like *All My Children, General Hospital, One Life to Live*, and *Young and Restless* have presented debased role models and situations to the American public. Such shows normalize, legitimize, and justify extramarital affairs, divorce and remarriage, premarital sex, and unfaithfulness. They all seem to follow a similar thread: a young girl and boy fall in love, are wedded, and have a happy first few years of marriage. Their first child arrives and they are having a happy life. Then, the lady meets an old boyfriend at a party. She has an extramarital affair with him. When the husband finds out, their family is broken. The wife marries her old boyfriend, the ex-husband marries someone from work, and so on. Meanwhile, the children are largely ignored or are left alone to process the implosion the so-called mature adults have wreaked on their family.

According to Pew Research center, the historical audience for soap operas have been poor women. Even as recently as 2013, Pop Matters reported that, "political correctness and supposed shifting demographics be damned, daytime TV is still all about women. According to a recent Pew research report, 73% of daytime talk show audiences are female.… Regular viewers of daytime talk shows are less educated than the public as a whole. Among this group, just 19% have four-year degrees, 26% have attended some college and 54% have a high school diploma or less education… About half (51%) have family incomes of less than $30,000, while three-in-ten have $30,000-$74,999 incomes. Just 12% have incomes of $75,000 or more.'" Clearly, America has not been affected equally by soap operas. The traditional target audience of poor women remains today. This is an issue because these are the women who are most in need of the stability a nuclear family brings.

So, what is the main problem with soap operas?

First, they create despicable role models. The heroes and heroines of the shows lie, cheat, and perform all manner of immoral and condemnable acts against their own spouses and children. This is a problem because human beings are subconsciously wired to try and imitate what we see others doing. If a child grows up in a family that condemns smoking, he will very likely not smoke. If a child in a school sees all his friends smoking, he will very likely also smoke.

This effect is known as the mirror neuron effect in psychology. Essentially, we can train our brains to behave, feel, or think a certain way by simply watching others do it. Researchers have found that viewers of on-screen programs connect strongly with the emotions in those programs. These researchers remarked in *Time* magazine that mirror neurons could possibly form the basis of social behavior. One researcher even compared mirror neurons to DNA in terms of their importance in influencing human development (Jaffe, 2007). It is a no-brainer that if men and women see other men and women on their TV screens having affairs with old friends for emotional closeness or divorcing their spouses to begin another romance, the viewers will be strongly affected and subtly influenced to copy that behavior. In this way, soap operas have proven to be a dangerous weapon against stable family structure and contribute to the epidemic of divorce.

Second, soap operas create unrealistic expectations in the minds of viewers. Statistics generally find that 45%-50% of divorcing couples cite unrealistic expectations as a reason why they are divorcing (National Fatherhood Initiative, 2005). Soap operas are adept at cultivating unrealistic expectations among both men and women as to what they should expect from a relationship and what is normal or healthy for married life. Soap operas glamorize and normalize selfish, adulterous, spoiled, brat-like behavior which can be picked up by their viewers. As Dr. Jeremy Nicholson remarks, "You may very well have a skewed perspective about sex and relationships from the constant, biased, media bombardment... [I] f you do, … you have simply been misinformed and misguided, which has resulted in beliefs that will not help you find love (2013)."

At 8:00 PM, when both parents and children are home and like to watch TV, what are the programs that are running on American TV? *Melrose Place*, *Wings*, *Roseanne*, *Cheers*, and *Desperate Housewives*—all of which have adulterous content. This is a problem because children are not able to filter what they absorb through mirror neuron behavior (Jaffe, 2007). Nielson reported that 9 million children or more viewed *Jerry Springer* weekly, a nasty program which featured wives swapping couples (Jerry Springer himself once remarked that it was a stupid program).

Movies have also contributed to the family breakdown. Sixty years ago, movies tried to showcase the importance of marriage. Consider the 1961 successful Disney film *The Parent Trap*. In this film, two identical-looking girls meet at a summer camp and discover that they share the same parents. They realize that although they are identical twin sisters, each one was taken by one parent in a divorce 12 years earlier. In the movie, the twins have very emphatic views on divorce. At the beginning of the movie, one girl mentions to the other, "It's scary the way nobody stays together these days." The other responds, "Why soon, there'll be more divorces than marriages!" How prophetic!

You can probably guess the plot; the twins switch places and try to bring their parents back together. Later, when they reveal their true identities, one of the girls tells her mother, "I think what you and Daddy did to us children is lousy! I think it stinks!" She is upset with her parents for having broken up her relationship with her twin sister simply because they had arguments in their marriage. I think this movie correctly reflects that children have a right to grow up in a married, stable family household.

Three decades later, *The Parent Trap* was already outdated. Consider the 1993 successful film *Mrs. Doubtfire*. In this film, a loving father is separated from his children because his wife wants a divorce (he doesn't) and the court prevents him from meeting with the children more than once a week. The father does everything possible to try and rebuild his relationship with his family; he gets a stable job and works hard, he finds a home for himself, and, to top it all off, he dresses up as a housemaid to be the hired help to have more time with the children. However, his wife gets a new boyfriend—an old, handsome classmate who is a bachelor.

At the end of the film, the parents do not get back together, and the family stays broken. The judge, furious with the father for dressing up as a housemaid, decides to punish him by preventing him from seeing his children further. Nobody in the film, whether lawyers or judges or even the children's mother, bothers to ask the children what they want (they want the family to remain intact). The children are pushed aside and told to deal with whatever the so-called mature adults determine. At the end of the film, the father remarks to another girl whose family has split that it would be nice if her parents got back together, but there are all kinds of families, so it is OK. This ending is completely ridiculous. A family is only a family if they are together.

In 1996, a very similar film to *Mrs. Doubtfire* was released in India in the Tamil language titled *Avvai Shanmugi*. The movie in India followed a similar plot to the English version: a wife divorced her husband because she was upset with his joking, casual, laid-back demeanor. She takes custody of their only child, a girl, with her. The father does everything possible to try and rebuild his family, and, just like in *Mrs. Doubtfire*, he dresses up as a housemaid to have more time with his daughter. There are two differences between the Indian film and *Mrs. Doubtfire*, however.

First, in the Indian movie the mother does not get a new boyfriend after she divorces her husband. She has already been wedded once and even though she felt that the marriage did not work, she does not try to indulge herself. Second, at the end of the Indian film, when the mother finds out the extreme measures that the father took to be with her and her daughter, she reweds him. The Indian film mimicked the humorous elements of *Mrs. Doubtfire*, but rejected the broken family ending. *Avvai Shanmugi* was a box office hit in India and it depicted correctly that a united nuclear family is worth saving and is the appropriate end goal. I bring it up because it shows how different the media and culture was between India in 1996 and the United States in 1993.

In more modern movies, things have gotten even worse. Just like in soap operas, many modern movies provide poor role models or unrealistic expectations about married life. For one thing, whenever sex is depicted in a modern film, it is almost always between unwedded partners. It is not part of a wedding. The marital relationships in modern movies are also more likely to be temporary or to portray satisfaction and feelings as the primary drivers of a relationship (as opposed to contentment or commitment).

You may be wondering why I spend so much time on media. I do so because the trash which is shown in media today is having and will continue to have detrimental effects on society, but we have become so desensitized to adultery in the media that we do not notice it. I will make a comparison to illustrate that what you sow, you will reap. Imagine that you know a young boy. When he gets home from school every day and turns on the TV, the shows he watches depict flashy young rogues wielding guns and shooting innocent people for fun. When he watches movies, they are about slick young folks who take out their anger by gunning down kids in schools. When he plays video games or surfs the internet, he is bombarded with these images of cool people shooting innocent kids.

What will happen to this boy? One day, something will make him angry, and he will think it is okay to go and shoot up a school. This is not fiction. It has been documented that the Sandyhook Elementary shooter, Adam Lanza, played a computer game called *School Shooting* (Pilkington, 2013). (In this computer game, one plays a school shooter who must enter a school and try to kill as many students as possible). Investigators generally agree that Lanza was desensitized to cold-blooded killing through what he saw in video games and media (Katersky, Kim, 2014). As one medical doctor has put it, if exposure to murder and violence creates murderous and violent young people, how can we dare say that exposure to adultery and infidelity will not create adulterous and unfaithful young people? (Grant, 2003) In fact, violent media has such an effect on viewers that Nemours health was prompted to issue an article to parents warning against letting children and teens see violence on-screen. If you sow bad behavior and role models among the people, you will reap it.

Perhaps this is why a poll of 10–16-year-olds found that "82 percent said television shows should teach right from wrong" (Stepp, 1995). Meanwhile, "a large majority—77 percent—said TV too often portrays sex outside of marriage." Regardless of whether or not we are willing to admit that TV has such a dramatic effect on children's sexual behavior, the evidence is already clear. A 2004 study found that: (1) teens who watch a lot of television with sexual content are more likely to initiate intercourse in the following year, (2) television in which characters talk about sex affects teens just as much as television that actually shows sexual activity, and (3) sex on TV was often presented as a casual activity without risks or consequences (Collins et al). The same results were found in a similar study by Canadian doctor Christina Grant (2003).

The negative effects do not end there. A 2017 review of media's effect on children by Professor Elizabeth McDade-Montez observed that "a number of researchers have documented that what children are exposed to through media affects a variety of health behaviors including sexual activity, substance use and aggression." A 2009 study by Boston Children's Hospital found that "for every hour the youngest group of children watched adult-targeted content over the two sample days, their chances of having sex during early adolescence increased by 33 percent. Meanwhile, the reverse was not found to be true-that is, becoming sexually active in adolescence did not subsequently increase youth's viewing of adult-targeted television and movies." In essence, this means that sexualized media causes children to engage in sexual behavior. It also shows that it is not perverted children or children who have sexual problems who are seeking out this media; rather, sexualized media is introducing the problems to the children. Sexualized media pollutes the minds of children.

Why is it a problem when media causes earlier sexual behavior among youth? It is because the association between early adolescent sexual activity and divorce is very clear. Teenagers who begin having sex at a young age when they are not wedded will be more likely to divorce a spouse to whom they are wedded later on in life. In addition, it has been well documented that the younger an individual begins engaging in sexual activity, the more likely they are to have children out of wedlock, experience poverty, and have multiple weddings. Since media fuels adolescent sexual activity, it is arguably also fueling later divorce.

The last form of media which I would like to discuss, which also contributes to divorce, is the Internet. Now this is not surprising. After all, the internet contributes to practically everything which is good or bad in our modern American society. Whether it comes to spreading news (real or fake), providing health information or conspiracies, and distributing entertainment or pornography, the internet can be used for pretty much anything. Why? Well, the internet is, by itself, a morally neutral entity. It is only as good or as bad as how people use it. For this reason, I will not spend much time on the internet, except to point out a few features.

First, I would like to address pornography. Years ago, when adults wanted to access lewd content, they had to exert time, energy, and money at an adult bookstore and buy either books or magazines which contained such content. You probably did not find many 12-year-olds in there, and unless you or your parents actively went to find such content, you would not be exposed to it. Nowadays, however, such content can infiltrate right into your living room without your knowledge or consent. This is because the modern tendency is to put responsibility for what is viewed on the internet on the user and not on the provider. Providers claim that viewers have discretion to watch or not watch, so the providers are allowed to put whatever they want on the internet.

However, this is ridiculous reasoning. We do not let heroin dealers stand on the corner and claim that people have the discretion to buy or not, so the dealers should be allowed to stand and sell wherever they want. Some things are so evil and so socially and morally detrimental that we as a society do not even give them a forum to be accessed. In America, we agree that these items are terrible enough that there is no circumstance under which people can have them: heroin, cocaine, short-barreled shotguns, and human trafficking. However, we tolerate an all-access pass to pornography via the internet. Internet access to pornography should not be permitted. In the same way heroin sellers cannot stand in a public, all-access place and sell heroin, pornography sites and distributors should not be allowed to keep their filth on the Internet where anybody can access it.

Second, I would like to address websites which encourage or promote infidelity (such as *Ashley Madison*). These sites connect spouses who want to cheat with one another. If there was a website which connected drug dealers to drug users, we as a society would be absolutely outraged and disgusted. We would shut it down. So why do we let websites that promote affairs destroy our marriages and our families? They should be shut down as well.

Media is not just a product of culture; it helps create the future culture. What kind of culture do you want your kids to grow up in? Do you want them to grow up in a culture that is similar to your favorite soap opera? Do you want them to have the personalities and attitudes of soap opera characters? Do you want them to grow up in a culture where divorce, extramarital affairs, and rampant premarital sexual activity are prevalent?

Or do you want them to grow up in a culture where stable family life, committed marriages, and spousal fidelity are valued? You know what your answer is; you know what is best for society. It is time for American media to change. The future of the family depends on it. In the same way American media helped fuel societal acceptance (and later, societal rejection) of smoking, it has the power to fuel societal acceptance or rejection of divorce and premarital sexual activity.

While the First Amendment of the United States Constitution grants the right to free speech, citizens should be protected from indecent material in grave circumstances. This is already recognized and widely accepted in the case of terrorist propaganda; it is not permitted to be broadcast freely but rather is censored for the sake of the common good. In fact, the Supreme Court has generally ruled that the government can prohibit speech which "threatens or facilitates violence in a more specific or immediate way" (Killion, "Terrorism: Free Speech Considerations", Congressional Research Service, 2019). Adulterous media, online pornography, and services like Ashley Madison are specific and immediate threats to the stability and wellbeing of American families, and therefore should be restricted in a similar way.

CHAPTER 16

WITH GREAT POWER COMES GREAT RESPONSIBILITY

"Children have more need of models than of critics."
- CAROLYN NELSON

The role model who can have the greatest impact on children is not an actor, teacher, politician, sports star, or religious leader. It is not a businessman or a reporter. It is not a TV host; it is not a repairman. No, the role model who has the greatest impact on a child are his parents. Children learn from their parents before they learn from anyone else. Actions speak louder than words. Parents must embody the values which they want their children to learn. The absence of responsible parents in the home contributes to the breakup of the nuclear family.

Let me ask you a question: would you want your daughter to be divorced before she turns 50? Would you want your son to be unfaithful to his wife? Would you want your kids to be involved in crime? Would you want your kids to be fathers and mothers when they are 16 or 18? Do you want your kids to swear constantly? You probably answered no to all of these things. But it is not enough to say to your children, 'no, you can't do that' or 'no, you can't have that.' Words are not enough.

Your children need to *see* you stay wedded and faithful, they need to *see* that you are honest and respectful and chaste. Only then will they have a true role model to look up to with respect and pride and say, 'that's what I want to be like.' You cannot just say, 'I don't want that for my kids' and then do it yourself. If you get divorced or cheat on your spouse or do a crime or have children out of wedlock or swear, your kids will have a hard time understanding why they should not. They can probably barely resist picking up bad habits from their friends; it will be impossible for them to resist picking up bad habits from their own parents! Whatever you do not want to see your kids doing, you should not do yourself.

Children need role models. In good homes, the father represented strength of discipline and firmness in love. He led the family in religion and charity. The mother represented tenderness and love, an example of self-sacrifice and hard work. They provided children with characters of ethics and discipline. While the role of parents may have changed in modern society, one part of their role which has not changed is that they must be characters of these ethics and disciplines for their children. But that does not seem to be the case. Today, parents dole out children to schools, day care centers, and sports teams. The children find characters to look up to in those settings, but usually not ones of ethics and discipline. The parents often find that their children are like a field which has been left to itself and is now spoiled with weeds.

There is a common misperception that the only responsibility a wedded couple has is to each other. However, this is not true. The wedded couple also has a responsibility to society and to their children. What sorts of responsibilities? First, there is the responsibility of the wedded couple to stay together. In this book, I explain how society suffers greatly from broken marriages. So, second, society has an interest in having a wedded couple stay together. Third, there is the responsibility to raise mature, polite, curious, and pleasant children. Children suffer greatly from the instability of broken marriages. Thus, children also have an interest in their parents staying together as a married couple.

One large contributor to the rise of divorce is the social acceptance of single motherhood. Single motherhood should be rare, not a commonality. Families need fathers! The writer Irving Kristol once noted that children in a household often admire their fathers even if their fathers are away from home for large portions of the day at work. Why? He mentioned that fathers, even if they are not very gregarious or even if they are tired when they come home, command a certain level of respect and awe. In addition, even if the father was away from home for large periods of the day, there was still the 'crucial element of his visibility at home'—in essence, his presence makes a significant impact in the children's lives. Of course, anyone who has lived in a family could probably tell you that. It is undeniable that the father's presence at home is required to help build a stable family.

What I point out here is that this is natural and good for a nuclear family social structure. I also point out that even the U.S. government recognized the value of the father's presence at home. During World War II, there was a campaign to 'Bring Daddy Home.' The military favored drafting young single men over married men; when it came time to send men home, the military again favored fathers over single men. Why? The military understood that it should not deprive wives and children of their husbands and fathers any longer than was absolutely necessary.

At the time of World War II, at least 183,000 American children lost their fathers when they were killed in combat (Van Ells, 1998). In 2021, according to the US Census Bureau, *18.4 million* children were growing up without a biological, adoptive, or stepfather in their home (U.S. Census Bureau, 2021). We are not at war with Nazis, yet ten times the number of children who lost their fathers in World War II are without fathers today. Where are the fathers? They are divorced or separated, absent from the lives of their children and families. While the U.S. government tried to "Bring Daddy Home" in World War II, there was no such push in the 1970s or 80s as divorce and separation skyrocketed. There is still no such push today. A policy favoring and promoting fathers to be at home with their families is needed now. Absence of fathers at home is an absence of parental responsibility, which contributes to the break-up of the nuclear family.

The next level of parental responsibility involves influencing or guiding the behavior of their children, especially in their children's relationship with a boyfriend or a girlfriend. In 1963, when I came to America, I stayed with a host family. One evening, the host family took me to a dinner at a colleague's house. When we were finishing dinner, the colleague's daughter received a phone call from her boyfriend asking her to go out that evening. She asked her father for permission; he granted it on the condition that she came home before a certain time. We were sitting around and talking and drinking tea when that time came, and on time, the boyfriend and the girl came to the front door and she came back into the house. What I point out here is that the parents of the girl not only took responsibility for their daughter's behavior but also for the boyfriend's behavior. When they set a rule, not only the daughter but the boyfriend was expected to obey it. Such parental responsibility is vital for a family to thrive. Absence of such parental responsibility causes the nuclear family to fail and breakup.

Any athlete who wants to be good at their sport must be disciplined and responsible. Any student who wants to do well in school must be disciplined and responsible. Any parent who wants to see their family thrive and succeed must be disciplined and responsible. And any society which wants its citizens to be engaged, happy, and healthy citizens must be disciplined and responsible. This is a law of nature. Yet when it comes to sexual morality, we are often scared to be disciplined or to demand that others be responsible. This has led to rampant illegitimacy, hookups, breakups, heartache, and loss of family life. Nevertheless, we are told that to intervene in others' sexuality would 'suppress' their humanity. This shows a clear misunderstanding of what disciplined and responsible is.

In modern culture, discipline and suppression are often confused.

Discipline is a necessary form of intervention to correct a behavior. For example, if a child steals something from a store, the father is obligated to discipline the child in some manner, usually by making the child return the stolen item and by punishing the child. This way, the child realizes what pain he has caused, and he is deterred from stealing or causing pain again. Contrary to some modern opinions, spanking a child can be necessary and appropriate discipline. Why? Discipline is driven by loving motives. Remember that love is when you want what is best for someone even at the cost of your own self-interest. A parent wants what is best for their child; they want their child to be honest. Thus, a parent may discipline their child in the hopes that the child will do what is best for himself or herself (be honest) once the disciplinary intervention is completed. This will make the child more responsible in the future.

Suppression is an intervention taken by means of coercion. Suppression is an incorrect and immoral form of intervention. Suppression is different from discipline because suppression is undertaken due to selfish reasons. A corrupt leader may suppress dissent among the people because he wants to retain his power. Suppression may look different within a household. There is a story of an atheist who kept his son inside the house so that he would not hear about God from the neighbors' children. This is an example of suppression; the atheist was preventing the child from going out for a selfish reason, namely, that he did not want the child to entertain belief in something which he did not believe in.

Within a household, discipline is permissible and will probably be necessary at some point. Suppression is unacceptable and intolerable. Both the husband and wife are authorized to discipline their children. A father or a mother can make their child stay home from a baseball game because he didn't finish his homework properly. Neither are authorized to suppress their children. Similarly, neither the husband nor the wife is authorized to suppress each other. The husband cannot make the wife vote for a politician she does not want simply because he wants his party to win. Neither can she do so to him. Hence, spouses are not to suppress one another or their children, whereas they may discipline their children.

In modern American culture, people are too afraid to use discipline on their own children. They worry that if they discipline their children, the children will not love them. However, this is a wrong belief. Although in the short term a child may take issue with their parent's discipline, in the long run the character improvements that discipline brings will actually make the child more grateful for their parent's disciplining (Wright, 2015)(Young, 2017). If the parents fail to discipline the child in small matters at a young age, they will have lost the ability to improve the child's behavior in much larger matters at a later age (Zamora, 2003). "When spoiled youngsters become teenagers, they're more prone to excessive self-absorption, lack of self-control, anxiety, and depression," notes Dan Kindlon, a professor at Harvard University (Kam, 2009). Refusing to discipline children creates dysfunctional, selfish adults who have trouble adapting to and empathizing with the needs of others. Discipline is a central part of stable family life; we must bring it back if we wish to bring back responsible adults and stable nuclear families.

In summary, children need strong role models. The best role models are their parents within the context of a strong nuclear family.

CHAPTER 17

FREEDOM
IS NOT FREE

The next causes for nuclear family instability are freedom and secrecy. In American society, freedom is prized above all other virtues and values. This has a historical basis; after all, America had to win its freedom from a world superpower and then defend that freedom several times, especially in wars. America's founders expressly sought to ensure that every individual American has freedoms which the government cannot take away, including freedom of speech, freedom of the press, and freedom of religion. By itself, this is all good. However, in the last several decades, I observe that Americans have begun divorcing personal freedoms from personal responsibilities. This is a mistake.

Archbishop Salvatore Cordileone once remarked that many modern freedom movements advocate "an extreme version of the theory that personal freedom is absolute, has no boundaries, and is responsible to no law other than the will of the individual" (2006). Doesn't this sound familiar in America? Alexander Solzhenitsyn, the Nobel Prize winner, once noted that "what you add to the truth, you subtract from the truth." We have added and added and added to what personal freedom means and have thus actually subtracted from what it means. We have forgotten what our rights really give us and what they do not. Although Solzhenitsyn was strongly critical of the communist ideology, he did not abstain from calling out what he saw as moral errors in American culture. In 1978, he remarked, "Two hundred or even fifty years ago, it would have seemed quite impossible, in America, that an individual could be granted boundless freedom simply for the satisfaction of his instincts or whims…[But now,] destructive and irresponsible freedom has been granted boundless space."

Perhaps no one has better insight into the interplay between freedom and responsibility than Lee Kuan Yew, the former Prime Minister of Singapore. Some call him a brutal, repressive control freak (Sleeper, 2015), while others call him a liberator and founder of a civil and orderly society (Cheng, 2015). Nevertheless, what is uncontested is that in just two generations, he transformed Singapore from a dirty, poor nation into a clean, attractive country where technological and financial success thrived, even in comparison to other developed countries in the world. Under Prime Minister Yew, unemployment in Singapore dropped from 13.5% to 1.51%, which many consider an economic miracle. Most people do not contest that Prime Minister Yew was able to identify the problems in Singapore and solve them; they only contest that he addressed these problems too harshly. So, when Minister Yew identifies that a culture or society is doing something which could degrade it or damage it, it is wise to pay attention to his observations.

What does Prime Minister Yew think about America? He has mixed views; for example, he thinks that the United States will retain entrepreneurial dominance over China because American culture allows people freedom to express creative thoughts whereas the Chinese communist society frowns upon it. However, Yew is more critical about some other aspects of American culture.

In 1994, Yew gave an interview which was published in my local paper, the *Pittsburgh Post Gazette*. In that interview, he identified that American civic society was vulnerable to breaking down because it had expanded individual rights to the point where individuals could behave or misbehave as they pleased without consequences, thereby destroying an orderly society.

Yew pointed out that every man has evil urges and tendencies inside of him which must be headed off, prevented, or stopped. In a society which emphasizes personal responsibilities, a man must possess a moral sense of right and wrong and stop the evil inside of him from taking over him. This prevents him from damaging those close to him and hurting the greater society. Yew observed that in American culture, individual freedom has been turned into a dogma, yet personal responsibility has been diminished.

Yew warned that this created a society where a man could do what was wrong at the expense of the society. This would, in the long run, actually reduce individuals' freedoms. Without an orderly society, individuals would no longer be able to enjoy basic freedoms. For an example, consider that in our modern society, pornography websites can distribute lewd content on the internet under the claim that they are exercising their freedoms. Meanwhile, there are no consequences to these companies; the government does not punish them or regulate them and rarely puts any sorts of limits on them.

In the long run, although these companies get great freedom, the American society suffers and each individual American gets less freedom. How? Today, your average American person cannot use the internet without worrying that some filthy advertisement or some mistyped words could land them on a site where they—or even worse, their children—do not want to be. Your average American mother must now worry that her kids are being exposed to it and that her husband is watching it. The average American teenager is now being targeted by these companies when they use the Internet. So, while these companies have gotten greater freedom, everyone else in America has to be more watchful, more suspicious, and more cautious—everyone else has lost freedoms.

On the other hand, while many of Yew's policies seemed to be overly oppressive by emphasizing personal responsibility, many Singaporeans felt that his policies actually gave them greater personal freedoms (Cheng,

2015). As Cheng noted, those who smuggle drugs get executed and those who molest women get whipped. I would certainly agree that this restricts the drug smugglers' and molesters' personal freedom. However, as Cheng goes on to say, this has resulted in greater freedoms for Singaporeans to enjoy. They can walk on the streets in the early morning hours without having to worry about getting robbed; they can leave their doors unlocked and their windows open; women can travel alone without worry; parents can send their children to school without concern. The average Singaporean does not have to worry about being exposed to porn or drugs. So, while some people will have their individual rights restricted in certain ways, this approach results in greater freedom for everyone else. I have witnessed this first hand. I walked the clean and organized streets of Singapore freely without concern for my personal safety.

We actually do behave the way Yew advises in other areas of our life here in the United States. For example, we take away people's rights to live in their own house when we put criminals in jail. We do not let felons buy guns; that is a restriction of personal freedom. We do not allow child molesters to get jobs in daycares. Yet, we do not look at these as 'restrictions on personal freedom.' Why? Because we recognize that although those people had their personal freedoms limited, they also had personal responsibilities. When these individuals did not use their personal freedoms responsibly, they lost them.

So why is it in American society a man can cheat on his spouse but there is no legal repercussion? Why is it that a porn vendor can sell pictures of naked 18-year-old kids but there are no repercussions? Why is it that we punish a college student for stealing a bottle of wine, yet that same college student has the 'personal freedom' to have sex with multiple partners? Our society has mistaken what personal freedom and personal responsibilities entail. As a result, our society has suffered. The breakdown of the nuclear family is a symptom of our inability to match responsibilities with freedoms.

Let's consider another analogy. What was your instinctive urge the first time you sat in a sports car? You probably wanted to slam down the gas pedal and see how fast the car could go! I mean, it's a sports car! But if you were in a parking lot or a driveway or a back road or even on the highway, you were not able to simply gun the engine. You had to follow the speed limit. What a bummer! You could not do what you wanted. A reasonable person would agree that this 'repression' of your urge to drive fast was actually a good thing. While you may have wanted very badly to drive the car from 0 to 100/mph as fast as possible, it is much safer and better for society and for yourself that you do not.

However, a radical freedomist would take a different view. They would argue that it should be a personal right to drive fast. After all, it's your car, so you have the right to use it how you want. America grants other kinds of rights-you have a right to free speech—and a right to petition the government—and a right to freedom of assembly. You also have a right to privacy, if certain Supreme Court cases are considered. According to the radical freedomist, because you have all these rights, you really can do whatever you want, provided you have an excuse for which right you are exercising at the moment.

While you might be seeing green lights, no matter how badly you want to gun the car to see how fast it will go, the only color you will see in the end is red. Your 'rights' are 'rights' insofar as they also burden you with responsibility. The government and society at large do not allow you to do what you want. So even though you may feel an unquenchable urge to zoom in your sports car down the highway at 100 miles an hour, you cannot. You do not have the freedom to do something so reckless or so dangerous as speeding when you want. No matter how burdensome you find traffic laws and the 'rules of the road,' you assume the responsibility to follow them simply by stepping into any car.

Similarly, you assume the responsibility to follow certain methods of behavior simply by living in a society. These include the responsibilities to respect others' well-being and freedom. You are only granted a driver's license once you agree to the responsibility to operate your vehicle in a safe manner and after you demonstrate competency with operating said vehicle. Similarly, you only get personal freedoms if you assume responsibility to exercise those freedoms in a respectful manner and after you demonstrate that you can do so maturely and competently. This is necessary not just to protect your freedom and safety but also to protect the freedom and safety of others.

Americans have misinterpreted freedom as saying that people are free to do what they want. But this is not true! Freedom grants people the right to do what they ought to do or what they should do. For example, our right to free speech only allows us to speak up when we should or when we ought to. Our right to free speech allows us to call out a bad law passed by the government or an unjust organization. It does *not* give us the right to walk into a theater and start yelling, "Fire!" and then claim, when the police arrest you for public disturbance, that you were exercising your right to free speech. Your right to free speech does not allow you to run down main street with a gun screaming at people, "I'm going to shoot you! I'm going to shoot you!" **As Americans, we do not have any rights which allow us to do what we want, when we want, the way we want; we only have rights that allow us to do what we ought, when we ought, the way we ought.** That's it! The sooner Americans realize this, the sooner we can start repairing what is wrong with our society.

One other point which must be addressed is that privacy does not equal secrecy. Your right to privacy does not give you a right to secrecy. Again, a right gives you the ability to do what you ought without repercussion. Your right to privacy gives you a right to do what you ought (like teaching your children the rules of your house), but it does not give you a right to do what you should not even if you want to (like dealing drugs out of your living room). Americans today think that if something is done in secret, then it should be protected as something in private. But this is not the case! If you do something that harms society in secret (like dealing drugs), then you are no longer protected by privacy laws or by rights to privacy. You are now answerable to the larger society for your misdeeds. Similarly, if you are cheating on your spouse, having multiple sexual partners, or not giving your children the attention they deserve, while this may all be occurring in secrecy, your right to privacy no longer protects you. You have no right to continue your poor behavior; in fact, society has the right to restrict your behavior.

CHAPTER 18

FAR FROM HOME

Thomas McCaulay once observed, "the measure of a man's real character is what he would do if he knows he would never be found out."

The United States was once an agrarian economy. One of the features of an agrarian economy is that people live further apart from each other, dotted around the countryside. In an agrarian community everyone knows everyone else. As I mentioned earlier, when people live in an area where they maintain close relationships with the area friends and family, they are much less likely to commit any sort of misbehavior (theft, adultery, murder, etc.) because their neighbors and family would find out. Close relationships to friends and family have a very dramatic effect on the way they live their life.

However, in larger towns and cities, people do not know one another. There are more people in close physical proximity, but these people are not having close relationships with one another. People in cities and larger towns have less knowledge of what is going on in others' lives. In this environment, you can keep misbehaviors like theft and adultery private. Even though the same number of people may find out, you will not be as dramatically affected, if at all.

As an illustration, I lived in a small town called Cresson in Pennsylvania for 35 years. The total population of Cresson was only 1,900. In that small town, everyone knows everyone. When I go to the post office, I know the people who work there. In fact, the clerk who weighs my mail for postage knows the street on which I live. When I go to the local bank, the tellers ask about both of my children. After I return to Cresson from a trip away, the cashier at the local grocery store asks me about my trip as she scans my food purchases. In summary, the townspeople know one another and each other's personal business.

Conversely, in New York City, a city with a population of approximately 14 million, an individual can walk down the street and not know anyone whom he or she passes. Social control is greatly lessened—for example, an individual can freely walk into an adult bookstore without anyone taking notice of such behavior. However, if you live in a small town like Cresson, then there is a greater deal of social control that influences decisions and behavior. Individuals in Cresson who enjoy respect and a higher standing are less likely to enter into an adult bookstore where others will notice and talk about such behavior. Before I lived in Cresson, Pennsylvania, there was an adult bookstore in that area. The adult bookstore was burned down. No adult bookstore opened thereafter in that area. In a culture like Cresson, Pennsylvania, the ability of an adult book store to survive and thrive was low. By contrast, a single borough of New York City that covers the same area as Cresson has, on average, 2 adult bookstores.

Let's compare decision making and behavior in these two communities. Assume the same temptation to commit adultery is faced by two individuals: one who lives in New York City and the other who lives in Cresson, Pennsylvania. The individual facing the temptation to commit adultery in Cresson, Pennsylvania is more likely to resist and decide not to act upon that temptation because the behavior will be noticed and talked about. Conversely, the individual in New York City is more likely to act upon and commit adultery because it is more likely to go unnoticed. As a result, threats to stable family life are likely to be more successful in New York City as opposed to Cresson.

Thus, there is a control mechanism which is present in small, tight-knit communities. People are more likely to know what is going on in other's lives and the inhabitants of that town are more likely to intervene. Consider the classic *To Kill a Mockingbird*. In this American court story, a black man is accused of committing a crime against a white girl in a small town called Maycomb. A white lawyer, against the advice of his community, represents the black man and shows in court that he is innocent. Instead, the town ne'er-do-well, Bob Ewell, is shown to be guilty. From that point on, everyone in the town knows Bob Ewell is guilty and treats him accordingly. Even though the white lawyer, Atticus Finch, loses the case, he gains new respect throughout the town because everyone knew he was willing to fight for the truth at court. Because the town was so small, if another person like Bob Ewell tried to come to town, they would quickly find strong social rejection. The size of the town acted like a control mechanism to prevent more people from becoming like Bob Ewell. Instead, the cultural environment encouraged people to adopt the behavior of Atticus Finch–by the end of the story, the Sheriff and even Atticus' neighbors are behaving more altruistically like him.

It has been well documented that as jobs become less agrarian and more technical, more and more people are moving to large towns, large cities, and sprawling suburbs. As more people move to societies which exert less influence and control over their behavior, the more and more they are able and willing to misbehave. It is a simple side effect of large cities and towns that social control mechanisms are lessened or dissipated. A Bob Ewell is much easier to miss in a city like New York than in a town like Cresson.

CHAPTER 19

FEEDING THE CROCODILE

"An appeaser is one who feeds a crocodile
hoping it will eat him last."
- WINSTON CHURCHILL

What does it mean to appease? To appease means to grant concessions, often at the expense of principles or right standing. It is a way of surrendering ground to others in order to create a conciliatory environment. In this chapter, I present two kinds of appeasement, sugar-coating and bending over backwards. These kinds of appeasement contribute to the breakdown of the nuclear family.

One kind of appeasement is sugar-coating, that is, calling some evil something other than its real name to make it more palatable. For example, in pre-emancipation America, slavery was often referred to by proponents as the 'peculiar institution' (Merriam-Webster, 2022). This allowed them to advocate for treating humans like animals and selling men into bondage by simply saying such human beings had been put into a 'peculiar institution.'

By this title, the pro-slavery proponents showed that they actually did feel interior qualms about slavery; they could only silence those qualms by calling slavery something other than what it was. The slavery supporters understood something fundamental: if you sugarcoat something to make it more appeasing, it becomes more acceptable. If 'peculiar institution' was a more appeasing terminology than slavery, then use it! It would make slavery more acceptable. The black evil of slavery would hopefully be whitened by the new choice of words to describe it.

The other kind of appeasement is bending over backwards, that is, giving in to external pressure to do something that is not right. For example, probably every American parent has approached the grocery store's checkout line to see rows and rows of bright-colored candy bars arrayed temptingly on tiny shelves. Of course, the candy bars are not set at an adult's eye level—that is where the magazines are—but they are set at a child's eye level. Why? Because intelligent businessmen have figured out what every parent dreads: when a child sees those candy bars on the shelves, they will want one. Oh boy, will they want one.

I am sure that every American has heard or seen or experienced a child crying or sulking in the checkout line to get a candy bar. But let's make it more personal. Imagine that you are walking down the checkout line and your four-year-old sees a Snicker's bar sitting there. "Can I have it?" they ask. What would you say? Most people would recognize three things: 1) the candy bars at the checkout line are priced a lot higher than the candy bars further back in the candy aisle in the store, 2) the candy bar is not healthy for the four-year-old, and 3) if they say 'yes,' that four-year-old kid will ask again the next time they come. So, what would most people do? Most people would say no. And while the child might be sad or sulk or even throw a full-blown tantrum, most adults would hold their ground and say no. And what do you find? After a while, your kids don't ask. They have learned that they are not going to get it. For those adults who said 'no' to the four-year-old, they have not yielded to appeasement. Although it may appear cruel to say 'no' to that four-year-old at the checkout line, in the long run it is better for the child not to have that candy bar.

Pretty much every American today would agree that sugar-coating the word 'slavery' to hide its evil nature is bad. And pretty much every

American would agree that yielding to your kid's demands for a checkout-line candy bar is bad. After all, we despise rich slavers and spoiled brats. But when it comes to another area—namely, our sexuality—most Americans turn a blind eye to the exact same kinds of appeasement.

Consider the word 'adultery.' Adultery actually refers to any kind of sexual activity with someone who is not your spouse. In other words, two college students sleeping together for one night are committing adultery. The boy is an adulterer; the girl is an adulteress. Unwedded friends having sex with each other are committing adultery. If an unwedded couple is having sex with each other, they are committing adultery. A person acting for a pornography video is committing adultery. A wedded person having an affair is an adulterer. Now these all may sound harsh, but that's the definition.

However, we have come up with all kinds of terminologies to sugarcoat and appease illicit sexual activity. It is because we do not want to admit that when people are committing adultery, they are committing adultery. We no longer want to call people adulterers or adulteresses. So now, when two college students sleep together, we say they have 'hooked up.' When people have sex before marriage, we call it 'premarital sex.' When unwedded friends have sex, we call the arrangement 'friends with benefits.' When unwedded couples live together, we call it 'cohabiting.' An adulterer or adulteress who makes porn is called an 'adult film actor.'

'Adultery' is only used now to refer to spouses who are cheating on each other. But even then, we hardly ever refer to such people as adulterers anymore. What does all of this new terminology do? Just like for slavery, it begins to 'whiten' the evils of adultery. It muddles up the picture; it distorts one's view. It helps people cover up the evils they are committing and hide them behind a curtain of complicated terminology. From 1800 to 2010, usage of the terms 'adultery,' 'adulterer,' and 'adulteress' have decreased dramatically (Google Ngram Viewer, 2020). In the same time span, 'premarital sex,' 'cohabitation,' 'casual sex,' 'hooking up,' and 'friends with benefits' all went up dramatically in their usage (Google Ngram Viewer, 2020). All of this terminology puts even slavery supporters to shame. Why, they could have called slavery 'enforced labor,' 'involuntary servitude,' or better yet, 'job skills training.' Today, if I was to call a college student who slept around an adulterer, he would probably hit me and accuse me of defamation by using inappropriate words.

Why do we sugarcoat adultery? I submit that it is because we know, in our heart of hearts, that it is wrong. We know that adult film actors, friends with benefits, and hooking up is all wrong. We know it does not lead to intimacy; we know it does not lead to love; we know it causes family breakup, mistrust, and divorce. We know it is evil. We know all these things, but we do not want to face the truth. So, we hide behind big words and hope that one day, the illicit sexual acts will become as white as the new words we use for them. But this cannot happen. Evil is evil, whether we like to call it that or not.

Our health clinics, pharmacies, governments, and schools commit the other kind of appeasement by bending over backwards to accommodate illicit sexual activity. I'm sure you've heard the spiel, "It's better to wait to have sex. But if you do choose it, make sure you use protection." This is like telling slave owners, "Slavery is wrong, but if you're going to do it anyway, make sure you give your slaves food." It is also like telling your kids, "Shouting for a candy bar is wrong, but if you're going to do it anyway, make sure you do it quickly and get it over with."

No! Slavery is wrong no matter how nicely the owner feeds his slaves. Giving in to a child's tantrum for candy bar at a checkout is wrong no matter how quickly they do it. Similarly, illicit sexual activity is still wrong no matter how much you 'protect' yourself or your partner. Rather than changing people's behavior to eliminate cheating or friends with benefits or other illicit sexual activities, we have changed our laws. We punish drunk drivers more than we punish cheating spouses. On college campuses where drinks and drugs are mixed with sex, we refuse to intervene, but there are national campaigns to prevent you from putting plastic bags in your child's reach. In the same way that pre-Civil War American culture was full of hypocrisies when it came to slavery and the value of the human person, so is our modern culture full of hypocrisies when it comes to sex and the proper role and value of sexual activity.

Appeasing leads to acceptability. If you appease your child by giving them a candy bar when they scream, then they will learn that it is acceptable to scream to get their way. If you appease slavers by selling men into a 'peculiar institution,' you will begin to accept that peculiar institution. And if you appease adulterers and adulteresses by turning a blind eye to their evil sexual behaviors, you will teach them that such behaviors are acceptable which allows such ill behavior to continue. Such behavior is a cause for the breakdown of the nuclear family. If, however, you don't give an inch to their behaviors, you will stop them.

CHAPTER 20

THE RISE OF RELATIVISM IN EDUCATION AND CULTURE

What is the purpose of education? William Bennet, the United States Secretary of Education under President Ronald Reagan from 1985-1988, proposed that education should have three goals: to build knowledge, to build skills, and to build morals. This view has been shared by virtually all proponents of education (Sloan, 2012). Bennett proposed that curriculums should abide by three C's: content, choice, and character. In other words, he advises that curriculums have correct content, that students have choices regarding which subjects to study and which curriculums to use, and that the moral character of students is built by the curriculum.

However, American schools have always had trouble with teaching morals. One reason is that morals are controversial; at one time in the 1800s, a child taught about slavery in the North would receive a very different moral standard than a child taught about slavery in the South. Another reason is that it is relatively easier to teach people knowledge and skills and set them up for a career than it is to teach them right and wrong and set them up for a good life. If anything, morals should be given more time than knowledge and skills; children should be given time to ask 'why?' and 'why not?' But, in an effort to stay out of hot water, teachers and curriculums tried to address morals by staying neutral—that is, by not addressing them.

This led to a new cultural idea called relativism. I find that relativism is widely held in America today. It is the belief that each person should come up with a personal set of morals and ethics and that he and he alone is responsible for determining and enforcing those ethics. Relativism is founded on the assumption that the only universal rule is that there are no universal rules—if you think abortion is wrong, then fine by you, but if I think that it is OK, then I am also right. In the past, philosophers agreed that there is a universal set of morals, even if they disagreed on what that set contains. For example, philosophers used to believe that it was wrong for any individual to commit murder, regardless of whether that individual personally felt that it was wrong or not. Relativism has done away with these traditional views.

Relativism is lethal to a society because it teaches everyone that anything can be right or wrong simply depending on your point of view (Austin, 2012). Relativism leads to a lot of contradictions. Consider the following: a policeman can decide that murder is wrong, so if he does not want to commit murder, OK for him. Yet a gangster can decide that murder is OK, so if he wants to commit murder, OK for him. According to relativism, both of them are correct!

Any American who has been educated should be able to see the contradiction in relativism and laugh at it. After all, relativism says that if a slave thinks slavery is wrong and if a plantation owner thinks slavery is right, they are both morally correct! Or, when Hitler killed the Jews while certain Polish communities saved the Jews, both were morally correct! I think even a 5- or 6-year-old who has been educated in morals could tell you that only one of them can be correct, and a 7- or 8-year-old could probably tell you which one.

Bennet argued that teaching knowledge and skills without teaching morals would create doctors, mechanics, lawyers, businessmen, and other professionals who were only rooted in work and money, not relationships or ethics. If such people did not believe that there was a true purpose to life or that there was even a truth at all, then they were free to do what they liked. This meant that a businessman can rationalize to say, "I will pay my workers a low wage. I think that is enough." However, the same workers can rationalize to say that their wage is too low and unfair. Or "Why should I take care of the environment? I do not care about it. Let those who care follow their own moral standards. They cannot enforce those standards on me. I do not believe in them." Or, a white person could say, "Blacks are inferior to me," and, under relativism, they would be correct!

Relativism is wrong; Bennett is correct. Schools which teach skills and knowledge without teaching morals will result in a narrow interest in work and money alone, not ethics or relationships. So, what would happen? You would create a culture focused only upon work and money and material acquisitions but falling apart in terms of relationships and ethics. Such a culture would become relativistic (everyone's morals are correct) and materialistic (everyone should work hard and get money to acquire more stuff) but become less unified and less charitable towards others.

We are seeing evidence that this has happened in America. And to see that evidence, I believe that you need look no further than the state of marriage today: it used to be that when you said, 'until death do us part,' everyone expected that you would keep your wedding vow until you died. But today, thanks to relativism, people who are getting married can suddenly pop out at any time they want and say, "I said 'until death' but I do not actually believe that I have any moral obligation to keep my promises. Instead, I think that the only moral obligation I have is to myself. So goodbye, spouse!"

Or look at racism. As I write this book, white supremacy, which was dying before, seems to be making a resurgence. I blame relativism. When Martin Luther King marched, parents and teachers could tell their kids, "Martin Luther is right!" and their kids would listen. But now that everyone believes that truth is what you want it to be, when a black person says, "All people are equal," a white supremacist can sneer, "Oh really? But your truth isn't the same as mine. In my truth, white people are better." Now how can a child hear these two rationales and reconcile their differences with relativism? He cannot! So, he can either walk away saying both are right (which is what relativism wants) or he can stand up and say that the white supremacist is wrong because there is a universal moral law which says all people are equal (which is what relativism hates).

Relativism hurts the institution of marriage. That is undeniable. It has increased the number of divorces; it has decreased the importance of relationships, and it has decreased the importance of keeping promises. I do not think that anyone would disagree with these statements (if they are a relativist, they have to say, "You're right," and if they are a rationalist who believes in truth, which is everyone else, then they would look at the data and say, 'By golly, you are right!').

CHAPTER 21

SEX EDUCATION

I propose that relativism has severely crippled more than just marital ethics, racial ethics, environmental ethics, and social ethics. I argue that the lack of morals in school and the subsequent rise of relativism has damaged one field of ethics more than all others, and that is sexual ethics. Sex education in America today is taught without any reference to morality. This approach contributes to the break-up of the nuclear family because a fundamental moral code is required for the nuclear family to exist and thrive.

Remember that schools do not teach morals? But they teach knowledge and skills, so the result is skilled, knowledgeable people who care about money and careers but not about relationships and ethics. Humor me with this question: what would happen if schools taught about some subject (subject X) without, of course, teaching the morals surrounding Subject X? Logically, I expect our view of subject X would become corrupted.

Now humor me some more. What if subject X was sex? What would happen? I expect by logical prediction that the result would be students and professionals who were focused on money, wealth, and materials goods, but also sex. In addition to being relativistic and materialistic, they would become sexually hedonistic (make sexual pleasure a god). You may be thinking nervously that it would be a bad idea for schools to teach skills, knowledge, and sex without teaching ethics or morals. You would be right;

it is a recipe for disaster. Yet that is exactly what we are doing in America today.

Let's begin with why America decided it needed sex education in schools. In 2009, *Newsweek* published a report detailing the history of sex education in America (Cornblatt). The report tracks the origin and evolution of sex education in America. The first seeds were planted in the 1890s as urbanization quickened and more Americans moved into cities. Before, during, and after World War I, sexually transmitted infection rates began spiking in cities rife with crime (like Chicago) and within the United States military population. In 1918, the US government began the first sex education program; it was not aimed at children but at soldiers and its goal was to educate soldiers about sexually transmitted diseases (STDs) and sexually transmitted infections (STIs) and how to avoid spreading them.

Within the next few years, however, the rates of STDs had become sufficiently alarming as to draw the interest and concern of the American public. In 1919, the Department of Labor's Children's Bureau began pushing for soldiers to receive sex education earlier. In fact, the Bureau suggested that the STD rates among World War I soldiers could have been prevented if those soldiers had received sex education earlier, such as when they were in school. The author of the report declared that it was cruel for society to withhold sexual information from adolescents and youth which could then cause them to be ill-informed and result in poor choices.

So, in the 1920s, sex education was introduced into American schools. In the 1930s, the US government became involved in sex education in schools; the Office of Education began its own training and curriculum development. From the 1940s to the 1960s, sex education spread throughout America into not just middle and high schools but also into colleges and universities. In the 1960s and 70s, however, opponents of sexual education (who usually objected on religious grounds) began leading a campaign against teaching children sex education. They argued that it did not emphasize ethical responsibility while teaching about sexual behaviors, thereby leaving children with more sexual knowledge then before and with no guidance except their own experimentation.

This movement was in turn opposed in the 1980s when the AIDS epidemic began gripping America. Suddenly, citizens were urging governments and schools to take action. Their response was to mandate AIDS education in schools with the hope that this sex education would stop the AIDS epidemic. The sex education developed and deployed at this time was called 'abstinence-based,' or 'abstinence, but…,' referring to its tendency to promote a message along the following lines: "abstinence is the best form of not contracting sexually transmitted diseases, but if you do choose to have sex, use a condom and a contraceptive." Today, 'abstinence-based' and 'abstinence, but' programs have come under fire for not achieving the goals of sex education (more on that later). This has triggered a shift towards another form of sex education known as 'comprehensive sex education' (Planned Parenthood Action Fund, 2020).

Now that I have run through a brief history of sex education in the United States, I would like to discuss what its goals were and are. When sex education was first conceived in the 1920s, it was designed to reduce the number of STIs in the American population. That goal has remained largely at the forefront of sex education, whether in regards to AIDS or other STIs. It was also supposed to help adolescents delay sexual activity longer. Modern sex education also has other stated goals. For example, under President Obama, sex education was reformed to also address reducing teen pregnancy. Meanwhile, others are pushing for sex education to provide more information about healthy relationships and consent (Fay, 2019).

With these goals in mind, I will next analyze whether sex education has actually met its goals. Well, results have been mixed. The number of cases of AIDS in the US has dropped by about two-thirds since the 1980s

(HIV.gov, 2019). However, the Center for Disease Control (CDC) reports that every year, there are 20 million new STD cases reported, half of which occur among people ages 15-24 (HealthyPeople.gov, 2014). About 110 million Americans had contracted an STD by 2014 (MedicineNet, 2014). Considering that there were 317 million Americans in 2014 (Schlesinger), this meant a disturbing one out of every three Americans had contracted an STD! The number of teen pregnancies has gone down, but sex education did not appear to affect whether students were sexually active or the age at which they became sexually active. This led several prominent sources to denounce 'abstinence-only' and 'abstinence, but' sex education as ineffective and outdated (Stanger-Hall and Hall, 2011) (UPenn, n.d.) (Planned Parenthood, 2020).

Some organizations, most notably Planned Parenthood, the Guttmacher Institute, and Advocates for Youth claim that the failure of 'abstinence-only' and 'abstinence, but' sex education lies in the word abstinence. They claim that teaching abstinence is morally rigid, outdated, unachievable, undesirable, unattainable, and unrealistic (Planned Parenthood, 2020) (Guttmacher Institute, nd) (Advocates for Youth, nd). They claim that it is idealistic to expect young people nowadays to abstain from sex until marriage. Thus, since nobody is going to wait that long, they think is better to remove the abstinence message promoted in sex education. On top of all of this, these organizations claim that if society does not give young Americans information about condoms or contraceptives (and where to get these services), these students will unwittingly transmit STDs, get pregnant, or have other sexually-related troubles.

Planned Parenthood and the Guttmacher Institute want Americans to endorse a different kind of education, which they term 'comprehensive sex education.' In a nutshell, comprehensive sex education would be a form of uncensored sex education. Schools would teach children about every kind of sexual activity and position, every kind of contraceptive and condom, and every method of sexual service provided by sexual health clinics. The idea here is that if children are informed on everything that they could possibly know about sex, this will help them make better decisions about their sexual lives. Of course, it is rather convenient that Planned Parenthood and the Guttmacher Institute would benefit greatly from this arrangement—after all, these students are potential Planned Parenthood customers. However, I am more interested in analyzing the thought process behind their logic.

Planned Parenthood presents a very convincing narrative, one which many people seem to agree with. However, I offer an alternative theory, one which I believe is much better backed by social evidence from America and from around the world. I believe that the problem with 'abstinence-only' and 'abstinence, but' sex education is not that it teaches abstinence. I believe that the problem with sex education lies in sex education itself.

You may have noticed a very strange assumption in all of the prior government decisions regarding sex education. The experts seemed to believe that educating students about their sexuality would naturally encourage moral sexual practices (Huber and Firmin, 2014). In other words, there seems to be a belief that if we teach students more knowledge, they will somehow naturally understand how to be more responsible and ethical with that knowledge. According to this kind of thinking, if people are making bad sexual decisions, it is because of ignorance (they don't know enough about sex). Thus, to prevent people from making bad sexual decisions, we just need to teach them more about sex sooner in their lives. Hopefully, by giving middle schoolers and high schoolers more information about their sexuality, society would have less transmission of STDs, less teen pregnancy, and fewer related societal ills.

As Planned Parenthood puts it, "Sex education is designed to help young people gain the information, skills and motivation to make *healthy* decisions about sex and sexuality throughout their lives" (2020, emphasis mine). Advocates for Youth says, "Young people have the right to lead healthy lives, and society has the responsibility to prepare youth by providing them with comprehensive sexual health education that gives them the tools they need to make *healthy* decisions. [Comprehensive sex education] must provide young people with honest, age-appropriate *information* and skills necessary to help them take personal responsibility for their health and overall well-being" (Bridges and Hauser, 2014, emphasis mine). Again, take special note of the assumption these organizations are making: if we simply give people more information, they will somehow make better decisions.

However, I strongly question this assumption. Simply giving people more information about something does not automatically make them more responsible or healthy. You must also teach them *what to do* with that information. This is like thinking that if we teach our children more about nicotine products, they will suddenly stop smoking or vaping. According to this line of thought, children smoke or vape because they are ignorant. If we taught them about cigars, cigarettes, pipes, snus, and vapes, this overload of information would suddenly make them want to stop vaping. You can probably see why this assumption is flawed—without teaching children the consequences and responsibilities regarding tobacco decisions, this education will probably instead encourage them to try even more nicotine products! Simply handing people more options does not make them more responsible unless they are also told how to use those options responsibly and morally. Simply making sex education less and less censored will not automatically teach students better decision-making skills about sex.

The US education system wants adolescents to be instructed in how to stay healthy, live responsibly, and make good decisions. Now all of these are good things. I want everyone to learn these things. But, as I mentioned previously, it is impossible to teach someone how to stay healthy, live responsibly, and make good decisions unless the content is grounded in a solid moral base. You can give students information about anything you like, whether it is money, sex, tobacco, or racism. Without teaching morals to the students at the same time, this information download will not help them make better decisions.

Consider the organization Alcoholics Anonymous. How does this organization help people who are addicted to alcohol learn how to live normal, alcohol-free lives? It uses a 12-step approach which first teaches the participant to ground themselves in moral certainties, evaluate where they are in relation to those moral certainties, and then take steps to improve their behavior. This 12-step approach, by grounding itself in morals, has managed to save thousands of former alcoholics' lives (Walters, 2015).

Similarly, it is possible that any sort of educational program, whether about sex, disease, violence, or entertainment, if grounded in solid morals and encouraging students to evaluate and discuss morals, would be able to achieve similar beneficial results. However, modern sex education is not grounded in morals. Because of this, I find that it does not encourage healthy behavior, personal responsibility, or good decision-making. In fact, it does quite the opposite. I identify five fundamental flaws with sex education as it is taught in America today. It does not matter whether it is 'abstinence, but' or 'comprehensive' sex education—these flaws are still present and contribute to the breakdown of the nuclear family.

1. Fundamental Flaw #1- Sex Education Assumes that Abstinence is Impossible

First, is it abnormal or impossible for people to abstain from sex before marriage? According to the Guttmacher Institute, the answer is yes. The Guttmacher Institute claims that 99% of Americans have pre-marital sex, so it is unrealistic for sex education to focus solely on abstinence. Rather, the Guttmacher Institute advocates for sex education that also addresses how to use contraceptives and condoms, saying that this will be more realistic to what the population needs (Guttmacher Institute, 2006).

However, there are a few problems with this line of reasoning. Foremost, this line of reasoning ignores that in America up until the 1920s, it was very uncommon for anyone to have pre-marital sex (ibid). Were Americans from 1776-1920 having multiple partners? No. So, the first takeaway is that it is certainly *possible* for a society to exist without pre-marital sex. In fact, American society, with its guaranteed liberties and freedoms, has spent the majority of its existence without pre-marital sex. Even if we take Guttmacher Institute's numbers at face value, Americans have only been engaging in premarital sex in appreciable numbers for less than 100 years.

Well wait, you might say. *That was then; times have changed. Isn't it impossible to expect abstinence before marriage in modern times?* Once again, the answer is no. Consider that even if the Guttmacher Institute's statistics are correct and that 99% of Americans have had premarital sex, this is not the norm around the world. As recently as 2016, more than 40% of Japanese adults reported being virgins (Aoki). Note that this includes all adults—it means that there is likely an even higher percentage of adults who are waiting/have waited until their wedding to have sex. In the same year, around 30% of Chinese adults reported not having sex before marriage (just 25 years earlier, that number was around 80%) (Buckley, 2016). In 2018, researchers in Indonesia found that almost 90% of the population was not having sex before marriage (Berliana et al). In that same year, 98% of single women in India and 90% of single men in India reported not having pre-marital sex (Kundu and Bhattacharya)—this study also used cross-analysis methods to eliminate biases in reporting.

From this data, it is glaringly obvious that around the world, regardless of religion or culture, abstinence before marriage has historically been the overwhelmingly most common practice. Thus, it is incorrect to claim that abstinence before marriage is impossible; humanity has done it that way for thousands of years all around the world. Moreover, even today, with all of the glamorized, sexualized media content spilling out of the West into the rest of the world, virginity rates have remained practically unchanged in countries with strong cultural or religious ties (only in China, which has diminished its cultural ties and broken its religious ties, has there been such a dramatic shift).

2. Fundamental Flaw #2- Sex Education Defeats Its Own Purpose

The second flaw with sex education is that it perpetuates the problems it tries to solve. How? Pretend that you are teaching a class of teenagers about nicotine use. You show them how to roll and smoke cigarettes, how to fill and smoke tobacco pipes, how to load and vape e-cigarettes, and how to roll and smoke cigars. When you have taught the teenagers everything there is about the topic of nicotine use so they are "well-informed," you tell them that they should not smoke or vape—but if they do, there are ways to "reduce the risk" so they "don't get caught."

Now some of those teenagers may be curious and some may have already smoked a cigarette or vaped before; do you know what these teenagers will do? Since you have taught the teenagers how to make and use nicotine products without being caught, some of them are going to do it! Rather than reducing the number of teenagers who smoke or vape, you have reduced the barriers they faced to smoking and nicotine use.

If you truly want to reduce nicotine use among teenagers, stop teaching the teenagers about the different kinds of tobacco products and how to use them. If you stop teaching about tobacco products and how to use them, this increases the chances that impressionable teenagers will not hear about the different methods of nicotine use and decrease the probability that they will ever use tobacco. Similarly, if you want to decrease the occurrence of premarital sex, stop teaching young people in school about sex. This will increase the chances that the young people will not hear about sex and decrease the probability that they will engage in that activity.

As a point of reference, consider a historical example. In the United States in the 19th century, the South remained racist for a longer period than the North. How do you think the South was able to remain racist for so long? Schools reinforced the racial creeds of society and helped children retain the racism. Similarly, how can you expect to teach teenagers explicit content about sex (the how to), remove personal responsibility (if you're going to do it anyway...), and then expect them to not have unrealistic desires or bad behaviors (what? you did it? oh, ok)?

If I told you, "Don't murder...but if you do, wear gloves so they won't lift your fingerprints to catch you." Or "Don't post racist comments online—but if you do, make sure you use an anonymous account so it can't be traced to you," how can I hope to discourage you? If I am teaching a teenager sensual content, which will activate their pleasure response (that's basic science), and then tell them they should not engage in it BUT if they do, they can do it in x, y, and z way, how do you expect to discourage premarital sex, teenager sex, or STD transmission?

The 'abstinence' education which says, 'abstinence, but' defeats its own purpose. Let's consider an analogy. Children are very cognizant of what adults expect of them. If you tell a child, "There are cookies in the jar on the counter. Don't eat them while I'm gone," what do you expect will happen? Most children will not touch the cookies while you are gone. A handful of children might—but they will know that what they are doing directly violates what they should be doing. And when you come home and inevitably find out cookies are missing from the jar, they know there will be a reckoning. You would be able to use the opportunity to teach them self-control, perhaps by giving them a talk or by putting them in timeout; next time, they would be less likely to take the cookies while you are gone.

But if you said, "don't touch the cookies while I'm gone, but if you do, make sure you protect yourself from some of the consequences by putting something at the bottom of the jar so when I look inside, it does not look like anything is gone," what do you think is going to happen? By planting an idea of how to circumvent the system in the child's mind, they are more likely to do it! And some children, who would not have done it anyway, might be interested in trying to see if they can really do it and get away with it! Similarly, any sort of abstinence message which says, "Be abstinent! But if you cannot, here are 10 ways to protect yourself from some of the consequences (the physical ones, not the societal or emotional ones) and here are 10 things you can use so your parents do not realize anything is wrong," this abstinence message will not be effective.

3. Fundamental Flaw #3- Sex Education Cannot Condemn Anyone

Sex education teaches nothing if it does not include morals. The message from Planned Parenthood is that abstinence education has not made any progress, so abstinence is impossible, and the abstinence-only message must be abandoned. I think this is an odd conclusion.

Sex education cannot teach children how to behave well if their parents and the culture are teaching them a bad behavior. As one middle school teacher put it, "How can I stand up there and preach abstinence when these kids' parents are living with someone but are not wedded?" If a child's mother has had three live-in boyfriends, teachers are afraid they may inadvertently condemn the parent in the eyes of the child or appear to be shaming the parent (Nazario, 1992, Wall Street Journal).

In other words, how do you teach children to wait to have sex until after the wedding when their parents are not doing so themselves? There is no possible way for American schools to teach sex education in a way that will instill in children the morals that we as a society want (e.g. don't have sex when you're 13) without offending or embarrassing or casting a negative light on some of us. Why, then, do we insist on saddling schools with an impossible dilemma? Sex education should not be their responsibility; it should not be in their realm.

I was once watching the show *America's Got Talent* and one of the contestants, a comedian, came onstage. Before she began her routine, the judges asked her some questions about herself. She revealed that she was a marriage counselor at her church—and that she had been divorced three times. After she said that, she laughed and waved her hand, saying, "Life is hilarious!" Now there are many things I could say about this, but let's start with this analogy: if you learned that your child' new school bus driver crashed their previous three school buses, would you want your child to ride in the bus driven by the driver with such a poor driving record? Probably not.

I would not want to take a marriage prep course to find out that the instructor had been divorced three times. I would wonder, *wait, you're teaching me this stuff, but you don't actually do it yourself? Then how do you expect me to follow it?* I find that a similar issue has pervaded American schools. One of the side effects of divorce on society is that teachers are also getting divorced. A 2015 study by the Census Bureau found that 30% of postsecondary teachers have been divorced; the number was virtually the same for all other kinds of teachers and teaching assistants.

Traditionally, children hold their teachers as role models. So, when a child finds a role model and learns that that role model has been divorced, what will it show them? I am not implying that divorced teachers stand up in their classes and say, "Get divorced! Divorce is great!" I'm just pointing out that if someone the child respects is divorced, it may make them consider it in their mind—the same way seeing a football player or musician touting a certain product can influence them to buy that product. Our teachers are not pure and innocent; they are part of the outside world that they inhabit. Thus, it is unwise to entrust them to teach children to make good choices in an area of life that the teachers themselves may not have made good choices in.

4. Fundamental Flaw #4- Sex Education Presumes that Abstinence is Repressive

Abstinence is not repressive or backwards. Society has always imposed moral standards on sexual behavior—there has always been 'good' and 'bad.' Most cultures (including the USA) condemn rape. So, is the USA repressive in that way?

Should Americans have a problem with shame? Institutions like the Guttmacher Institute, Planned Parenthood, and Advocates for Youth say that it is wrong to discourage or condemn premarital sexual activity because it is 'shaming' those children who have premarital sexual activity. They say that 'shaming' someone is wrong; that making someone feel shame is wrong. They tell horror stories of children who were so ashamed of finding they were pregnant or had an STD that they committed suicide or made other frightening decisions as a result.

I would note that these institutions got one thing right: shame is a very powerful force. It can drive a person to despair over the deeds they have done. But shame can also stop a person from making a bad decision when nothing else—either rational arguments or love or common sense—can do so. So, is it right to say that feeling shame is wrong? Is it right to say that making someone else feel shame is wrong? I would say no. If you have done something wrong, then it is appropriate for you to feel shame. You should be ashamed of your action or decision. If someone else has done something wrong, then it is right for them to feel shame.

Consider this—in July 2020, while the coronavirus pandemic was raging in the United States, a couple walked into a grocery store wearing bandanas that bore the Nazi swastika. They did this to protest the orders to wear facemasks. I argue (and many people would agree) that the couple should be ashamed of themselves. It is wrong to walk around brandishing the symbol of a totalitarian nation which murdered millions and which our forefathers shed blood to fight in a twisted demonstration of freedom.

Let us take this back to premarital sex. Should young people be ashamed when they have premarital sex? I think they should. (*Gasp*). If it is wrong, then it is wrong, and they should be ashamed about it. The key is not to tell them that it is alright so they feel better; the key is that they should accept their shame and stop making bad decisions. It is wrong to assume that shame will always drive our children to despair and suicide. Shame is a natural way to motivate us to improve on something we have done wrong. Telling our children that they should never feel ashamed or uncomfortable is doing them a disservice.

5. Fundamental Flaw #5- Parents Should Teach Morals; Schools Cannot

Some argue that there should be no limits to sex education, like the National Education Association (NEA). The NEA has advocated for sex education to begin in kindergarten. Kindergarten? Why stop there? Why don't we just start teaching the kids sex education the instant they're born? It will make sure they are 'well-informed' so they can make 'healthy decisions regarding their sexuality.' Or, why don't we go one step better and start teaching them while they're still in the womb? You may be laughing, but realize this—any rational person would admit that there is an appropriate age and time to introduce sexual topics to a child. I would also add that there is an appropriate place and there are appropriate persons to introduce sexual topics—and for most of those topics, the appropriate place is the child's home and the appropriate persons are the child's parents. Who else is most qualified to give their children good moral instruction?

Sex education in schools must be modified because what is taught is not sex education, but rather sexual immorality. Currently, sexual education is for the purpose of avoiding STDs. Former sex educators have revealed that they addressed topics such as what it means to masturbate, what is oral sex, and what is vaginal and anal intercourse along with other kinds of sexual experience. These educators were told that their audience of middle school children were already doing all these kinds of behaviors, so their job was simply to tell them how to do it safer (Olohan, 2019).

This approach does not prevent STDs but overshadows traditional moral values. Instead, sex education should include that responsible sex is waiting for sex until after your wedding and only with your spouse. This is the safest sex! Students should be taught that exercising discipline and chastity by postponing sex is best for your future. The biology of sex should be taught in a morally acceptable rather than a feigned morally neutral manner. Birth control and condoms should not be given to schoolchildren as a responsible way to handle sex. The sex education curriculum must be reformed.

A large percentage of the American population thinks that it is necessary for schools to teach sex education. I disagree. Do schools need to teach a fish how to swim? Sex is an instinct, just like eating and drinking. Parents are the ones who teach their children how, when, and what to eat and drink; in fact, we look to parents to teach their children what is healthy to eat and drink. I believe parents should teach their children about sex. Parents are perfectly capable of doing so; they have experience, or they would not have kids!

Some people claim that parents teaching their children is a problem because parents might not tell children about the "whole spectrum" of sexual activities, like bathing together or oral sex, or tell their children about condoms or birth control. I propose that it is the parents' decision! (Gasp). We let parents decide what deserts their kids can have and how much quantity they can have. We do not impose upon schools the job of teaching children about the "whole spectrum" of deserts, from ice cream to brownies to cakes. It is not the school's responsibility to make sure that kids are 'well-informed' about the 'whole spectrum' of deserts. Likewise, allow parents to decide what to tell their children about sex. This is not the job of sex education in schools.

If schools want to teach anything, they can teach chastity education. Chastity should be promoted for all unmarried people. There are certain things that are necessary for human life, such as food and water. Sexual activity is not necessary for a person to live their life. Therefore, young people must be introduced to the virtues of discipline and chastity. Children should be taught that a family consists of a father, a mother, and biological children (and/or adopted children). All children must be taught that a physical union between a male and a female counts as a marriage, regardless of commitment level and regardless of the wedded status of the spouses.

Children should be taught that real love is sacrifice. Saying, "I love my wife," means that the husband will do anything for her needs, even if that requires him to give up other things. The more intense the sacrifice, the deeper the love. Love demands commitment, which means staying true to the oath of lifelong marriage, until "death does us part." Commitment requires contentment, which means being happy with what you have. Instead of desiring qualities that are absent in your spouse, you need to be satisfied with the qualities that your spouse has and focus on improving yourself. All these truths should also be incorporated into the curriculums of elementary, middle school, and high school courses. Introducing these truths into the school curriculums will expose children to the necessary elements to create a strong nuclear family for themselves. Failure to teach these truths in the school curriculums will not equip today's American children to adopt and adhere to the fundamental moral principal's of a stable nuclear family life.

CHAPTER 22

CRAZY COLLEGES

When a school teaches knowledge and skills without morals, the results are corrupt intellectuals. When a school teaches knowledge, skills, and sex without morals, the result is intellectually brilliant, morally hollow, sexually promiscuous students. That is found on any college campus in America today. How do I know they are brilliant? I find them to be brilliant by the technological advances of the last decade. How do I know they are sexually promiscuous and morally hollow? Well, when my grandson recently did his orientation at a large state university, he learned that 75% of the students drink alcohol underage and that 25% of females on campus reported being a victim of sexual violence. 75%! 25%! These are terrible rates! These numbers are reflective of the nation's colleges (Pauly, 2019). These statistics reflect an environment inhabited by morally hollow, sexually promiscuous students.

While most schools have eliminated the teaching of morals, a few have quietly encouraged corruptive, immoral behavior. For an example, look no further than college dormitories in America. When I went to college back in the 1960s, there were guys-only dormitories and there were girls-only dormitories. Dating was as common then as it is now, but pre-marital sexual activity was much less common. Thereafter, colleges and universities began mixing male students and female students in student housing. First, they began male students on one floor and female students on the next floor.

Then, they put rooms with male students and rooms with female students on the same floor. Today, male and female students can share the same dorm room at many colleges, including the University of Pennsylvania, Oberlin College, Brown University, and Standford University (The Associated Press, 2008)!

It is ludicrous to pretend that there is some benefit to higher education by moving male and female students into such close living quarters. In 2009, Rueters reported on a study which found that coed dormitories had, on average, double the rate of sexual promiscuity and more than double the rate of binge drinking when compared to non-coed dormitories (Norton, 2009). Pornography use also increased in these co-ed dorms (LiveScience, 2009). Dr. Brian Willoughby, the lead researcher, noted that the shift from single-sex dormitories to co-ed dormitories was part of a larger move away from the traditional notion that colleges should act as substitutes for parents and enforce rules on students' social behavior. In other words, it was because colleges had decided that they should act as places for students to do what they wanted, rather than as places for students to learn responsibility. He added, "This transition to co-ed housing has happened without an evaluation of its effects"—in other words, we have no idea what this will do to students' long-term physical and social health, to say nothing of society's health or the nuclear family's health.

Now anybody could tell you that the purpose of a university of higher education is to turn students into scholars. So why have our colleges and universities made decisions which are turning our students into promiscuous individuals? As Gallagher notes, "Young adults are affected by their environment, including any cues adults give them about what kind of behavior is expected." The move of colleges and universities to co-ed dorms for no logical reason or benefit to education shows that they are subtly encouraging drinking and sexual misbehaviors among students—or at least turning a blind eye. How could we expect this to not result badly?

When I visited some eminent college and university dormitories in the 80s and 90s, I asked some of the students whether they thought co-ed housing might encourage immoral behaviors. "Definitely not," they replied. "Don't you trust us?" "No, I don't," I responded. "You are not a piece of stone that cannot have feelings. You are a human being made of flesh. If you put iron and magnets together, what do you think will happen?" If you put male and female students together at a young age and mix in drugs, alcohol, porn, locked doors, and no supervision, what do you expect is going to happen?

One student perhaps gave a better justification than the just-trust-me line; he responded, "Well, isn't morality a private matter?" While he perhaps took the time to make an argument rather than an evasion, his argument is still shallow. Sexual ethics, like all ethics, is a public matter, not a private matter. Ethics of lying, cheating, killing, and making money are all considered to be public matters because they have public consequences. Sexual behavior has resounding public consequences; those who drink alcohol and engage in sex are more likely to suffer from diseases, those who mix alcohol and sex are more likely to experience a sexual assault or rape, and those who engage in sexual behaviors with multiple partners are more likely to contract and spread sexually transmitted diseases. So, colleges and universities are wrong. They cannot back out of discussions of morality or let students do what they want. Colleges and universities should be on the forefront of teaching responsible moral and ethical decision-making.

Let me put it this way: if you walked into a neighborhood and saw rundown houses, broken windows, rusted cars, stray dogs, broken fences, and unmaintained lawns, would you want to live there? Would you want your kids to be educated in that environment and live in that environment? You wouldn't. This is because a physical premise can help reveal to you the moral and social tone of that environment. So, when the physical sleeping premises at universities seem designed to create environments of lax standards, lax oversight, and lax morals, why are we content to sit idly by and let our college-age children live in that environment?

Why is it that we allow higher education institutions which are publicly funded to ignore morals? It is well within the public interest to develop college and university graduates with good morals. Why do we throw the responsibility back to the homes and the parents? Why is it that when a college or university begins to show a hint of morality, we refuse to support it with public funds? Why are we scared of teaching morals to college and university students? What do we have to lose? We clearly have much to gain.

CHAPTER 23

REGARDING RELIGION

Do you know who George Washington is? That question may sound absurd; of course, you know! He was the first President of the United States! He was the Commander of the Continental Army! He basically laid the foundation for America to be a democracy, free from tyranny, with peaceful transitions of power!

Although you probably know all this about George Washington, you probably do not know that in his 1796 Farewell Address, he wrote "Of all the dispositions and habits which lead to political prosperity, religion and morality are indispensable supports. In vain would that man claim the tribute of patriotism, who should labor to subvert these great pillars of human happiness, these firmest props of the duties of men and citizens. The mere politician, equally with the pious man, ought to respect and to cherish them. A volume could not trace all their connections with private and public felicity. Let it simply be asked: Where is the security for property, for reputation, for life, if the sense of religious obligation desert the oaths which are the instruments of investigation in courts of justice? And let us with caution indulge the supposition that morality can be maintained without religion. Whatever may be conceded to the influence of refined education on minds of peculiar structure, reason and experience both forbid us to expect that national morality can prevail in exclusion of religious principle."

This is a jam-packed statement; let's take it apart. First, Washington claims that religion and morality are 'indispensable supports' of prosperity. Any man who subverts these two 'great pillars of human happiness,' even in the name of patriotism, would be severely damaging the nation. Religion is not for pious men alone to respect, but also for other higher-class individuals, such as politicians. Washington remarks that without a sense of religious obligation, the rights which Americans enjoy regarding property, reputation, and life, would all be put in jeopardy. And Washington was not convinced that a society could maintain a proper sense of morality without religion. Indeed, he declares that the national sense of morality would decay if separated from religious principles. In essence, George Washington believed that it was virtually impossible for a society to remain morally upright and prosperous if it attempted to separate morality from religion.

And so, we come to the first and perhaps greatest role of religion in a society—it can inject moral values into a person's day-to-day life in a way no other institution can. Religion can be a means of dictating behavior and guiding human relationships in a way that no other organization can hope to achieve. Most people would agree that religions can have a strong effect on individuals' lives. However, a growing percentage of Americans are distancing themselves from religion.

One reason often cited by these people is that they do not see religion helping society. However, a quick examination of the historical records, along with empirical evidence, shows that while religious organizations have occasionally committed grievous atrocities, the majority of religions have helped rather than hindered the wellbeing of adherents. In fact, research is essentially unanimous when discussing the benefits of religion. Religion has been praised by the National Alliance on Mental Illness (Greenstein, 2016), Psychology Today (Feldman, 2018), Time Magazine (Walsh), Forbes Magazine (Fisher, 2019), and the Heritage Foundation (Fagan,

1996). Some, like Fagan, lay out how religion is indispensable to social stability; others, like atheist Stephen Asma, believe that religion provides things which natural or human laws cannot (New York Times, 2018).

Without religious organizations like the Catholic Church, society would not have universities, the Big Bang theory, the Gregorian Calendar, non-profit hospitals, social justice, or the scientific method (Marcel, 2016). For every Galileo situation (where the Church directly opposed the idea of a heliocentric world), there are ten Gregor Mendels (a Catholic monk and the father of genetics), Albert the Greats (a Catholic monk who developed the scientific method), and J. B. Macelwanes (a Catholic priest who pioneered seismology). The idea that the universe has well-ordered laws that could be discovered came from the Christian faith and laid the foundation for the Enlightenment (Woods, 2011). Without religion, none of the philosophical, scientific, or mathematical discoveries of the Babylonians, Greeks, and Persians would have survived to the modern world. In short, religion has been largely beneficial, not detrimental, to the well-being of modern society (Finegan, 2018).

Why do I bring religion into a book about the break-up of the nuclear family? The answer is, *how could I not bring religion into a book about the break-up of the nuclear family?* There is no force, organization, institution, or establishment on the face of the earth which can either discourage or promote nuclear families quite like religions. Any book about nuclear families which does not address religion's role as a cause and potential solution is incomplete. It is foolhardy to exclude religion from any conversation about the nuclear family.

Without religion, who can say that men and women should be married? Who can say that a married man and woman should remain faithful to each other? Who can provide these directives and also provide the necessary support to make it happen? I do not think it is government. It is religion. Why? Because government authority is dependent upon the will of the people. A government, specifically a democratic government, necessarily asks the question, 'what do the people want?' and then tries to provide it. This is how a democracy runs. However, religious authority is not dependent upon the will of the people. A religion does not ask 'what do the people want?' but asks 'what is morally correct?' or 'what does God want?'

How is this beneficial? Consider that in a democracy like the United States, slavery was allowed when a majority of the people in America thought black men were not truly men. Because a democracy asks, 'what do the people want,' it can become an instrument of oppression or immorality if that is what the majority of the people want. A democracy can be floated about on the winds of cultural change.

Perhaps this is why John Adams, the second President of the United Sates, stated, "We have no government armed with the power capable of contending with human passions unbridled by morality and religion. Avarice, ambition, revenge, and licentiousness would break the strongest cords of our Constitution, as a whale goes through a net. Our Constitution was made only for a moral and religious people. It is wholly inadequate to the government of any other." Adams was absolutely correct; for years, America broke the Constitutional right that every man is equal and treated black men as inferior because the democracy acted on the immoral will of the majority of the people. Adams recognized that if there is no higher moral code or authority, a democracy will be carried away by the wishes of the people, even if those wishes are wrong.

However, things are different in a religion. Religions all claim that their authority comes from a higher, constant source—either from a God or gods, or from some other spiritual power or law. This means that a religion has one quality which a democracy does not; by asking 'what is right?' or 'what does God want?' rather than asking 'what do the people want?' Religion is able to avoid the pitfalls of uncontrolled popular opinion.

It was on religious grounds that the abolitionists made their case against slavery. They claimed that God had created all men equal, and this moral code was constant and higher than any law created by the US democracy. Thus, a religion could say that when the US democracy treated black men as inferior, even if this was the will of the people, it was still wrong. Fundamentally, a religion looks in a completely different place for a standard of behavior than a government. A government looks to the people (or, in a dictatorship, looks to one man). A religion looks up to heaven and tries to determine what the standards of behavior are up there; if the standard of behavior is that all men are equal, then a religion strives to adopt that same standard and prescribes that same standard to its adherents, regardless of how popular or culturally unacceptable that is. If you do not agree, ask yourself why Communist Russia and China destroyed organized religion as one of their first moves. They understood that religion could teach people truths about freedom and liberty which they did not want their people to know. Once they destroyed organized religion, they were able to create whatever laws they wanted—even if those laws were unjust.

I can give a historical example of how religion can dramatically affect the social life and wellbeing of a society. Consider the role of women in the household and in the society. Before the time of the Catholic Church, women were treated as inferior to men in practically all cultures and societies. When the Christian religion began in the Roman Empire, it was largely dismissed by powerful and influential men as a "women's religion." Why? Because it advocated for the equal treatment and dignity of all human beings, including women. Essentially, the Christian religion claimed that Jesus Christ had shown them the higher moral reality of the universe—and it did not tolerate unequal treatment of the sexes (Finegan, 2018). Perhaps it is no surprise that women flocked to this religion.

Today, the influence of the Christian religion in making women equal to men is undeniable. It was in the Christian nations that women were first held to be equal to men; it is in the Christian nations today where women are free to exercise their rights. I bring this example to show that religions can do something for society which nothing else can: they can point humans to a transcendental reality or truth which requires them to behave in a moral manner. Religions have an authority which other institutions simply do not have. My main takeaway here is that religions are vital. We can delve into a historical debate about the good things and bad things religions have done, but they are positioned to help improve things in a way nothing else can by virtue of the way they search for truth in reality.

I strongly believe in a moral reality which is higher than governments or man-made laws. This means two things. The first is that we do not get new moral realities. We have the same moral realities for all times, for all places and for all people. All men are equal. Women and men are equal. Slavery is wrong. Racism is wrong. The nuclear family should be supported. These are all moral realities.

The second thing is that our societal changes in behavior are because we either live up to the moral realities we ought to have lived up to in the first place (like with slavery) or we abandon moral realities we ought to keep upholding (like the nuclear family). One cannot claim that the abolition of slavery was because we achieved a new moral reality—slavery has always been wrong and will always be wrong. Similarly, one cannot claim that premarital sex and divorce are because we achieved a new moral reality—these have always been wrong and will always be wrong.

What do religions do for society? All religions throughout the world have one thing in common: they have established a code of conduct for right human living which is prescribed to adherents of that religion. Religions provide a moral framework regarding personal behavior and act as corrective forces for human behavior. They provide a moral compass that defends, respects, and stands by truth and create a moral power which is higher than expert power, governmental power, or military power in the hearts of adherents. Religions refresh, remind, reinvigorate, revitalize, and reinforce moral values, rather than simply doing the will of the people. Culture reflects the way we behave and think. Religion is able to have a strong influence on this.

It is no secret that strong religious affiliation and church attendance decreases socially undesirable behaviors in a population, including drinking, smoking, and theft (Adamczyk et al., 2017) (Cengage, 2020) (Jang, 2019). The Pew Research Center has well-documented evidence that a growing proportion of Americans have become 'nones,' meaning that they adhere to no religion at all. There are also growing numbers of atheists (those who believe there is no God) and agnostics (those who neither believe or disbelieve in god or religion, neutral) in the US.

The data seems to indicate that a large part of our modern social ills, from premarital sex to divorce, lie in the gradual dissolution of religion in the United States. For example, a 2018 study by the Pew Research Center found that a large percentage of atheists, nones, and agnostics (usually 11-13%) were cohabiting and that as many were married as were single. Meanwhile, the percentage of self-identified Mormons, Catholics, Jews, Methodists, and Episcopals who were cohabiting was much smaller (usually 2-3%) and a clear majority were married. A Pew Research Center study on Catholics found that those who actively practiced their religious beliefs had a 31% lower divorce rate than non-religious individuals (Betts, 2018). In 2015, another study by a University of Connecticut Sociology professor also found that divorce rates were higher among nones than among most religiously-affiliated groups (Wright, 2015).

Why is it that religions seem to foster marriages and nuclear families? Well, this is nothing new. Philosophers and religious down the ages have always respected marriage as between one man and one woman. They have always supported and promoted such marriages. Why? Was it because they were ignorant bigots? I do not think so. I think that they had their thumb on a natural law of humanity: the strongest and best weddings are those between one man and one woman, and a strong nuclear family requires one of these to thrive.

There is a memorable passage in the Bible regarding marriage and divorce. I think it very applicable to today's society: Matthew 19: 3-12.

Some Pharisees approached [Jesus], and tested him, saying, "Is it lawful for a man to divorce his wife for any cause whatever?" Jesus said in reply, "Have you not read that from the beginning the Creator 'made them male and female' and said, 'For this reason a man shall leave his father and mother and be joined to his wife, and the two shall become one flesh'? So, they are no longer two, but one flesh. Therefore, what God has joined together, no human being must separate."

They said to Jesus, "Then why did Moses command that the man give the woman a bill of divorce and dismiss [her]?" Jesus said to them, "Because of the hardness of your hearts Moses allowed you to divorce your wives, but from the beginning it was not so. I say to you, whoever divorces his wife (unless the marriage is unlawful) and marries another commits adultery."

[His] disciples said to him, "If that is the case of a man with his wife, it is better not to marry." Jesus answered, "Not all can accept [this] word, but only those to whom that is granted. Some are incapable of marriage because they were born so; some, because they were made so by others; some, because they have renounced marriage for the sake of the kingdom of heaven. Whoever can accept this ought to accept it."

Let's take this scripture piece by piece. First, the Pharisees ask Jesus if divorce is permissible for any reason. He eloquently says no, with the argument that God created humans as male and female at the beginning, that they were designed to be unified, and that once they have chosen before God to become unified through marriage, no man can break it.

The Pharisees are surprised and say that Moses the prophet allowed them to write bills of divorce, so why won't Jesus? Jesus retorts that Moses only allowed this because of the stubbornness of their hearts. In other words, the problem is not with marriage; the problem is with human stubbornness. Then it gets even better! Jesus' own disciples come to him and remark that if divorce is not permissible, then it is better not to get married at all (this is indeed a sentiment with echoes in today's culture, is it not?). Jesus again replies that the problem is not with marriage, but with human immorality; he says that some are incapable of living up to the marriage covenant for various reasons or forgo it for religious reasons. However, for the majority of people, it ought to be accepted. When you read that, you should be wondering why, in a country as rich, powerful and prosperous as the United States, there are so many people who do not accept this word. How can such a nation be unable to accept something so simple? How can so many people proudly go around saying they are not able to accept something so simple?

There is another memorable passage I would like to delve into regarding Jesus and marriage. It involves a time when Jesus was speaking with a woman at a well. This is from John 4: 16-18:

"Jesus said to her, "Go call your husband and come back." The woman answered and said to him, "I do not have a husband." Jesus answered her, "You are right in saying, 'I do not have a husband.' For you have had five husbands, and the one you have now is not your husband. What you have said is true."

Jesus is pointing out that even though the woman does not have a legal (or moral) husband at the time, she has had several husbands by physical union. This passage confirms that a physical union between a man and a woman creates the relationship of marriage. The woman at the well has had physical union with five separate men and Christ recognizes all of them as her 'husbands.' Today in our society, men and women pick up someone of the opposite sex and have physical union with them at their convenience—yet we fail realize that each physical union creates a marriage, whether we admit it or not.

It was Lucretius who remarked, *tantum religio potuit suadere malorum.* That is Latin for 'To such heights of evil has religion been able to drive men.' I mentioned earlier that religions look to the heavens rather than to the people when synthesizing moral doctrine. However, there are two errors one can fall into with this approach. The first error is when a religion does not truly find a piece of moral law as intended by God, but creates one itself- the false doctrine problem. The second error is when a religion ignores the true moral law intended by God in order to go along with popular opinion- the appeasement problem.

Religion has committed both errors throughout history, and religion will continue to do so until the end of time. Since I am writing primarily for an American audience, I will give examples from the Christian religion.

Some Christian churches have altered their doctrines regarding marriage. The original divorce doctrine accepted by all Christian churches originates in the Catholic Church. Specifically, divorce was not permitted by Christ in any case except in situations expressly specified by Christ; Christ said an unlawful marriage was considered to mean lewd conduct or abandonment and eligible for divorce. Some Christian churches have committed the false doctrine problem. The Orthodox church teaches that while Christ 'generally prohibited' the practice, divorce was an acceptable option in a "broken and virtually nonexistent marriage" (ReligionFacts, 2017). What on earth is that language supposed to mean? Marriages either exist or they do not, much the same as your head exists or it does not. There is no such thing as a 'virtually nonexistent' marriage; while the bond between the spouses may be bruised, strained, or otherwise damaged by the conduct of the spouses, it does not make the marriage any more nonexistent than bruising your head makes it disappear.

In addition, while Christ condemned remarriage after civil divorce as 'adultery,' the Lutheran Church created its own views on remarriage, which is an example of the false doctrine problem. According to the Evangelical Lutheran Church of America, "remarriage can be an opportunity to use wisdom gained from the past to create a new relationship of loving commitment and joy" (ReligionFacts, 2017)(see Eleventh General Convention of the American Lutheran Church *Teachings and Practice on Marriage, Divorce, and Remarriage*). This is completely misunderstanding what a marriage is. You can use wisdom gained from a friendship to make better friendships in the same way you can use wisdom gained from one job to do better at a later job. However, you cannot use wisdom gained from one marriage to help make a subsequent marriage better. You can only be married to one person of the opposite sex at any time.

Then there are Christians who have committed the second error- the appeasement problem- by ignoring the truth in order to accept or pay lip service to cultural fads. A glaring example is in the use and distribution of contraception. In 1968, contraceptives like the Pill had just been developed. Congregations were turning to their pastors asking for permission to use these new drugs. In that year, Pope Paul VI released a document entitled *Humanae Vitae*, or Of Human Life. Most people expected him to bow to the demands of the Catholic faithful and allow the use of contraceptives in marriage—but he did not. Rather, the Catholic Church opposed the use of contraceptives by the faithful. In fact, Pope Paul VI made four predictions of what would happen to the world and culture at large if contraception became widespread:

1. First, he predicted that this would "lead to conjugal infidelity and the general lowering of morality."—in other words, more people would be unfaithful in their relationships and the general moral standard of society would fall.

2. Second, he predicted that man would lose respect for woman and "no longer (care) for her physical and psychological equilibrium" to "the point of considering her as a mere instrument of selfish enjoyment and no longer as his respected and beloved companion."—in other words, men would begin to see women as 'cheap' and 'easy' avenues to their own pleasure, and would no longer bother with caring for them in the long term.

3. Third, he predicted that contraception would become a "dangerous weapon... in the hands of those public authorities who take no heed of moral exigencies"—in other words, that harsh governments would force citizens to use such drugs and other technologies as part of efforts to control or repress population growth.

4. Fourth, he predicted that man would come to think that he had complete control and dominion over his own body—in other words, that he would think that he had absolute right to do whatever he liked with his body and whatever he wanted to his body, even to the point of sterilizing it, without being answerable to anyone else. Source: Professor Janet Smith, University of Dallas

All other Christian churches, however, disagreed with the Catholic Church's position in *Humanae Vitae*, or Of Human Love. Within 15 years of the publication of *Humanae Vitae*, all of the other Christian Churches approved the use of contraceptives by their adherents. Today, 60 years after the publication of *Humanae Vitae*, it is worthwhile to ask what the effects of contraceptive use has been. When the Christian Churches caved to the culture, did Pope Paul VI's predictions come true? Absolutely yes!

Overwhelmingly, social scientists agree that all four predictions have come true (Langr, 2019) (Morana, 2018) (Castaneda, 2018). And so, we find that when religion bows to peer pressure – the appeasement problem-disaster results.

Responsibility, hell, and sin have all become bad words in today's churches. They are not used because the churches do not want to offend anyone. The clergy no longer instill a sense of sin because they confuse this with being intolerant or guilt-tripping.

A frog put in boiling water jumps out. However, a frog placed into warm water that slowly heats will cook to death. Similarly, children today are raised in a society, a simmering environment, that tolerates sexual sins. This environment blinds them to the reality of what these sins do to them and others. This environment helps them incorrectly believe that premarital sex is not wrong. It also makes it easier to believe in the inferiority of marriage and virginity because both are portrayed as unreasonable and unattainable. Pastors and bishops do not address unpopular truths because they are afraid of becoming unpopular and losing attendance, thereby losing collection/ donations. Pastors and bishops should summon the courage to correct the behavior of their faithful.

Religions do not require churches—the essential is the moral truth, not the building. Lose the building if you have to, but always stand up for the truth. Jesus did not come to appease or bow to cultural pressures. Jesus taught, leave your possessions! Treat your neighbors like yourself! Tell the truth! Jesus came to shake and revolutionize the status quo. Appeasement is not a service, but a disservice.

Christians do not live up to what they were told by Jesus. Jesus said clearly that what God creates, no man can break. (see Matthew 19:6 and Mark 10:9) When a man and a woman are married, they cannot break the marriage because God made it and so no man can break it. It is a paradox that the evil of divorce has become an accepted, common way of life in a

Christian, affluent, highly educated nation like the United States. How is this possible?

Now the blame does not lie entirely with religion. There are some places where government or society or courts have taken religion out of a conversation where it should have been included. Consider the notion of the separation of Church and State in the United States. It was designed to prevent governments from taking over or controlling religious institutions. That's it. It was not designed to prevent morals from taking over the government. Recall what John Adams declared—"We have no government armed with the power capable of contending with human passions unbridled by morality and religion. Avarice, ambition, revenge, and licentiousness would break the strongest cords of our Constitution, as a whale goes through a net. Our Constitution was made only for a moral and religious people. It is wholly inadequate to the government of any other."

There has to be a moral compass to the nation. When cultural elite like university professors, media, court judges, and celebrities spurn religion and throw it out as a moral compass, they may say that they want no religion telling them what to do. This is folly! You cannot throw out the Christian religion and hope not to replace it with something. When you get rid of one set of morals, you have to substitute it with another. Government can try to fill the void, but it cannot—it is not steadfast, it changes. The nation needs a firm solid moral foundation! What is the foundation? Today, the foundation is relativism, an ideology founded on the belief that all beliefs are equal (except, of course, any beliefs that say relativism is wrong).

Intellectual arrogance does not equal wisdom. America thinks it can replace religion with some "be good, and do justice" sort of approach. America cannot. The only acceptable moral compass is one which prioritizes virtuous living. Yet the concept of virtuous living has disappeared from public discourse. Let me make this clear: we do not get new moral realities.

We just don't. We either live up to the moral realities we ought to have lived up to in the first place (like abolishing slavery) or we abandon moral realities we ought to uphold (the disintegration of the nuclear family).

Gone is our understanding of religion's vibrant role in sustaining marriages, nurturing children, and strengthening families. Gone is our appreciation for religion as the basis for individual self-initiative, social quietude, and voluntary obedience. Once upon a time, illegitimacy, broken families, crime, and welfare were addressed by churches and religions. Now, Americans have relinquished those responsibilities to the state. Religious institutions have either abdicated their responsibility or been stripped of it (Supreme Court rulings took religion out of schools). The State is incapable of dealing with moral issues—it has no moral authority, only legal authority.

The social functions once held by religion cannot be taken over by a government which moves according to the current popular trends and wants of the society. Who has the guts to come and tell when wrong is wrong? Churches are the best-positioned institutions on the globe to instruct the people. Churches can best bring healing and help to the people. It is quite possible that the rise of crime, drugs, alcohol, and teen pregnancy is the result of the decreased role of religion in America today.

"Without God, life has no purpose, and without purpose, life has no meaning. Without meaning, life has no significance or hope." –Pastor Rick Warren, in The Purpose Driven Life

Albert Einstein said *"Science without religion is lame, religion without science is blind."*

CHAPTER 24

THE BLIND
LEADING THE BLIND

What is an expert? According to Merriam and Webster, an expert is 'someone with the special skill or knowledge representing mastery of a particular subject.'

If someone needs advice about marriage, who would one ask? Marriage experts. Marriage experts include marriage counselors, marriage therapists, doctors, psychologists, psychiatrists, sociologists, priests, and pastors.

But there is one problem with being an expert—there needs to be something for the expert to solve for them to make a living with their expertise. An expert in physical wellness, a doctor, must have sick people to conduct a thriving medical business. For marriage experts to exist, there needs to be a crowd of married couples who are having problems with their marriages. Otherwise, there is no need for such marriage experts. When the marriage and nuclear family is stable, the marriage experts have no one with problems to treat.

And so, we discover the dilemma of treatment: the doctor who cures his patient will no longer get business from that cured patient. Obviously then, you hope that your doctor is selfless enough to sacrifice making money and wants to cure you for your wellbeing. Similarly, the objective of any well-intended marriage expert should be to help cure the marriage of whatever is troubling it. The marriage expert should be selfless enough to lose the potential fees and instead seek the solution of the problems ailing the marriage.

However, too many of today's marriage experts thrive on the continuous existence of marital problems. Too many marriage experts today help marriages come apart but do not put even minimal effort into helping them stay together. Let me give you an example.

When I lived in Bethlehem, Pennsylvania, a student of mine at DeSales University was working with me one day. Let us call him Dave. While talking with Dave, I asked him what he planned to do with his future. Dave told me that he was studying to become a marriage counselor, a marriage expert. I asked Dave why he wanted to become a marriage counselor. He responded, "A lot of money." When I asked him to explain, he remarked that all he would have to do was take a certification test and then open an office. People would come to him with all kinds of family and marital problems and he would just have to listen. The more sessions they came for, the more money he would make. Easy! He told me that he would make sure to bring them for as many sessions as possible so they would pay more money.

I cannot think of anybody who would willingly want Dave to be their marriage counselor. He clearly has no interest in the wellbeing of marriage, only in the amount of money he can make. Would you go to a doctor who charged you for as many appointments and tests he could just so he could rake in the big bucks? I do not think so.

But what about marriage counselors like Dave, who plan to get all the legal credentials, but are still focused on the money? Clearly, what they are doing is immoral. The goal of any marriage expert should be to save the marriage, not to make money.

Unfortunately, even marriage counselors who do not have money as their primary motive may not be effective at keeping a marriage together. A 2005 article in the New York Times found that common marriage counseling techniques only improved about 50% of marriages.

In addition, those couples that did benefit often lost the benefits within a year. The article mentioned that many marriage counselors either give up on the marriage and tell the couple to divorce or drag out sessions for weeks on end. Four years after counseling, 38% of couples were divorced. If a 'cure' for a disease had this kind of failure rate, we would not call it an effective choice of treatment. In addition, a 2015 PsychCentral article found that divorce rates for practitioners of psychotherapy, including marriage counselors, were higher than for the general population. This led the author, a licensed marriage therapist herself, to wonder why so many of the counselors who give marriage advice are doing so despite having a broken marriage themselves. This was echoed in a 2012 Huffington Post Contributor article (Doyle).

Dr. Tim Gardner, a graduate professor of counseling, explained that there are many reasons why marriage counseling may not work. First, he has found that many counselors tell couples to 'get out of' their marriage. He suggests that this defeats the point of counseling, especially when the counselor gives up before the couple does. Second, Dr. Gardner mentioned that marriage counseling is often based on theories which have not been tested or which are better suited to individuals, not couples. This was consistent with analysis by the New York Times (2005). Third, Dr. Gardner mentioned that marriage counseling will not work if the couple is closed off to becoming more virtuous individually. Couples cannot focus on the other partner becoming better—they must focus on they themselves becoming better. Once again, it seems that moral living is the requirement for strong marriages! Psychotherapy cannot replace this, and if it does not cultivate individual virtuous living in the marriage, then it is useless.

How can I say this? Well, I would like to point out that the best marriage advice I have ever seen given comes not from psychotherapists or marriage counselors. Instead, it comes from a couple's best friends and parents. Sometimes, good advice can even come from priests, pastors, or other religious and social leaders who are not influenced by cultural fads. None of these individuals provide psychotherapy or psychoanalysis for a fee. However, these are the individuals who are best able to strengthen a marriage.

Why is this? Once again, I think that it is because virtuous living is what makes a marriage strong. Since parents, good friends, priests and pastors are all capable of enhancing how virtuously you are living, they are all able to have a direct impact on strengthening your marriage. In fact, I would argue that they have a much better and more direct impact than a marriage therapist who focuses on vague theories rather than morals. Intellectual ability (or intellectual arrogance) is not a substitute for the reasonable and pure advice of good friends, family, pastors, and priests. Even the greatest expert who knows all the theories about marriage will not be able to solve social decay without first being able to distinguish between good and evil.

Case in point: In 2007, I was reading the *Morning Call* newspaper in Allentown, PA. I brushed across an article by a marriage adviser, Jeanne Phillips (also known as Dear Abby). She is an American advice columnist with a net worth of $5 million. Her advice columns are syndicated in about 1,400 newspapers in America with a combined circulation of more than 110 million copies. *Dear Abby's* website receives about 10,000 letters per week, seeking advice on a large variety of personal matters.

In this particular edition, Jeanne Phillips had received a question from a 28-year-old woman who had been dating a 26-year-old man for four months. The woman and the man had a discussion about sex while on a date, and the woman learned that the man was a virgin. She also learned that it was "important for him to find a girl who had 'never been with anyone' either." The woman honestly revealed to him that she was not a virgin and had made poor choices in high school which she regretted, and that she wished to wait until marriage to have sex again. When she asked the man if he wished to continue dating, he replied "'I'll think about it.'"

The man decided that he still wished to date the woman and still liked her. However, she felt 'devalued,' and told Jeanne Phillips that if she had known about the man's standards in the first place, she never would have dated him. She wrote to Jeanne Phillips asking what to do. Jeanne Phillips responded with acid against the man, saying "Cross him off your list as husband material. Your friend may be self-conscious about his lack of experience or his old-fashioned values. It's the old double standard, and even some men who have sown acres of wild oats feel this way. While most men today have more sophisticated thinking about sex, the one you are dating has his heart set on a 'sweet old-fashioned girl.' If that's what he wants, it's his privilege—provided he can find one. As for you, it was your bad luck to get involved with someone whose values are different from your own, but that's the luck of the draw. Please don't take it personally. It's time to move on."

Now I would like to take this advice by Jeanne Phillips apart piece by piece. First, Jeanne Phillips accused him of being "self-conscious about his lack of experience or his old-fashioned values." Yet, I would point out that it is the woman who is feeling self-conscious about her poor decisions and is subsequently feeling devalued by shame. The marriage counselor should say that while shame is a natural feeling that accompanies poor choices, the woman should not let it affect her view of her own value (obviously, the man was willing to move past her mistakes, so she should too!). Instead, the marriage counselor says that the woman should "[c]ross him off your list as husband material." For a man to remain a virgin until he is 26 years old shows he has an enormous sense of self-control and discipline. In fact, it would probably be best for the woman to marry someone who successfully held himself to his strong moral standards!

Jeanne Phillips also accuses the man of holding a "double standard" by remaining a virgin himself and desiring a wife who was also a virgin. She clearly shows that she has no idea what a double standard means. The man is not holding himself to one set of conduct and then expecting a stricter set of conduct from the woman! In fact, while he desired a woman who was a virgin, he also remained a virgin himself! This shows that while he may have had high moral standards for his future wife, he held himself to the same standards. If there is any double standard involved, it is because the man was still willing to date the woman and like her even after he found out she was not a virgin! He was cutting her slack even though she did not hold up to the rigorous moral standards he had prescribed for himself!

Jeanne Phillips also claims the man wants a "sweet old-fashioned girl." Where did she get that from? The only thing he asked for was a girl with equivalent moral standards—and, when he found out that the girl he liked had not lived up to those standards but was willing to try to do so, he decided to continue dating her! He did not ask her to wear a skirt or dress, stay at home rather than work, or occupy herself with household chores alone.

Jeanne Phillips also makes a mistake by writing off morality as a fashion. She thinks one set of values is wrong because it is "old-fashioned" and another is correct because it is new-fashioned or "sophisticated." This is ludicrous. At the time of slavery, the intelligentsia undoubtedly saw themselves as "new-fashioned" and "sophisticated," while they saw their detractors as "old-fashioned" supporters of racial equality. But the "sophisticated" white supremacists were still morally wrong! Like I said before, moral standards do not change. We either live up to them or we fail to; we either understand them or we do not. When the man held himself to be a virgin and decided to continue dating the woman when he learned she was trying to stay pure, he showed that he was indeed a man with correct moral standards. He had chosen to take the harder path but compassionately forgave and accepted those who did not and were striving to make it back.

Writers and advisors like Jeanne Phillips can have a devastating effect on a society. They can help make people vilify those who are really heroes and can desensitize the population to things which are evil and wrong. Instead of complementing virtuous behavior, Jeanne Phillips devolved into unprofessional attacks on a moral person.

Often, when it comes to articles like these, it is not the question which is troubling but the answer. Consider another situation which appeared in the same column by Jeanne Phillips (the daughter of the first Jeanne Phillips) in 2015. A woman wrote to her saying that she had found out her boyfriend had been sleeping not just with her but with two other woman and had potentially infected them with STDs. He had claimed he had been tested regularly but had been lying. The woman lamented that all three of the girlfriends were wondering whether they would ever be able to trust a man again.

Ms. Phillips responded correctly with a gentle admonition ("Now might be a good time to re-evaluate whether premarital sex is worth the headache and the heartache."). However, she also gave some wrong advice, saying that of the consequences that result from premarital sex, "an inability to trust is among the least of them. If a man doesn't protect his partner, it's up to her to protect herself—both from pregnancy and from sexually transmitted diseases, which are rampant." This is wrong. How can the author say that the real problem is that the woman should protect herself because the man won't? How can the author say that the inability to trust is 'among the least' of the problems? What the author *should* say is that any man who won't protect his wife by abstaining from sex with anyone but her is not worthy of her. What the author should say is that any premarital relationships which cause an inability to trust are wrong—premarital sex foremost among them.

Americans are unique among many cultures because they tend to rely more on outside experts to tell them how to live their lives, rather than asking other family members or friends. While this can be a good thing, experts are not always right about everything. Consider these four humorous examples of American experts being wrong about something:

1. The Airplane: "The (flying) machine will eventually be fast; they will be used in sport, but they are not to be thought of as commercial carriers"—Octave Chanute, 1904. Just 10 years later, on Jan. 1, 1914, the first scheduled passenger airline service began operating between St. Petersburg and Tampa, FL. It became immensely popular, selling out tickets 16 weeks in advance of its daily flights (Sharp, Space.com, 2022).

2. The Automobile: "The ordinary 'horseless carriage' is at present a luxury for the wealthy; and although its price will probably fall in the future, it will never come into as common use as the bicycle"— The Literary Digest, October 1889. By 1908, Henry Ford had started mass production of the Model T, and his competitors soon followed. The 1920s established Ford, General Motors and Chrysler as the "Big Three" auto companies (History.com, 2018).

3. The Television: "While, theoretically and technically, television may be feasible, commercially and financially I consider it an impossibility, a development of which we need waste little time dreaming"—Lee DeForest, 1926. In 25 years, televisions became affordable household items and were purchased en masse by the American middle class. This opened the door to new methods of entertainment and news sharing that transformed the 1950s (Woollen, nd).

4. Human Surgery: "The abdomen, the chest, and the brain will be forever shut from the intrusion of the wise and humane surgeon"—Sir John Erichsen, 1873. Only 14 years later, in 1887, a Philadelphia native and Jefferson Medical College graduate, Dr. W. W. Keen performed the first successful brain tumor surgery. He removed a meningioma from a 26-year-old man experiencing

headaches, seizures, and aphasia, earning renown as "American's first brain surgeon" (Aker, 2022).

These four examples are not exhaustive of the number of times experts who made supposedly well-informed predictions were incorrect. These examples are relevant to showcase that experts are not always correct, whether it comes to travel, technology, or health. Therefore, experts who give advice on marriage are not always correct and their guidance should not be relied upon outright as accurate and correct.

In my experience, the best experts you should consult are your parents. This is because the parents have known their child since birth and are the best people to consult when looking for a life-long spouse. They know their child physically, emotionally, behaviorally, and psychologically. They know the child sometimes even better than the child themselves.

When you think about it, a society where there is no work for marriage experts would be a very strong society indeed!

CHAPTER 25

RAINBOWS AND PONIES

"Anyone who believes that permanent romance in a relationship is a perpetual possibility is doomed to perpetual disappointment." –Scott Peck (Further Along the Road Less Traveled, 2010).

"You don't marry one person; you marry three—the person you think they are, the person they are, and the person they are going to become as the result of being married to you." --Richard Needham (You and All the Rest, 1986)

What is the purpose of dating? It is supposed to be a method for helping you get to know the other person. However, right from the start, I suppose that this is a virtually impossible task. You cannot ever know somebody perfectly. Who they are and who you think they are differ. You can know someone kind of well, you can even know someone very well, but you cannot know someone perfectly.

Why do I bring this up? I bring this up because of a common question a couple asks themselves during a divorce. That question is 'Had I known?' It takes many forms. "Had I known that he or she had this attitude towards money, would I have married them?" "Had I known that he or she liked this activity, would I have married them?" "Had I known that he or she had this opinion or political view, would I have married them?"

See, here is the thing: there is always something that you will not know about your spouse. You cannot know them perfectly. Things will be revealed after your marriage which you did not know before, things as benign as your spouse liking hot sauce to as serious as your spouse having a different outlook about finances. But I do not think that the reason marriages fall apart is because one spouse did not know enough about the other. I think that asking, 'Had I known?' is the wrong question. Rather, I think that the reason marriages break up is much more often because one or more of the spouses had an unrealistic expectation of what marriage should look like. Allow me to explain.

I have come across a very common theme in my research on divorce. When you ask the spouses why they divorced, more often than not, they will say that their spouse changed dramatically from the time they were dating to the time they were divorced. "He/She's not the same person I married," they will say. "He/She is not like before. He/She used to be so caring and fun. Now they are so serious, and they always get into fights with me."

On the surface, this may sound like a perfectly good reason for a couple to separate. That person is not the same as the person you married? Well, you married that older person, not this newer version. You loved that older model, not this newer one. Surely you cannot be expected to hang around.

However, I think that this line of reasoning is fallacious. You cannot expect people to be the same always. That is unfair. People change. It is ridiculous to think that once a person has become an adult, they are done growing and changing. That is absolutely not true. They may lose interest in some things (like soccer) and develop new interests in other things (like golf). It is completely unfair to demand that your spouse remain exactly the same as the person you dated. Nobody can be the same old person you once knew. It is better to think of a person as a verb, not a noun. They are always becoming something new (and hopefully, someone better—more on that later).

I think it also follows that no relationship stays the same. Just like a person, a relationship is better thought of as a verb than a noun. It changes over time. Just because a relationship or a person is changing, this does not signal that something is wrong. In fact, it usually signals that something is right. Marriage is a huge step in a person's life. It is a huge step in a relationship. It is unrealistic to expect that your spouse and your relationship with your spouse will stay the same after the marriage as it was before the marriage. This is simply not the case. As stated in the humorous quote at the beginning of this chapter by Richard Needham, your spouse will certainly change, not least as a result of being married to you.

So, if you should expect your spouse and your relationship with your spouse to change after marriage, what kinds of changes should you expect? You may have noticed how I mentioned earlier that changes should be for the better. I will expound on that now. The goal of any person, whether married or single, should be virtuous living. This does not change after marriage. Both spouses should be trying their best to become more virtuous. This is the kind of good change that is healthy for a marriage.

People suffer from this vague idea that they can improve their relationships by 'working on them.' That is false. You improve your relationships by working on yourself. If you yourself become more virtuous, your relationships will improve as a byproduct. Similarly, if both spouses are committed to becoming better people, the marriage relationship will change, and the people will change, but they will change for the better. This kind of change is both necessary and healthy for any relationship, including a marriage.

The next set of unrealistic expectations that people take into marriage come, I believe, from dating. Earlier, I praised the merits of dating, but here I will also point out some of the glaring deficits of the process. Dating gives a couple an unrealistic picture of life together. In the dating process, the couple is not living together, and they are not sharing many responsibilities which will be faced as a married couple. A dating couple's relationship usually consists of fun and games. They go out to dinner; they go to see movies; they dance together at parties. However, a married couple must also face the realities of working for a living, raising children, and managing a household. While a dating couple can go out to dinner every Saturday night, it is more likely that a married couple will spend their Saturdays taking a child to a soccer game. The life which the couple enjoyed while they were dating cannot be the same life they enjoy while they are married.

Is this a bad thing? No. If the couple realizes that the environment in which they date cannot be the same as the environment in which they live as a married couple, then it is unlikely that dating will harm them in this way. If, however, the couple expects their relationship after marriage to perfectly mirror their relationship while dating, they will be sorely disappointed. Does this mean that a husband will never take his wife out on a date after their marriage? Of course not. It simply means that married life cannot be the same as dating life.

Is this a good thing? Yes. I suggest that a relationship between two people where everything comes easy and everything is rosy is hardly a strong relationship. After all, success is a lousy teacher. In this sense, a couple's feelings for each other while dating are not the true metric of how strong the relationship is. On the other hand, a relationship between two people that has weathered some serious headwinds is a much stronger and more mature relationship. In fact, I would contend that a couple who have raised children together, filed taxes together, and lived in a house together have much more in common than a dating couple that likes to go bowling.

In sum, the role of dating partners must change as they become spouses and assume new roles in marriage. My answer to "What happened to the person I married?" is that he or she is different because they *must* be different. You and him or you and her must change from one type of relationship to another type of relationship. All of this will result in change. But change is not a bad thing.

I would like to contrast dating with arranged marriage as I defined it (pg 93). In arranged marriage, in most cases, the spouses do not have a dating relationship with each other prior to the wedding. (Recall that they get married because the parents decide that the two will be compatible with each other). One benefit of this arrangement is that they do not have to experience the transition of roles from boyfriend and girlfriend to husband and wife. This may save them from developing serious unrealistic expectations of what the marriage should be compared to dating. Perhaps this is one reason why arranged marriages have lower divorce rates than love marriages.

One thing I point out is that you cannot escape the reality of change by not getting married. There is this strong illusion among some people that if they cohabit but do not get married, then they will not have to face a situation where their married lives differ from their dating lives. Or, they think that if changes does occur, since they are not tied down by marriage, they will be able to separate and leave easily. These couples worry that marriage might 'ruin their happiness' (King, "Would Marriage Ruin our Happiness?" 2014).

This is a travesty. Why is the idea of committing to love somebody no matter how they change such a scary idea for so many Americans? People change all the time; often it is for the better! Once again, I point out that change is not a bad thing, either before marriage or after it.

People are not clones of each other, either before a marriage or after. Even two clones will be at least slightly out of sync if they run a wheelbarrow race. Similarly, in marriage or in any relationship, even between identical twins in the same family, there cannot be complete blissful compatibility all the time. In marriage, just as in any relationship, both must adjust behavior to meet the needs of the marriage. Living in the past is childish, and you cannot expect that you will not have to change yourself. Asking someone why they are different from who they were before is wrong. It is selfish to demand that someone stay the same as you knew them, that they not change at all. It is unrealistic to think that you yourself will not change; you will. In fact, you should be working to change yourself for the better.

'OK,' you may be saying, 'people becoming better is all well and good. I can handle that kind of change. I can handle the realities and responsibilities that come from raising children, sharing finances, and managing a household. But what if the change in my spouse is something I do not like? Or what if I learn something I do not like (maybe my spouse likes to play video games every day, even if the dishes are not done)?' These are valid concerns. These concerns, or similar concerns, are part of every marriage. Does this mean the marriage failed? Absolutely not! If the couple tries to address these, even in a heated manner, does that mean that something is wrong? Once again, change and even conflict do not mean that the marriage is doomed (Hill, 2018) (Wong, 2019) (Syrtash, 2020).

I think that many experts have already addressed how couples can have a conversation, even a heated one, about a change or conflict in their relationship which they would like to address (Hill, 2018) (Wong, 2019) (Syrtash, 2020). However, one advice which these experts do not mention is that couples should feel comfortable speaking with their parents about how to manage difficulties or challenges in the marriage. After all, their parents probably had similar changes or challenges that arose from raising children, sharing finances, or managing a household. The parents probably have a wealth of advice on how to manage a maturing relationship.

The last unrealistic expectation I address is that you can 'get' the perfect spouse. You do not 'get' the perfect spouse. Similarly, there is this misperception that you can 'make' your spouse the perfect spouse (if only they would listen to you!!). That is also wrong. The only person you can truly change is yourself. The only thing you can do is **become** the perfect spouse. That is where the emphasis should be in our modern culture. You become the perfect spouse. You do not 'get' the perfect spouse.

CHAPTER 26

PAPARAZZI AND POOR ROLE MODELS

"Scandal is the coin of the contemporary celebrity. It keeps the public interested." Richard Corlis, Time Magazine

Have you ever wondered what makes someone famous? Why is it that Tom Hanks is a celebrity today, whereas you have never heard of Joe and Jane Doe out in Nebraska? Celebrities are born when society gives honorable recognition to those who have achieved something great. Scientists, engineers, actors, musicians, inventors, athletes, and many more are examples or role models who can be motivators to others. As a society, we admire their accomplishments. The media highlights these people. We want to be like them.

Consider Mahatma Gandhi, Michael Jordan, or Albert Einstein. Everyone knows who these people are; everyone knows how these people made an impact on the world; virtually everyone is inspired by or hopes to follow in the footsteps of these great people. Even on a smaller level, we create celebrities. At colleges, we announce our Dean's List, we declare which graduates are *summa cum laude*, we feature prize-winning students in newspapers. This culture teaches us to aim high and do right. This entire culture of celebrities can spread benefits and have a positive effect on society.

On the other hand, society is very intentional about who we do not praise. Have you ever seen a college announce the names of its dropouts? Do you see newspapers praising the people who have committed burglary within the past week? Have you been to the theater and seen movies glamorizing Nazis or communism? No. Why? Our society intrinsically understands that we do not want to be like them. We do not want to emulate or praise such people.

However, what happens when the media praises someone of questionable status? What happens when we praise something that is wrong? The answer is that society can quickly become confused about what proper, decent behavior looks like. When the wrong people are praised, society takes a turn for the worse. Just look at how praise for Hitler and *Mein Kampf* helped fuel his rise to being made Führer of Germany.

Our modern celebrities are a classic example of this. While they have many praiseworthy qualities that deserve the media's attention and praise, their marital lives are poor. Many celebrities get married 3, 4, 5, or more times. Why is this? Even if you think that it was reasonable for them to have 1 'bad' marriage, how can they have 3 or 5 'bad' marriages? Is their method of finding someone to marry just that incredibly flawed? Or do they simply have no understanding or respect for what the institution of marriage truly means? Just like an ordinary person's wedding vows, celebrities promise to be married for *life*, in good times *and* bad. Why, then, do so many celebrities untie the knot?

Consider Britney Spears and Jason Alexander, who had their marriage annulled a mere 56 hours after it began. Then there is Carmen Electra and Dennis Rodman, who began their divorce proceedings a mere 10 days after getting married. Another example is Dennis Hopper and Michelle Phillips, who divorced 9 days after marriage. Then there is the endless list of celebrities who have been married and divorced repeatedly. There's Larry King, Leana Wood, William Shatner, James Doohan, Nicolas Cage, Harrison Ford, Mickey Rooney, Reese Witherspoon, Kim Kardashian, Madonna, Ryan Reynolds, Angelina Jolie, Johnny Depp, Ashton Kutcher, Nicole Kidman, George Clooney, Jennifer Lopez, Mariah Carey, Usher, and Tom Cruise. In fact, a study found that A-list celebrities have a divorce rate double that of the standard British and American populations (Benson & Azim, 2016).

How did we get to this? When did it become the norm among our role models to get divorced and remarried 2, 3, 4, 5, or more times? What does it mean to them to say 'forever' and 'I promise' and 'I do' when they do not marry forever, do not keep their promises, and do not do what they said they would? Today, to enjoy watching an actor or actress' entertainment, you have to navigate their messy private life. Do we want our children to be learning from this? Even the most ardent sexualist would agree that they do not want their child to be divorced 5 or more times. But instead of questioning or outright rejecting this immoral, unfaithful, contradictory behavior, our society has appeased such celebrities by keeping silent. Why? We do not have to take this from our role models.

So where did this start? Let's go back to the 1950s and 60s when American film was just beginning to be well-established. At that time, there were two actresses in particular who helped create an atmosphere of acceptance in Hollywood regarding sexual promiscuity and divorce. These two women are Marilyn Monroe and Elizabeth Taylor.

In 1962, Marilyn Monroe was invited to sing at President Kennedy's birthday party. Though she was only 36, Monroe had already been married and divorced 3 times and had established a reputation as a sensuous actress. I think it was completely out of place to give Monroe this honor. Why? Marilyn Monroe had made a career out of undressing before the camera. She dedicated her life to being sexually revealing. Some people think that Monroe helped 'sexually liberate' women, but I do not agree with this. I think that Monroe helped create an environment that defined women by their sexual appeal and nothing else—a legacy which later female actresses were forced to submit to (San Miguel, 2016) (Israelsen-Hartley, 2017). In my opinion Marilyn Monroe is an unrealistic and poor role model for society, and I submit that elevating her to such a high status sends the wrong messages to both men and women.

Sadly, just as Marilyn Monroe made a career from hyper-sexualizing herself, many others did too. The 1961 and 1967 Academy Awards went to Elizabeth Taylor. This actress changed husbands like handkerchiefs—she was married eight times and divorced eight times with seven husbands. Sadly, the more divorces she had, the more famous she became. At least twice, she cheated on her current husband and seduced another woman's husband into having an affair (the most notable of these was Richard Burton while filming *Cleopatra*). Divorcing husbands became an asset. Her products sold well. She became famous. She got lots of awards. Is this the model for society? Even if you are a feminist, would you have liked seeing your husband torn away from you by a seductress and then watch as she became *famous* and *rich* by selling the sordid details to the press? I highly doubt so.

What happens when the media projects immoral behavior as a standard of acceptability? This makes dishonorable things appear as honorable. This blurs the distinction between right and wrong, virtuous and unvirtuous.

When Elizabeth Taylor died in 2011, Good Morning America hailed her as making 'enduring contributions to the world.' One person commented that she was a cultural touchstone. How ridiculous! This woman's life is not a model to follow. While she may have made praiseworthy charitable contributions, the fact remains that she tore apart several marriages by seducing another woman's husband. The fact remains that she cheated on her own husbands many times. The fact remains that Elizabeth Taylor had no qualms with doing what was wrong.

Other Hollywood celebrities have given senseless reasons for their divorces. Consider Jane Fonda, who was divorced three times before getting a boyfriend in her 70s. In an interview with Oprah, she claimed that she had not felt intimacy with her many husbands, but had felt intimacy with her boyfriend, which was why she was in that relationship (I wonder why she married men she did not feel intimate with, but let us continue). Jane Fonda said she did not feel guilt or shame because she was raised in a household that had abuse and her mother committed suicide.

What a way to abdicate responsibility! She blamed her father and mother for her own poor decisions. Jane Fonda admitted to having regret about leaving her children from her marriages to be cared for by governesses and people other than their mother. She should! When a Hollywood couple breaks up, it is not just the spouses who are affected. What will happen to their children? Will they ever know or love their real parents, or will they simply be given a governess?

Another strange excuse came from Jennifer Lopez, who was married three times. She claimed that she does not 'count' her first two marriages because they were short (Mizoguchi, 2019) (Kamp, 2019). This is a delusional statement. Once a person says their marriage vows, then they are married. There is no such thing as a marriage that 'didn't count.'

It does not matter if someone has a celebrity lifestyle, it does not matter if someone has a big fairy-tale wedding, it does not matter if someone looks good or not, if they cannot keep their promises. This is the main problem with the rampant Hollywood divorces we are seeing: our role models are breaking their promises to remain faithful forever, to love forever, to be there in good times and in bad. Earlier, I mentioned that the true measure of your love for another person is not how you behave when you have all the good feelings for them and times are good, but how you behave when you have lost feelings for them and times are bad. The current Hollywood culture creates an unrealistic picture of what a healthy marital relationship should look like. Where then should we look for standards? From where should we create our expectations (which I discussed earlier)? Obviously, we should not use celebrity marriages as a model. There is something wrong happening in Hollywood.

I would like to move away from immorality of celebrities and focus on another type which has very real and lasting consequences: immorality of high officials. Specifically, I mean politicians.

Among our early presidents, we wanted moral leaders, leaders who were impeccable in honesty. George Washington, America's first President, was expected not to tell a lie. He did not lie. America could and did trust him. How about Abraham Lincoln? Same thing. America could and did trust him. In return, the American people respected and honored both George Washington and Abraham Lincoln. Even today, Americans and people all around the world respect and honor these two former presidents of the United States.

Today, Presidents publicly lie in office and commit adultery, most notably Bill Clinton and Donald Trump. The worst part is that such persons lie and commit adultery with impunity or no consequences. This immoral behavior reflects poorly on the Presidents; it reflects poorly on America and Americans because the people elect and support such candidates for the Oval Office. Failure to reverse this trend now will result in this immoral behavior becoming a way of American life. Some would argue that such immoral behavior is already the way of life in America!

When George Washington and Abraham Lincoln were President, we expected them to hold their office in high honor and behave properly. Today, it is no longer a given that our politicians will do so. Consider how many politicians of high status from both political parties (D-Democrat and R-Republican) have been recently convicted of sexual offenses: Senator John Edwards (D-ran for President), Senator Larry Craig (R), Governor Eliot Spitzer (D, New York), Senator Gary Hart (D-ran for President), Senator John Ensign (R), Senator Al Franken (D), President Bill Clinton (D), Representative Newt Gingrich (R-was speaker of the House of Representatives), and President Donald Trump (R). And this is just a small sampling!

If such prominent leaders are committing adultery, lying, and cheating in front of the public eye, what lesson does this teach our children? It is horrifying to watch one political party defend their own President's promiscuity and then attack the other party's President (the Democrats defended Clinton and attacked Trump, the Republicans attacked Clinton and then defended Trump). American congressman, senators, and other public officials are becoming infected with lying, adultery, and other vices.

If our American leaders are engaging in marital infidelity, then ordinary citizens will too. After all, a leader's moral shortcomings will negatively affect everyone around him. We cannot relegate these matters to the politicians' 'private business' and therefore fail to interfere. If we do not condemn such illicit behavior, but accept our politicians' weak excuses, how can we refuse to accept the same weak excuses from our spouse, children, family, or friends? A public servant is accountable to the citizens he represents in the same way one spouse is accountable to another or children are accountable to their parents. As Thomas Jefferson so aptly put it, "When a man assumes a public trust, he should consider himself public property." If we should expect good behavior of celebrities, we should expect even better behavior of political leaders.

Everybody hates guilt and sin. Today, these words are considered taboo. But we need those words in our vocabulary. Why? They give a frame of references for guiding personal behavior. You need some sort of compass to determine whether someone is behaving properly or poorly. If someone feels guilt for committing a crime, then they know they have done wrong. Appease them and take away the guilt, and suddenly they do not understand why they cannot commit the crime.

We need to stop appeasing our political leaders and our celebrities. Again, while they may have done many good things for society, this does not excuse their sexual excesses or their marital infidelity. We should call out such improper behavior when we see it and reject it.

I submit that society should focus more on actors and actresses who were married only once, people like Norman and Peggy Lloyd (75 years), Karl and Mona Malden, Charlton Heston (Ben-Hur), Eli Wallach (The Godfather), DeForest Kelly (Star Trek), Robert Mitchum (El Dorado), Danny Thomas (comedian, founded St. Jude's Hospital), Denzel Washington, Jon Bon Jovi, Meryl Streep, Jay Leno, Michael Fox, Jamie Lee Curtis, Bob Newhart, Alan Alda (M*A*S*H), Martin Sheen (Gandhi), Bob McGrath (Sesame Street), David and Victoria Beckham, and Dolly Parton. These are celebrities who grace our society with their musical and acting talents, have donated to charitable causes and have also maintained an admirable personal life.

Consider the marriage of David and Victoria Beckham. After more than 20 years and four children, they are still married. When asked about his marriage, David told a reporter, "We stay together because we love each other; we stay together because we have four amazing children, and do you go through tough times? Of course, you go through tough times. It's part of relationships, it's part of marriages, it's part of having children, it's part of having responsibilities. Of course you make mistakes, and we all know that marriage is difficult at times...It is about working through it. We have come up against tough times. But we know each other better than anyone else knows us."

Notice how David Beckham used the words 'responsibility' and 'children' and 'working through' when he talked about his marriage. This is not someone who was only looking for fun or sex or enjoyment or personal fulfillment. This is someone who knows that marriage is a relationship that requires work and commitment, just like any other relationship, and that it requires a unique kind of love. Like I said earlier, the true measure of your love for another person is not how you behave when you have all the good feelings for them and times are good, but how you behave when you have dampened feelings and times are bad. In my opinion, David Beckham is worthy of praise not just for his soccer skills and Victoria Beckham is worthy of praise not just for her singing and dancing skills; the two are worthy of praise also because they have built a strong family and a strong and committed marriage.

The public campaign should feature these couples' faithfulness to each other, through good times and bad. Their stories should be broadcast in ads that are shared via television, social media, and newspapers. The American public should be able to see these celebrities' commitment to each other so that they can follow them as role models. In addition, there should be entertainment content, such as soap operas, music lyrics, TV series, movies, and books that center on stable family lives and healthy marital relationships.

CHAPTER 27

THE PROBLEMS WITH THE PILL

The Oxford Dictionary defines technology as "the application of scientific knowledge for practical purposes." Technology by itself is morally neutral. However, depending on how technology is used, it can take on a positive or negative morality. For example, dynamite can be used to build (tunnels, bridges, etc.) or even to sculpt (Mt. Rushmore). These are good and moral uses of dynamite. However, dynamite can also be used to kill others, like in the 1920 Wall Street Bombing (Andrews 2019). This is a bad and immoral use of dynamite.

A relatively recent and serious technological invention whose societal effects should be examined quite closely is the contraceptive pill. Since its introduction in the 1930s and governmental approval in the 1960s, the pill has changed modern American life just as much as inventions like the car, TV, radio, and smartphone—if not more.

Simply put, sex has always been a highly pleasurable activity. This is because sex is the method by which the human species replicates—it makes sense, then, that this encourages people to have offspring and keeps the human population alive and well. Sexual pleasure is very strong, but it often came with responsibility. For most of human history, when people engaged in sexual relations, there was the possibility that they naturally would have a child as a result.

Sometimes this level of responsibility made sex inconvenient, especially for premarital sex and extramarital affairs. If a woman engaged in sex outside of her marriage and became pregnant, people would know what she had been up to, resulting in social stigma. Similarly, if a man impregnated a woman who was not his wife, he might be legally or socially obligated to care for any offspring of theirs. Thus, certain men and women have wished to separate the sex from procreation—in other words, to get the pleasure without the responsibility of having a child.

This was exactly what the pill does. It uses synthetic hormones to fool a woman's body into believing it is pregnant. Thus, the woman does not ovulate (release an egg every month). The pill made it possible to separate sex from procreation. It is a voluntary form of temporary sterilization. Once sex and procreation were separated, it suddenly became possible for men and women to have sex without worrying about conceiving a child (almost—contraceptives still have a failure rate).

Today, the pill has been heralded as a boon for women. It is widely accepted and widely used, with some estimates saying that upwards of 90% of women will use it at some point in their lives. In addition, many consider the pill to have liberated women from traditional household roles and given them the ability to pursue higher forms of education (law school, medical school, college and graduate school) because they can have sex with husbands or other male partners without having to conceive and care for children.

However, while the pill may have done all of this, I point out that the pill did not just liberate women from having to bear and rear children. It also liberated men from having to care about their unwedded female partners after having sex with them. I also point out that the pill made extramarital and premarital sex much less costly because the chance of conceiving a child was less. The pill contributes and increases the divorce rates, thereby breaking up the nuclear family, because it increases both extramarital and premarital sex.

Before, at least illicit sexual behavior was dampened by fear of pregnancy. For those men and women who lacked the strength of moral character to not engage in premarital or extramarital sex, fear of pregnancy and resulting social stigma was like an arrow pointed at their heads. Fear of pregnancy and social stigma acted as a check against premarital and extramarital sex. Now, the pill has made such risk-taking much less serious. This enables men and women to have many sex partners before and after getting married, if they even get married at all.

It is well-documented that extramarital affairs are a leading cause of a divorce. In addition, it is well-documented that those who have premarital sex with multiple partners are more likely to divorce. Thus, it is not surprising that several well-controlled studies have isolated the simple cause-and-effect relationship that the pill has increased divorce (Fehring, 2015) (Marcen, 2012) (Greenwood et al. 2020).

Is it a good use of technology to satisfy our desire for pleasure without responsibility (or pleasure without consequences)? Sex is not a requirement for survival or self-actualization. The urge to have sex can go unfulfilled for long periods of time, unlike the urge to eat. This means it is natural and healthy for us to wait to have sex. Is the new instant gratification obtained by use of the pill good for us?

Dogs mate one with another and then go their own way. They have no knowledge of family and are motivated by pure instinct. Animals do not have a moral law in terms of where, what, when, or with whom. They do not have ethics. Shouldn't it be troubling that our own boys and girls are behaving the same way? Humans have a moral law. Humans have ethics. Humans have relationships. We must care about other people, or society falls apart!

We do not get new moral realities—we just do not. We either live up to the ones we ought to have lived up to long ago, or we abandon the moral realities we should still be following. Some people say that humans have been trying to prevent pregnancy forever and that humans have always wanted sex outside of marriage, so this means that monogamy or life without birth control is impossible. Others say that men used to be free to cheat while women were not, so now the shoe is on the other foot, and we should give women their turn. This is ludicrous! The moral ideal has always been one spouse for life and no sex until marriage. That is the moral ideal. We should be better at living it out today than before instead of using our ancestor's weakness as an excuse.

After all, history is rife with examples of one group racially discriminating against another. Does this mean that humans will always discriminate, and we should just stop trying to eliminate racial discrimination? Does this mean that we should now enslave all the former enslavers and make the former slaves the new taskmasters? No! There is the moral reality we should have always lived up to and must always live up to where all men were treated equally. Similarly, we should live up to a moral reality that sex within marriage is better for the spouses, better for the children, and better for the society. We should live up to a moral reality that tries its hardest to prevent divorce, not encourage it.

CHAPTER 28

THE DOMINO EFFECT

Sadly, the consequences of divorce are many and devastating both to individuals and to society. Perhaps the worst effects of divorce are borne by the children of a divorced couple.

An article by Annalise Walliker in the Herald Sun (April 5, 2017) reported that children of divorced or separated parents are more than 20% more likely to be abused. The research, undertaken by the Family Violence and Family Court Research Center at Monash University, found that divorce often leaves children vulnerable to child abuse, and that the children who are abused are then more likely to get divorced in the future. Vicious cycles like this repeat and create more problems for society. The researchers suggested that children whose parents were divorcing were likely under parental supervision less often, making them more appealing targets to perpetrators.

The third leading cause of death among teenagers (age 15-24) is suicide. Why do teens commit suicide? Most commonly, they feel depressed, hopeless, anxious, or trapped in a situation they cannot handle or control, making suicide look like the only way out. How does divorce play a role in teen suicide? A 2011 University of Toronto study found "that men from divorced families had more than three times the odds of suicidal ideation in comparison to men whose parents had not divorced. Adult daughters of divorce had 83 per cent higher odds of suicidal ideation than their female peers who had not experienced parental divorce." According to the lead author, " The association between parental divorce and suicidal thoughts in men was unexpectedly strong, even when we adjusted for other childhood and adult stressors, socioeconomic status, depression and anxiety." The researchers suggested that the loss of a father figure was the main driving force behind the increase in male-child suicide following a divorce (this was because previous studies found that growing up without a father has a negative effect on boys' development).

Simply put, divorce is usually a traumatic experience for everyone involved. A classic study by psychologists found that it is the second-highest psychological stressor (only behind the death of a spouse) in the life of a child (Lumen Learning). It is easy to see why. When a child finds out his parents are getting divorced, he or she will immediately wonder "What is happening? Who can I count on? What will happen to me?" The child will probably feel worried (because the future is uncertain), angry (because the parents will not be there for him/her), and/or embarrassed (because their family has 'failed').

Some experts used to believe that nothing would change once things calmed down after a divorce (Whitehead, 1993). They remarked that children would likely bounce back and suggested that joint custody would be the solution to the trauma of divorce. However, Harvard professor Robert Mnookin, formerly director of the Stanford Center on Conflict and Negotiation, compared joint child custody to carrying out King Solomon's threat to cut the baby in half. When a child is 'shared' by two parents, they may feel like an object bouncing around between two people without truly belonging with either of them. Joint custody is not a substitute for jointly raising children.

However, if joint custody has been a poor substitute for marriage, single parenting has been even worse. The Minnesota Psychological Institution reported that the absence of a father in a household often led to ten adverse outcomes "in a child's life: (1) Perceived abandonment, (2) attachment issues, (3) child abuse, (4) childhood obesity, (5) criminal justice involvement, (6) gang involvement, (7) mental health issues, (8) poor school performance, (9) poverty and homelessness; and (10) substance use." A 2017 NPR interview with Claudio Sanchez, a 30-year education expert, reported that 7/10 high school dropouts were fatherless children.

In 2017, Pew Research Center found that 25% of American children lived in a home with just one parent (Livingston, 2018). This was a higher percentage than in any other country in the world (Kramer, 2019). A whopping 81% of these children lived with a single mother, while the remaining 19% lived with a single father. Another 7% of American children lived with cohabiting parents. This translates into almost 24 *million* American children living with unmarried parents (Livingston, 2018). The effects have been particularly pronounced among minority communities. In 2017, just 7% of married mothers were black. Meanwhile, 30% of single mothers were black. Single black parents are overwhelmingly female (89%). Minorities are disproportionately affected by single parenthood: 52% of single parents are black or Hispanic.

A 2008 report from the journal *Demographic Research* estimated that before reaching the tender age of 9, 20% of US children born to a married couple and 50% of US children born to a cohabiting couple would see their family break up at least once (Kennedy and Bumpass, 2008). This led the Pew report to a crucial conclusion: "The declining stability of families is linked both to increases in cohabiting relationships, which tend to be less long-lasting than marriages, as well as long-term increases in divorce" (Livingston, 2018). In other words, the stability of the two-parent, married-for-life, nuclear family was being undermined by more temporary cohabiting relationships and by marriage-shattering divorces.

Single parenthood has been perhaps the most obvious consequence of divorce. However, while attitudes towards divorce vary, it seems that most people think the trend of single parenthood is bad for society. Indeed, this seems to be widely accepted across the political spectrum. A 2015 Pew Research Center poll found that 83% of Republicans/leaning Republicans and 56% of Democrats/leaning Democrats thought that increasing numbers of single mothers raising children by themselves was a 'bad thing' for society (Livingston, 2018). Is this true? What are the consequences of divorce for children?

First of all, single parents are much more likely to be poor. This economic deprivation is not surprising—rather than having a two-parent income or a single parent who can work a full day, single parent homes have a one-parent income, and the parent must juggle work with caring for children. Children in single parent households are much more likely to live below the poverty line. A Pew Research Center report found that 27% of single parents and 16% of cohabiting parents lived in poverty, much greater than the 8% of married couples living in poverty (Livingston, 2018). And a 2001 study found that a mere 30% of children from divorced families will receive financial support for college tuition from their family, compared to 90% of their peers from intact families (Vogel).

This is not surprising. After all, as reported by a 2014 review study, a woman usually loses 25-50% of her pre-divorce income when she gets divorced, yet she is generally given custody of the children (Anderson). Thus, it is not surprising that more single mothers live in poverty than married mothers, and single mothers stay in poverty longer than married mothers (Anderson, 2014). In fact, a Harvard study found that the greatest predictor of poor upward social mobility in several geographic areas of the United States was the increase in the percentage of children living in single-family homes (Chetty et al., 2014).

Why are divorced parents so often in financial distress? Well, first, the financial cost of a divorce is significant and can drain much of a couple's income and savings. A report by journalists Jae Yang and Janet

Loehrke in the February 26, 2017, edition of USA Today (using data from credit reporting company Experian) found that the average financial loss experienced by a divorcing couple was $19,922. The journalists noted that this primarily consists of litigation costs. For a couple who makes $40-80,000 a year together, this kind of bill can be a sizable cost, especially since the income post-divorce will be less than before.

In addition, most single parents expect that they will receive alimony or child support payments from their former spouse (Itkin, 2018). However, this is a notoriously unreliable source of income. As reported by CBS News, only about 50% of divorcing couples ever actually receive a custodial order that lays out who will pay for the children (Leefeldt 2019). And according to the Census Bureau, of those parents who are entitled to receiving child support, *less than half* actually received the full amount they were due, while almost a third received *nothing* (Census Bureau 2018).

The figures were even worse for the 1.6 million custodial parents in poverty: a mere 39.2% received full child support payments. To make matters more complicated, the average child support due to a custodial parent was a mere $3,447 per year, hardly enough money to raise a child on (Census Bureau, 2018). This may explain why 29.2% of custodial mothers and 16.7% of custodial fathers live in poverty (Census Bureau, 2018). Perhaps it is no surprise that researchers have found that marriage is an incredibly effective method at reducing child poverty (Fagan et al, 2003).

There are some who would argue that poor economic conditions are a major cause of divorce. According to this thinking, of course people live in poverty after divorce. They were poor before, that was why they divorced, and they will be poor after. However, this does not seem to be a logical deduction. In countries where the per capita income is well below the poverty level, the divorce rate is often much lower than in the United States. Additionally, the divorce rate in the US during the Great Depression, perhaps the time of greatest poverty, hovered around 10%. In addition, among poor early immigrant populations (the Chinese, Irish, Italian, and Polish) divorce rates were historically very low. Thus, the argument that poverty is the cause of divorce does not seem to be true. In fact, the reverse seems to be true. It was only after the 1940s, when the American economy was growing quickly and Americans became more prosperous, that the divorce rate also increased.

After a divorce, even as the single parent's financial resources have decreased, their expenses may have increased. A 2012 report on Retirement Security to the US Senate found that, on average, women lose 41% of their pre-divorce income through a divorce, while men lose about 23% (US Government Accountability Office, 2012). However, a custodial parent may now have to pay daycare, groceries, mortgages, school activity fees, and college tuition compared to the noncustodial parent. (Ellevest Team, 2018). In addition, the custodial parent must invest, save for retirement, and pay off interest on a house/car. Juggling all this is an impossible task for one parent alone; nature has not designed the family to be this way.

As a report by the US Department of Education summed it up, "Divorce reform was supposed to be a panacea for women trapped in bad marriages. It has trapped many of them in poverty." It is not surprising, then, that 22% of divorced spouses later regret splitting (Maloney 2016). Even if the government gives them support in the form of welfare, childcare, or tax breaks, it cannot replace their spouse. Perhaps it makes sense why divorcee Jane Gordon wrote "divorce has strengthened my belief in marriage" (Gordon, 2009). Maybe this is why other writers have also expressed their regrets over divorcing their spouse (Andrew, 2019) (Grazer, 2011) (Anonymous 2019, Good Men Project) (Anonymous, n.d., Leslie Cane Articles).

Divorce's domino effect extends far beyond economics. Parental divorce or separation has serious health effects on children. Children of divorced parents are more likely to be obese and have mental health difficulties. A

2019 study from the United Kingdom found that divorce or separation of a couple resulted in "increases in children's BMI [body mass index] and their risk of overweight/obesity," even when the study authors had controlled four other variables like age and gender. The authors concluded by warning that "parental separation [is] a process with potentially long-lasting consequences" (Goisis et al., 2019).

And this is hardly the strongest link that has been found between parental divorce and adverse child health consequences. A 2014 meta-analysis of 47 research studies remarked that "[studies] continue to document negative effects of father absence on child well-being" even when considering "rigorous approaches to handling the problems of omitted variable bias and reverse causality." The authors concluded with several dire statements: "We find strong evidence that father absence negatively affects children's social-emotional development," "we find strong evidence that father absence increases adolescents' risky behavior, such as smoking or early childbearing," and "we do find strong and consistent negative effects of father absence on high school graduation."

The researchers noted that there was little difference in the cognitive ability between children of absent fathers and children from intact nuclear families. In other words, the children from broken families were just as 'smart' as other children. So why did fewer graduate from high school, an important educational benchmark? The authors suggested it was directly because of the absence of their fathers, saying "we see the strongest evidence…suggesting that the psychological harms of father absence experienced during childhood persist throughout the life course…looking across studies, it is apparent that father absence can affect child well-being across the life course" (McLanahan et al., 2013). Others have suggested that many grown children must fill in as a 'caregiver child' and take care of both a psychologically distraught parent and younger siblings, leaving them without a social life, friend circle, or time to do homework (Wallerstein,

Lewis, and Blakeslee, *The Unexpected Legacy of Divorce*, Chapter 1, 2000).

But what if divorce is simply 'in the genes' of the parents—they are doomed to divorce because their genes make them more likely to do so? And what if children of divorced parents do poorly simply because of genetics, not because of the divorce? These myths have been dispelled by science. A 2010 decade-in-review article in the *Journal of Marriage and Family* stated, "Genetically informed studies indicate that most of the links between divorce and problematic child outcomes cannot be accounted for by passive genetic inheritance" (Amato, 2010). In other words, divorce, and the resultant problematic child outcomes, are not the fault of genetics.

Children of divorced parents are more likely to have issues with drug and alcohol abuse. A 2020 Lebanese study found that "adolescents whose parents are divorced or separated were more likely to have hazardous alcohol disorder (HAD) [and] greater dependence on cigarette[s] and waterpipe[s]" (Jabbour et al.). This followed a 2016 American study which found that "parental divorce/separation was associated with earlier initiation of alcohol use" among young adolescents.

Even worse, the authors found that parental separation/divorce drove children to begin drinking at younger ages and greater frequencies than stress, child psychopathology, a family history of drinking, or parental drinking. (Jackson et al.) A 2014 study found that "15/16-year-old adolescents who experienced early parental divorce were more likely to smoke cigarettes and use doping agents compared to their peers whose parents were continuously married" (Zeratsion et al.). The authors noted that the younger the children when the parents divorced/separated, the stronger their use of drugs.

Children of divorced parents are also more likely to be involved in crime. In fact, this link is powerful enough that the Federal Bureau of Investigation considers family breakup and divorce to be predictive "factors known to affect volume and type of crime in different locations" (Wisconsin

Department of Justice, September 2013). A 2015 crime study in the journal *Societies*, in discussing previous crime research, blatantly observed, "several studies have shown that parental divorce leads to offspring antisocial behavior and criminal convictions." After analyzing three generations and thousands of cases, the study also found that parental divorce resulted in significant increases in non-violent offenses by their children (e.g. theft), even when controlling for other factors like the parents' criminal history. The researchers surmised that this was because the "crimes committed by children of divorced parents [try] to compensate for the decreased economic resources [of the family]." The researchers concluded by suggesting that special care taken to help families stay intact could help deter crime (van de Weijer, 2015).

It is generally taken for granted among divorce experts that the children will spend most of their time with their mothers; even if she has joint custody with the father, it is sadly quite common for the father to never or rarely meet with the child (Anderson, 2014). Since the father is usually absent and the mother must usually work to provide for the children, they may have less parental supervision than before, resulting in greater opportunity to commit crime (van de Weijer, 2015). Researchers have also been able to rule out other factors which could link divorce and crime, such as 'bad' genes in the children making them predisposed to violence. In fact, a study in the journal *Developmental Psychology* was undertaken specifically to analyze this alternative explanation. In summing up their study, the authors flatly stated that their findings indicate "it is the actual experience of parental divorce (and remarriage), and not common genes, that drives the association between divorce and adolescent delinquency" (Burt et al., 2008).

It is not surprising that divorce and the break-up of the nuclear family has such devastating consequences. After all, a single-parent family structure goes against the natural order—like a bird trying to fly with one wing, too much balance and support is torn away. It would be impossible to continue going through all the evidence, data, and studies which have consistently and repeatedly shown that parental separation and the destruction of their nuclear family to be a bad thing for children. Thus, I shall conclude by letting the scientists speak. As a 2016 meta-review comparing children of divorced/broken homes with children of intact homes put it, "living in a nuclear family was positively associated with almost all aspects of well-being in comparison with the children with separated parents" (Vezzetti). Now, I recognize that not all children of divorced parents will face all these hardships. However, their risk is much higher because they do not have the stable family life which is vital to their emotional, social and physical development. After all, if a child sees their parents leaving each other, they may wonder if they are next.

While I have found media, schools, and politicians to be very receptive at combatting racism or gun violence, they have remained largely indifferent to the divorce and destruction of the nuclear family crisis. Many of these people have good intentions. For example, some think it would be worse to trap a child in a 'bad marriage' than having the parents get divorced. However, this does not seem to be the case except in marriages where violence or abuse are present (Anderson, 2014). Early studies to answer this question found that "adolescents from the [unhappy marriages] functioned similarly to those who would remain in [happy] intact families, but better than those in the… divorced group, suggesting that differences can be attributed to parental divorce and its accompanying disruption of family processes" (Earp et al., 2012). Similarly, it has been reported from other sources that following divorce, the new environment the children find themselves in (where they must shoulder burdens their parents formerly bore and navigate their parents' new love lives) is often not 'better' (Wallerstein, Lewis, and Blakeslee, *The Unexpected Legacy of Divorce*, Chapter 1, 2000). Finally, another study found that only about

5% of children reported having a good relationship with a stepparent (Vogel, 2001).

Some may take my discussion of the problems of single parenthood and family breakup as an insult or thoughtless moralizing to hardworking, disadvantaged single parents. As one author succinctly summarized it in the *Atlantic*, "Many people see the discussion as no more than an attack on struggling single mothers and their children: Why blame single mothers when they are doing the very best they can? After all, the decision to end a marriage or a relationship is wrenching, and few parents are indifferent to the painful burden this decision imposes on their children. Many take the perilous step toward single parenthood as a last resort, after their best efforts to hold a marriage together have failed. Consequently, it can seem particularly cruel and unfeeling to remind parents of the hardships their children might suffer as a result of family breakup" (Whitehead, 1993).

However, I emphasize that I am not trying to beat up on single mothers here. I am simply trying to present that divorce and family breakup has horrendous consequences in terms of private costs to the individuals that experience a divorce, particularly the children, and societal costs as well. As a society, we must not turn a blind eye to this reality. Similarly, we cannot put a Band-Aid over the problem or try to treat the symptoms alone (which is the current strategy). Instead, we must identify, recognize, and treat the cause. We must find ways to keep our families intact!

Up to this point, I have focused upon the private costs upon the children of a divorced couple. The children of divorce and family breakup are not the only ones who suffer. The adults suffer too. Studies which examine how adults fare after their divorce seem to show that they, too, can suffer from it—physically, psychologically, and emotionally (Anderson, 2014).

Again, I submit that there is no such thing as a purely private problem. All private problems have some way of affecting society, and divorce and nuclear family breakup is no exception. Sadly, the social effects can be extreme in some cases. In particular, I focus on an area that I believe has not been examined as thoroughly as it should be: mass murder and divorce.

Earlier, I mentioned studies which show that divorce and crime are linked. Personally, I have surveyed at how major crimes and broken families are linked. I have reviewed a sample of 59 famous mass murderers (serial killers, school shooters, mass shooters, etc.) in the United States between 1860 and 2018. For my purposes, a mass murderer is one who has committed or likely committed 3 or more murders (although many, especially the serial killers, may have potentially committed several unconfirmed murders.) I have found that the vast majority (86.4%—51 of the 59) of the perpetrators saw their parents' divorce/separate, experienced a divorce/separation themselves, or both.

These can be broken down further. Some of these mass murderers were bigamists (married a person while already legally married to someone else) in addition to murderers, like the first serial killer in the United States, H. H. Holmes (1860s-27+ victims), or the serial killer Albert Fish (1936-3+ victims confirmed, many more suspected).

Many of them watched their parents undergo a divorce or separation, like the first mass shooter in the United States, Howard Unruh (1949-13 victims), the school shooter Charles Whitman (1966-17 deaths-deadliest mass shooting at the time), the serial killer Edmund Kemper (1973-10 victims), serial killer George Howard Putt (1991-5 victims), murderer and grave robber Ed Gein (1984-11 victims, 2 murders—Gein became the inspiration for the Hitchcock thriller *Psycho*), serial killer Jeffrey Dahmer (1994-17 murders), serial killer Aileen Wuornos (2002-7 murders), serial killer Charles Cullen (2003-29+ victims), school shooter Jeffrey Weise (2005-9 victims), serial killer Carl Watts (1982-14+ victims), mass shooter Robert Hawkins (2007-8 victims), mass shooter Michael McLendon (2009-10 victims), school shooter T. J. Lane (2009-3 victims), mass shooter Bryan Speight (2010-8 deaths), mass shooter Scott Dekraai

(2011-8 victims), Norweigan mass bomber and shooter Anders Behring Breivik (2011-77 victims), Newtown school shooter Adam Lanza (2012, 28 victims—deadliest attack on an American elementary school), serial killer David Wood (1987-9 victims), kidnapper and rapist Ariel Castro (2013, 3 victims), mass shooter Vester Lee Flanagan (2015-3 victims), mass shooter Dr. Henry Bello (2017-8 victims), insane cult leader Charles Manson (1969-responsible for 9 deaths, possibly more), school shooter Nikolas Cruz (2018-24 victims—deadliest attack on an American high school), and mass shooter Dylann Roof (2015-9 deaths) (Sauer, 2015) (Biography.com, 2020) (Jenkins 2020) (Ramirez, 2006) (Montaldo 2019) (Koningsberg, 2007) (Knausgaard, 2015) (Solomon, 2014) (Manson, Biography.com, 2020) (Borden and Frankel, 2015) (Safranek, 2008) (McKelway and Williams, 2010).

A similarly mind-boggling number underwent a divorce or separation themselves, including serial killer John Gacy (1978-33 murders-Gacy held the record at that time for most murders by a single American), mass shooter Carl Brown (1982, 11 victims), mass shooter George Banks (1982-14 victims), mass shooter Joseph Wesbecker (1989-21 victims), mass shooter Gian Luigi Ferri (1993-9 deaths), mass shooter Mark Barton (1999-26 victims), serial killer Gary Ridgeway (2001-49+ murders), serial killer Anthony Hardy (2002-3+ murders), mass shooter Douglas Williams (2003-7 deaths), serial killer Charles Cullen, serial killer Carl Watts, serial killer Arthur Shawcross (1989-14 victims), mass shooter Jiverly Wong (2009-14 victims), mass murderer John Frazier (1970-5 deaths), mass shooter John Muhammed (2002-27 victims), mass shooter Scott Dekraai, serial killer Tommy Sells (1999-23+ suspected victims), mass shooter Robert Dear Jr. (2015-12 victims), mass shooter Dr. Henry Bello, and mass shooter Stephen Paddock (2017-928 victims, 61 deaths-deadliest mass shooting by a lone shooter in American history) (Halbfinger and Hart, 2003) (Assad, 2003) (Murder Victims, n.d.) (Squires, 2009) (Montaldo, 2019) (Berkes et al. 2017).

These are simply the mass murderers who had links to divorce or separation. Many of the other mass murderers I analyzed experienced the death of a parent, were raised by unmarried parents, were raised by stepparents, or adopted parents, were raised only to learn they were illegitimate children, or were abandoned by one or more parents during childhood. In fact, practically every mass murderer I assessed (58/59 or 98%) had some link to a broken family. Only one mass murderer—serial killer Judy Buenoano—had no links to a broken family.

I am not the first person to notice that mass murderers tend to come from broken homes. In fact, an in-depth analysis by Dr. Peter Langman, an expert in school shootings, found that 82% of school shooters grew up in dysfunctional families or without both parents together. This led him to conclude that the typical portrayal of school shooters as coming from "stable, intact, middle- to upper-middle-class families" was incorrect (Langman, 2016). A similar analysis using case studies of six mass murderers by Dr. Michael Cook found that divorce was a common link among them. In every case, either the parents were divorced/separated, or the shooters themselves had been divorced. Cook made sure to note, "only a tiny fraction of children of divorce turn into rampage killers;" however, he also remarked that these findings mean that the negative effects of divorce and broken families should be "shouted across the roof-tops" (Cook, 2017).

After every mass shooting, after every serial killer is caught, there are loud calls for gun reform (Nikolas Cruz, Stephen Paddock), mental health reform (Jeffrey Wise, Robert Hawkins), or criminal justice reform (Carl Watts, Tommy Sells). People talk about noticing the 'warning signs' before the attack and how they were missed (Adam Lanza, Charles Cullen). However, I am of the opinion that gun reform, mental health reform, or criminal justice reform can replace another essential reform which is even more badly needed: family stability reform.

While gun control, expanded mental health service, or improved criminal justice laws may be able to treat the symptoms (criminal behavior—rape, murder, etc.), the simple fact is that the true problem lies much deeper, inside the hearts of each of the mass murderers. It is from inside that the desire to kill, to rape, or to attack comes from. Is it a coincidence that family instability is linked to these desires? No, I do not think so. Every person longs to be recognized by others and to have an intimate relationship with others. When a person does not find this in their family, is it really so surprising that they try to find it elsewhere, in whatever twisted way they can?

Guns do not directly make criminals; mental health does not directly make criminals; poor laws or policies do not directly make criminals. The human heart does. I submit that the only way to truly stop someone from developing a criminal heart is to give them the validation and love they needed from the start, the love and validation that can only come from parents, from a spouse, from family. Fixing gun laws or mental health systems or criminal justice laws may help identify or stop criminals from committing crime, but if you want to stop people from even going down that path in the first place, you must first fix the family.

Crime may be the first major social implication of divorce and broken families, but it is not the only one. Divorce has larger social impacts than just crime. It also has drastic consequences for culture. It is not difficult to see why—after all, divorce strikes at the most basic unit of society: the family. It is hard to deny that divorce has had significant consequences for the family, and these have translated into significant consequences for society.

The first manifestation of this is the new family structures created by divorce. In the not-so-distant past, it was taken for granted that a family consisted of the biological father and mother and their children. Grandparents or other relatives might live with them for a time, but the nuclear family was well-defined. Everyone had a sense of purpose and belonging in this family structure because the roles were well-defined.

Divorce has created a much larger number of blended families—that is, families in which the parents live not just with children from their current relationship but also with children from previous relationships. Today, many spouses may divorce and remarry once, twice, thrice, or even more, having new children with new spouses each time. This results in a child having a different mother, father, or siblings over time. This has several key domino effects.

First, it is very confusing for the children to know who 'counts' as their grandparents anymore, let alone their aunt or uncle. Previous relatives may no longer 'count' as relatives because the parent who came from that family group has left the child's family. And if the remaining parent remarries, the child is suddenly introduced to a whole new host of relatives, who now 'count' as uncles, aunts, grandparents, etc. It is also hard to figure out your relationships with other siblings—the older one might be your full sibling, but the middle one might be your step-sibling, and the youngest one might be your step-step-sibling. Also, who is taking care of you now? Is it one of your grandparents? Or, is it now a stepparent? Or, a step-step-parent? Or, maybe a former grandparent? Who is coming to see you on the weekends anyway? Is it your dad or your former dad, your mom, or your former mom? What do they 'count' as now?

Second, it is very confusing for the spouses. Suddenly, new terminology is required to talk about the children—some are 'my children from my first marriage,' others are 'his/her children from his/her first marriage,' some are 'our children,' and some are 'the other guy's/girl's children.' With each step—that is, with each divorce and remarriage—this becomes more complicated.

Third, it becomes very confusing for friends of the family. Say you are friends with a woman and she gets married and has children. You grow to like her husband and children and become friends with them. Then she gets a bitter divorce. She remarries, and so does her husband. Now, you must figure out if being friends with the woman means you cannot be friends with her first husband anymore. Or, maybe, you can be friends with the children from her first marriage, but not from hers second—never mind that you were friends for many years.

Fourth, it becomes very confusing for the relatives of the family. If your brother marries a woman and they have children but later divorce, are you still the uncle/aunt of their children? Or, if the wife takes custody, do you suddenly fall out of their life as a relative? It is even worse if you are a grandparent and your son or daughter gets married, has children, and then divorces. Suddenly, if your former daughter-in-law takes custody of the children, do they still 'count' as your grandchildren? Even if they do, will you be able to see them again? How much of a role will you have in their life, or will they have in yours?

If all of this is giving you a headache, I am not surprised. Sadly, with every divorce and remarriage, these are exactly the kinds of heartbreaking questions which children, spouses, friends, and families must wrestle with. Is this a good thing for society? I overwhelmingly say that it is not. It is difficult for adults to process these kinds of questions—imagine, then, how hard it must be for the children! With each step, relationships between family members are severed, and new relationships are suddenly formed. Humans (particularly children, but adults too) are not designed endure this kind emotional turmoil. Like tape on a roll; we cannot stick equally well to any surface, be ripped off, and be stuck again. With every subsequent divorce and remarriage, with every subsequent breakup of family structure, not only are existing relationships weakened, but the ability to form new relationships is weakened as well.

How can a child continue to be carefree and trust that the 'new' dad is going to be the 'real' dad forever? The 'old' dad was not. How can you be sure your brother is going to stay with his new wife forever? He did not with the last one, even if that was what he vowed at the altar. If you are the spouse, how do you know that you and your new spouse will not get divorced just like your old spouse? With each stepparent, step sibling, step-step-wife, and so forth, the ability of a human to form long-lasting, committed relationships declines.

If the intimacy and trust of the relationships decreases, the authority weakens as well. Children can tell their new stepparent, 'You're not the boss of me,' 'you're not my mother,' or 'don't tell me what to do.' Similarly, how uncomfortable would it be for a mother to treat a child like her son even though he is not, or for a sibling to treat another as a sibling even though they are not? The more steps there are in the family structure, the worse it gets. The stepparents may not be able to discipline the stepchildren properly without creating animosity (Martin, 2011). A stepchild may feel resentment when a stepparent tries to encourage educational advancement or enforce a new house rule and may feel the stepparent is an imposter trying to take over from the 'real' or 'true' parent (Quinlan, 2015) (Bayless, 2014).

Is this unfair on the part of the child? Can you blame them? The stepparent may feel resentment that their spouse spends time with their biological children from the previous relationship (Frostrup 2020). Meanwhile, the children may have very little or no emotional attachment to each other. Or, in some rare cases (especially if the stepchildren are adolescents), they may feel sexual attractions to one another (Shark, 2019) (Godstone, 2017). One such child who experienced this begged others to recognize that "If both have children who are teenagers, we may need to recognize that they have hearts too" (Godstone, 2017). Or, the stepparent may feel sexually attracted to the stepchildren (Waterworth 2020) (Johnston 2019) (Williams 2020).

The house of a blended family is more like a group of people together (a club) rather than a family. How do you teach someone about lasting commitment, lasting relationships, or complete trust in an environment like this? How can someone give themselves to another in love and intimacy if they personally did not witness such relationships? What does commitment mean when there is none? The parents say, "Oh we love each other,"—and then, a few years later, "we're not in love anymore." What did we think this was going to do to our children? To our society?

The blind cannot lead the blind. I mentioned earlier that the dating couple often needs parental advice to make the transition from friends to spouses. However, if the parents are absent, or if the parents have been divorced, or if the parents are separated, then the parents do not have a wealth of advice from which they can draw. This leaves their children to learn about commitment and permanent relationships by themselves elsewhere.

When someone has divorced and remarried and divorced and remarried so many times, you make friends with them or interact with them knowing that one or both of them have committed adultery. Christ was very clear on this when He said, "I say to you, whoever divorces his wife (unless the marriage is unlawful) causes her to commit adultery, and whoever marries a divorced woman commits adultery" (Matthew 5:32). So how is it that in a Christian country like America today, divorce is so widely practiced and accepted? Why did we get so comfortable with adultery?

What used to be common sense in our country (if you get married, you are married for life, because that is what you promised) no longer makes sense to many people and is no longer common. However, it is still a moral reality. We do not get new moral realities; we either live up to the ones we ought to have lived up to before, or we abandon moral realities we ought to keep upholding. Even if you say that every divorce happening today was because the marriage was a mistake, doesn't that then beg the question of why so many marriages in as advanced a society as America are mistakes?

The modern culture of divorce does not live up to the moral realities of marital relationships and commitments that it should.

While crime and broken family structures are dangerous consequences of divorce, they are not the worst. Perhaps the worst effect of divorce is that it creates a vicious cycle. The children of divorced parents are much more likely to get divorced themselves.

How much more likely? A systematic review by researchers found that "if a woman's parents divorced, her odds of divorce increased 69 percent, while if both a husband and wife's parents divorced, the risk of divorce increased by 189 percent." This was no fluke result either—10 other longitudinal studies investigating the same topic over a period of 20 years found similar results (Epstein, 2019).

Why is this the case? Two major theories have emerged. The first theory suggests that couples who divorce were not able to communicate effectively or manage their marital relationship in a healthy way. Since their children did not witness effective inter-couple communication or marital relationship management, they are unable to maintain a healthy marriage themselves and get divorced (Epstein, 2019). The second theory suggests that children of a divorced couple simply lose confidence in the permanence of commitment and marriage (Pinsker, 2019).

As explained by Dr. Judith Wallenstein in her own research, "children of divorce are haunted by the ghosts of their parents' divorce and terrified that the same fate awaits them" (2005). Another study by researchers from Boston University and the University of Denver found that children whose parents had divorced had "both reduced commitment to marriage as an institution and lower confidence that marriages can remain stable" when compared to children whose parents stayed married (Whitton et al 2008). They also found "at the outset of their first marriages, women whose parents had divorced reported lower relationship commitment and less confidence in the future of their [own] marriages than did women from non-divorced families."

What is the net effect? As explained by therapist Sarah Epstein (Epstein, 2019):

"Children of divorce are at risk of responding to their fear of divorce in one of two ways. Some dive headlong into inappropriate, unformed relationships as a counter-phobic response to their fears. Others avoid relationships all together, and when in relationships, maintain a mindset akin to waiting for the other shoe to drop. They struggle to believe in the strength of relationships to weather difficult stretches, and many arrive ill-equipped to address a relationship's most potent challenges" (summarizing research including Wallerstein, 2005).

Whichever path the children choose, they are at greater risk for divorce. It has been well-documented that children of divorce often feel a need to look to outside relationships to satisfy the attention or love they lost through their parent's divorce, a phenomenon known as the 'father wound' or 'mother wound.'

Researchers have found that women whose father left them in childhood were at higher risk of looking to outside relationships to satisfy their longings for intimacy and love, making them more likely to engage in relationships (including sexual relationships) with men without evaluating them thoroughly to determine compatibility first (Schreiber 2017). This is thought to be the reason why daughters of divorced parents are more likely to engage in sexual activity at a young age or experience a teenage pregnancy (Ellis et al. 2003) (Newport Academy, 2019). This effect is certainly not limited to women. Other researchers noted how President Barack Obama's 2004 book, *Dreams from my Father*, spends 460 pages reflecting on Obama's father wound even though it had been 46 years since his father had left him (Miller, 2012). Clearly, while these 'wounds' may not be physical, they are certainly long-lasting and increase the chance of heartbreak or divorce further down the line.

One surprising finding of all this research is that children of parents who fought frequently but did not get divorced were no more likely to get divorced than children of parents who did not fight frequently and stayed married (Amato and DeBoer, 2004). In other words, while we in America have very negative views on couples fighting, this does not lead to higher divorce rates among their children. This is a far cry from the idea that 'unhappy' couples should get divorced 'for the benefit of the children.' In fact, divorce in a family itself is the only predictor of higher divorce rates among their children (Epstein, 2019). Researcher Nicholas Wolfinger, a sociologist at the University of Utah, explained these findings by writing, "All couples fight. If your parents stay together, they fight and then you realize these things are not fatal to a marriage. If you are from a divorced family, you do not learn that lesson, and [after fights] it seems like things are untenable. And so [when you fight in your own marriage], you bounce" (Pinsker 2019). Divorce, not discord, begets further divorce.

Other children, rather than chasing relationships, may be scared away completely. As reported by Reuters, when it comes to children of divorced parents, "Some of those children, later in life, don't want anything to do with marriage" (Pinsker 2019). As psychotherapist Ken Page explained it, "Your original loves are echoed in your current loves. If there's a really high degree of wounding, anger, or hurt in your childhood, you're going to be bringing that into your next relationship" (Saint Thomas, 2015). I submit that it is a glaring warning sign that something is wrong when the children in a society are afraid of having an emotional attachment to another human being because they are afraid it will not last. Further, I submit it is a glaring warning sign that something is wrong when the children of a society are afraid to be like their parents. And, it is a glaring warning sign that something is wrong when something that society has turned to for solving marital relationship problems (divorce) actually perpetuates those problems later down the line.

Of course, this is focusing on those children who want to get married. But a good number of children of divorced couples do not want to get married at all. For example, an anonymous writer told the Guardian newspaper what she concluded after her parent's divorce: "I'm 24 and I think marriage is pointless – and [I have thought so] my whole life…I associated marriage with separation and pain… my priorities right now are getting ahead in my career and buying my own place. And I don't see that changing for a very long time" (Anonymous 2019).

In addition to crime, broken family structures, and a vicious cycle of repetition, divorce has other negative effects on society. Consider that a divide forms between intact families and broken families. They are different in structure, and they are different in terms of lived experiences. Also consider that a divide forms between children from intact families and children from broken families. The children from broken families will have the bitter, terrifying experience of watching their family ripped apart, an experience not shared by children from intact families.

Children from divorced families may be confused or not understand why children from intact families are more willing to be trusting and committed to relationships. Or, children from divorced families may feel jealous of children in intact families. Similarly, children from intact families may not understand why children from divorced families have deep relationship anxiety. Divorced families and single parents also must rely on social welfare programs to make ends meet (Garfinkel and Zilanawala 2015). This could make them embarrassed when they must rely on public support while their neighbors who come from intact families do not have that type of reliance. Similarly, those who come from intact families may feel angry or cheated that their hard-earned money is going to pay for the consequences of divorce of another couple.

It is easy to see that divorce has so many negative consequences that it is time that we as a society find a way to stop it. Children of divorce are negatively impacted in numerous severe ways. The old notion that they would simply 'bounce back' from a divorce is simply false. Everything from their physical health to their emotional wellbeing to their educational achievements are impacted. They are not able to perform to their maximum capacity and are less productive to themselves and the society. In addition, with no role models of a healthy relationship, they may also get divorced, prolonging the negative effects on society. Everyone suffers when our children are emotionally stunted at a young age. Everyone in society stands to lose if our children cannot grow up in a stable environment where their physical and psychological need for a mother and father is met.

When crime is committed, the society not only pays for the damages, but must also pay for the imprisonment of the inmates and the workings of the legal system. Crime is bad for society, and divorce, which increases crime, is also bad for society. Not only are the potential talents of the inmates locked behind bars, but the society also ends up diverting attention and resources to dealing with the legacy of broken families when that attention and those resources could have been diverted to somewhere else—to cleaning up the oceans, for example.

Clearly, the private and social consequences of divorce are many. Society could perhaps withstand 5% of marriages being broken; perhaps it could withstand 10% of marriages being broken. But no society can healthily withstand the continued breakup of thousands of families and the ensuing costs this entails. The consequences of this are too great to ignore.

PART III
DEFEATING THE DRAGON

What Happens if We Fix (or Don't Fix)
the Problem?

CHAPTER 1

THE ROOT OF ALL EVIL

The root of the Nazi party was Adolf Hitler. Once he was killed, the Nazi party was dealt its stricken blow. Yet, Naziism, the ideology, still exists. Why? Because Adolf Hitler did a good job of quantifying who his enemies were: Jews, black people, Catholics, and all who opposed him. Even today, people still carry on those same ideas. To destroy Naziism, we must oppose the idea that these people are somehow inferior to others. Adolf Hitler is dead; killing him alone did not solve the problem of eliminating Naziism.

This means that our enemy in our current fight to restore the family is not a person. It is not even a group of people. Our enemies are not the men and women on their second or third marriage. Our enemies are not their children or stepchildren. Our enemies are not the college student partiers or the porn industry or prostitutes. Destroying these people will not fix the problem of the breaking nuclear family. We must destroy the ideology.

Our enemy is the culture of selfishness. The root of nuclear family breakdown is selfishness.

When a man or woman puts their own pleasure and desires first, they feel that it is better to break up a family and chase those feelings rather than stay and support their spouse and children. Our enemy comes from inside. We must fight our own selfish tendencies and desires to put our own wishes first.

In a culture that tells us that we deserve to have what we want, when we want, the way we want, we must fight back and realize that this is a terrible way to live, both for ourselves and for others. It is time to destroy the ideology of selfishness with an ideology of selflessness. It is time for us to put others' wants and desires before our own. People mistakenly chase a selfish lifestyle because it promises them satisfaction, but this is a mirage. They will never find satisfaction by chasing their whims. Instead, it is those who put others first that will find fulfillment and satisfaction in their lives.

Here is my proposal to America:

First, stop putting your own desires ahead of everything else. Stop being selfish. Second, put the needs and wants of your nuclear family members ahead of everything else, except God. Allow yourself to think about what is best for your spouse, your children, and your family life. Third, if you are a spouse in a marriage, decide today that you will work to make your marriage succeed. Be open to creative solutions. Be persistent in your quest. Examine how you can modify yourself to improve your marriage. Your marriage will thrive when you and your spouse each decide to change and improve yourselves from within. Fourth, if you are the child of a divorce, do not avoid marriage. Choose to be committed to a spouse for life in marriage. Be open to receiving the benefits, joys, and successes of a thriving marriage for yourself and your nuclear family. If America adopts this proposal, then the catastrophic path that the nation is currently travelling upon (explained in next chapter) will slowly evaporate. This solution will not be effective with attention for just one day. This solution will only be effective when the people of America decide to make a difference and commit themselves for their entire lifetime. Such a commitment for life will result in future generations being prosperous; there will be prosperity for the individual, for the nuclear family, for the nation and for the entire world.

CHAPTER 2

LEARNING FROM HISTORY

It is a well-known saying that those who do not know their history are doomed to repeat it. What this means is that humans tend to make the same mistakes over and over again. Thus, we can take lessons from the past and use them to make better decisions in the future. The mistakes made by previous civilizations can be used as a learning opportunity for current civilizations to avoid making those same mistakes.

There is a civilization which I find to have striking parallels to the United States. This civilization is Ancient Rome.

The ancient Roman Empire has been compared to modern America in several ways. For example, they are both roughly the same size by land area within their borders. They are both the largest and strongest world powers of their times and have a large influence on the rest of the world. Both are open societies that welcome immigrants and grant them citizenship, resulting in large cultural melting pots. Ancient Rome was governed by a unique set of laws that differed from the laws of nearby areas. Similarly, America also has its own distinct set of laws compared to other countries.

Ancient Rome had a large, mighty army and the United States has a large and mighty army. The Romans had the most advanced scientific and medical practices at that time. Likewise, the United States offers the most advanced science and medicine found anywhere in the world. Other areas in which the Romans excelled include the arts, literature, public infrastructure, theaters, and means of relaxation such as the swimming pool. Today, the United States excels in all these areas as well. Both civilizations profited from slavery, although the US outlawed slavery whereas Rome did not. (Anderson, 2009). Both refused to give women the right to vote, though the US suffrage movement corrected this whereas Rome never did.

In the area of government, it is no mistake that ancient Rome and contemporary Washington D.C. have many similarities. In fact, the Founding Fathers looked to the Roman Empire as a guide for what worked—and did not work—in creating a democratic society. Both civilizations incorporated checks and balances into their political structures to prevent the consolidation of power into one person's hands (Lewis, 2014). According to Dr. Kenneth Calvert, Professor of Ancient History at Hillsdale College, both civilizations relied primarily on local governments to resolve problems while governance from the capital city took a more behind-the-scenes role (Pullmann, 2018). In addition, both expanded citizenship to numerous 'outsiders,' resulting in racial and cultural intermingling.

Both the Roman Empire and America have senates as part of their government. The Roman emperor was the highest official and single leader while the President is the single leader of America. There are other strong parallels between Rome's greatest leaders and America's greatest leaders. For an example, let's examine Cincinnatus from Rome and George Washington from the United States. Both leaders were farmers who selflessly contributed their abilities to lead their countries in times of crisis, but then gave up their great power to return to their farms.

In addition to government and social structures, the general public in both civilizations had a strong adhesion to shared moral principles including honesty, bravery, and discipline (Sharp, JMU Research Journal, Vol 2, 2014). According to Dr. Calvert, these virtues helped both societies become dominant, strong world powers (Pullmann, 2018). Even if different groups of people were separated by wealth or race, the different social classes were unified around these values, leading to cooperation between them.

The Early Roman period, before 404 BC, had strong morals and family life that guided them. According to Dr. Richard Saller, a Professor of History, and former Provost of the University of Chicago, "Romans…took the essential family unit to be father, mother, and children. The central value binding that family together was *pietas*, which can be translated as affectionate devotion. Husbands and wives, parents, and children, were supposed to love one another" (2001, UChicago). Divorce in Rome, at that time, was difficult and rare; the first recorded divorce in Rome was in 268BC (Duran, *The Story of Civilization Part III,* 1944). Likewise, in early American history from the nation's independence in 1776 until the 1940s, family life in America was stable, divorce was rare, and virginity and chastity of men and women were honored.

However, once divorce became common in Rome, both women and men became more sexually promiscuous and abandoned moral ideals like *pietas* in favor of sexual pleasure and personal liberation (Saller, 2001, UChicago). Seneca, a famous Roman Senator, warned his compatriots that their behavior would result in the downfall of their society. He lamented that "they divorce in order to remarry. They marry in order to divorce" (Flurry, 2018). From 1945 onwards, family stability in America began to erode until the current time. Family life in America continues to decline today.

The similarities between ancient Rome and America continue. There are parallels between how Rome fell apart and how America is falling apart. First, leaders became self-interested and selfish (compare Roman emperors like Caligula and Nero to some current American politicians). Second, there was a general abandonment of strong moral principles among the general population (honesty, bravery, discipline); these were replaced with relativism and personal liberation. This loss of shared values resulted in estrangement between social classes and immoral behavior among both the powerful and the general population, resulting in the collapse of the Roman Empire.

The height of this disintegration occurred around 400 A.D (Duran, *The Story of Civilization Part III,* 1944).[4] Rome was destroyed in 476 A.D. I predict that if America does not change its current trajectory, it, too, will decline just as Rome did. The immorality in America today resembles what Rome went through in 400 A.D. Virginity and chastity among both women and men is scorned rather than honored. Today, divorce and unchastity are rampant in American culture, and family breakup is common. If America does not correct these problems, I predict that America's success and leadership role in the world will decline and then end. America will end up like the Roman Empire.

If the solutions in this book are not implemented and the warning herein is not heeded, then I predict that the following will result: A disaster, just like what happened to the Roman empire. The mighty Roman empire fell and ceased to exist. In the same way, America's status as the global leader will end. Many of the evil elements that caused Rome's collapse are the same elements happening today; specifically, perverted sex, unstable marriages, widespread homosexuality,[5] adultery, and divorce (Squires, 2011)(Pearse, 2014).[6] In short, the collapse of the Roman Empire occurred because of moral decay in its society. A nation rises and falls with the rise and fall of the nuclear family. Without strong nuclear families, each citizen is purely self-serving and the common good disappears. As the nuclear

---

[4] *The Story of Civilization: Part III, Caesar and Christ, A History of Roman Civilization and of Christianity from their beginnings to A.D.325,* Will Durant, Simon and Shuster 1944

[5] https://historynewsnetwork.org/article/138300#:~:text=A%20prominent%20Italian%20 historian%20has,hordes%2C%20sparking%20a%20furious%20row.

[6] https://www.roger-pearse.com/weblog/2014/01/17/did-moral-decay-destroy-the-ancient-world/

family disintegrates, so will America and so will the other societies around the globe that are embracing the same immoral practices.

If nuclear bombs drop across the US tomorrow, what will happen? Many sci-fi films (Mortal Engines, Love and Monsters) and videogames (Fallout) have tried to imagine life after the bombs. They feature polluted water, mutated organisms, burned-out landscapes, and guerilla fighting between rival factions. If we continue down our current path of family breakdown, the effects on ourselves and our nation will be similar. When the children of these broken families do not receive the nurturing and affirmation they need from their family, they will seek it elsewhere: in drugs, in gangs, in toxic relationships, or in other escapes. Everyone needs a strong nuclear family group; if they do not get it from their nuclear family, they will try getting it elsewhere. The effects of a nuclear family breakdown are like those of a nuclear bomb: the defects and mutations will live on in the survivors and their children.

CHAPTER 3

CAN DIVORCE EVER BE ALLOWED?

To save a human life, amputating a wounded leg or arm may be necessary. It is an undesirable solution, but a necessary procedure to save that life. Similarly, there may be limited and extreme situations where divorce is needed. In Jesus Christ's teachings, he stated that marriage is unbreakable except in the case of 'unlawful marriage' or, as other translations put it, 'lewd conduct,' 'unchastity,' or 'fornication.' Christ himself gave an extreme and limited situation where divorce may be appropriate.

Hence, I propose that divorce (or annulment for Catholics) should only be granted for marriages where spouses experience impotency, proven cruelty, adultery unconfessed in the Sacrament of Reconciliation, or grave lying before marriage. Adultery is an instance where a physical consummation occurs between one of the spouses and someone else. This does not include pornography, but it does include prostitution.

What do I advise for families that have already gone through divorce? Large numbers of Americans are now in their second or third marriage. Large numbers of American children have stepparents, stepsiblings, and step grandparents. So, what can these families do to improve family life in America? They cannot go back to their first marriage.

The best thing for them to do is twofold: first, they must treat their current marriage as their lifelong committed relationship. Second, they must remain actively involved in the lives of all their children, whether their own or stepchildren. They should give a commitment to care for all their previous spouses and their previous children. This kind of renewed commitment to their families cannot replace unbroken nuclear family stability, but it is a proactive and positive step forward for these families to improve the stability of their current families and to provide a good example for their children of starting anew.

CHAPTER 4
FINAL REMARKS

I acknowledge the enormity and complexity of the task of promoting stable nuclear families. It requires unified recognition of the problem and intensive action over time to correct it. I am confident that the American people can re-stabilize family life in this society. Americans are creative, resilient, and strong. When the American public was shattered by the terrorist attacks on 9/11 (2001), by the assassination of President John F. Kennedy in 1963, or by the natural disasters of Hurricane Irma (2017), they have always built back stronger after the destruction.

If the warning in this book is heeded, America will be a prosperous nation for all. There will be increased respect, happiness, safety, emotional wellbeing, and love. Because parents will have a deep sense of responsibility in their family lives, employees will be more productive, causing economic growth. Education will thrive because parents will be more invested in their children's future and more involved in their child's education and homelife. There will be more peace at home. Children will experience real, natural love. Even if parents scold or discipline their children, this will be within the framework of love and commitment that only a nuclear family can bring. There will be better psychological, emotional, and affectionate attachment among all the family members.

All human beings long for loving support, and the best support comes from intact, nuclear families. The children of stable families will grow much more disciplined with much better lifestyles than those in blended families. The enduring impacts on America from strong, stable families will be lower crime, better health for all, and more community involvement.

I predict that there will be individuals who resist and reject this positive change. This includes anyone who profits from the status quo, such as corrupt politicians, the pornography industry, marriage therapists, divorce attorneys, drug companies who sell antidepressants, and any other organization that benefits from the breakdown of nuclear families. The daytime soap opera and romance novel media, which make broken families look like a way to personal freedom, will lose viewership and readership as more consumers reject their lies about family life.

Nevertheless, Americans as a whole will greatly benefit. Americans are pioneering people. They settled the 'new world' and achieved heights and depths that other nations could not reach. America put the first man on the moon and put the cell phone and automobile into the hands of people all over the globe. Similarly, America can and should renew its support of stable nuclear families.

The new and predominant culture we ought to create can be glimpsed in the lives of Asian families. Asia has one of the lowest rates of divorce worldwide, with just 1 in 1,000 weddings ending in a divorce (Bain, 2015). There, abstinence before marriage is the norm. In countries like Sri Lanka, India and Indonesia, the divorce rate is lower than 2-3% (DNA Web Desk, 2022). Traditionally, Asian children highly value their parents' advice and counsel in the choice of a prospective spouse and in other family matters. It is generally recognized in the Asian culture that the parents know their children well and can identify what they need better than anyone else. Thus, Asian parents have a prominent role in arranging and participating in their children's marriages.

I propose that the Western cultures should adopt the family-centered emphasis of Asian cultures. I do not wish Westerners to dress the way

Asians dress or eat what Asians eat. Rather, I want them to observe and implement some of the values that Asians possess in their families. First, among these, is commitment. Once a man and woman are wedded in the Asian families, they are emotionally and physically committed. They understand this commitment to be permanent and unyielding. It is time for Western couples to bring the same level of understanding to their marriage. Rather than bailing on their relationships based on fleeting feelings, Western couples must learn to stay committed to their marriage no matter the circumstances.

Second, Western couples should emulate the importance Asian couples give to being involved in the lives of their children. Once the Asian wedded couple has children, they make their children the central point of their lives. Their primary motivation is to ensure their children's wellbeing by cultivating their children's talents and interests. This does not mean that the couple no longer enjoys anything together anymore; rather, they enjoy together the time they spend investing in their children. The interests of the children become the interests of the parents and the family.

Asian families also do not cast their children off or leave them alone once they are 18 years of age. The children never exit the parent's lives, even once they leave the house. The parents continue to visit and help their children through college and into their adulthood. There are open lines of communication. Rather than wanting to "get rid" of the kids, the Asian coupless want to keep their children. The African proverb "It takes a whole village to raise a child," is fundamentally true. Asian children are raised in a family structure that includes more than just their parents: grandparents, uncles, aunts, and cousins are heavily involved as well. However, in front of the whole village comes the parents first. Asian families understand that parental investment is the key to their children's wellbeing. This shared focus and vision in turn helps bind the couple together in love.

This does not mean that Westerners must practice arranged marriage as they do in Asia, but it means that parents should modify their current way of thinking and how they conduct themselves. I find that Western parents and Western culture places an overemphasis on how the young man and woman feel about each other rather than their level of commitment. Do they have a strong feeling of elation or physical attraction when they are around the other person? If yes, then, according to western culture, what they feel means they are in love.

I do not mean to completely discredit all feelings, but feelings are not the main consideration. Feelings can and will change, and the sense of elation and attraction can dwindle away over time. The couple needs more than just feelings to rely upon. The couple needs commitment. I am not proposing that young adults consent to marry based solely on their parents' recommendation. Instead, I am proposing a dynamic process that incorporates both the young person who wants to marry and their parents. In the end, while the young person's feelings may help influence the decision, there must be a long-term, lifelong commitment on the part of both spouses for a marriage to work and to endure.

America has traveled to the moon, but its families are destroyed. Americans must realize that running and maintaining a nuclear family is critical for the future generations to flourish. Once the family is gone, then the nation is gone. The freedom enjoyed in America must be responsibly blended with moral and ethical values such as chastity and discipline and commitment. These values must be imparted not only in the home, but in all walks of life—in educational environments, political arenas, religious institutions, and business centers.

I have been living in America for the last 57 years, more than half a century. I have witnessed dramatic changes in the social, cultural, spiritual, and technological areas. America is full of good-minded, virtuous people who should not lose heart. All Americans need to get engaged in creating a cultural change for the family. We cannot afford to sit aside at the expense of the future generations—our children, grandchildren, great-grandchildren, and descendants depend on it.

America can change. In my 57 years here, I have witnessed dramatic improvement in race relations. Before, black people suffered from Jim Crow laws. Today, black men can sit in restaurants, travel on buses, and attend concerts alongside white men. Before, special-needs individuals could not gain access into many buildings without walking up a flight of stairs. Today, there are handicapped parking spaces close to the entrance of buildings, ramps near stairs, dedicated bathroom stalls, and other facilities and amenities to make spaces accessible to special needs individuals. America has shown that it is capable of undertaking large-scale collective action to benefit its citizens. America can do it again.

America fought in World War I, World War II, the Korean War, the Vietnam War, and the Iraq/Afghanistan War. All these wars were fought in the name of keeping the nation secure. Today, we are facing a new war, one that is much worse. This war will not be fought within a foreign nation; it will be fought within our own. It is not another nation's homes and families that are being ripped apart and destroyed, but our own.

The bedrock of the American society, the nuclear family, is disintegrating. American families are broken and destroyed. In this war, the enemy is not across our borders, but is here within the nation. Together, we must identify and recognize this enemy. We must unite and mobilize ourselves to fight hard and unceasingly to stop the destruction of the nuclear family. We must fight to ensure that our children come home to stable homes and intact families. This war requires all of us to fight: women, men, business owners, political leaders, religious clergy, teachers, and children—in short, the whole society. It is not a war that will be won by shooting bullets or dropping bombs. It is a war that will be won in our hearts and minds to secure our families and homes.

The one thing I love about America is when the President takes the oath of office. In the oath he says, "so help me God." We all must invoke the help of God Almighty. I trust He will help us in this national movement to create and support strong nuclear families. Above all, I submit everything to Almighty God.

You cannot go back and change the beginning,
but you can start where you are and change the ending.
- C.S. LEWIS

BIBLIOGRAPHY

20 Actresses Who've Spoken About the Objectification of Women in Hollywood. (n.d.). Cafemom.com. Retrieved from https://cafemom.com/entertainment/199625-20_actresses_whove_spoken_out [No longer available]

2000 Surgeon General's Report. (2024, February 28). Cdc.gov. https://archive.cdc.gov/www_cdc_gov/tobacco/sgr/2000/index.htm

2000 Surgeon General's Report - Highlights. (1995, March). www.cdc.gov. https://archive.cdc.gov/www_cdc_gov/tobacco/sgr/2000/highlights.html

29 days: The story of Serial Killer George Howard Putt. (n.d.). Jeffdroke.com. Retrieved September 2, 2024, from https://jeffdroke.com/George%20Howard%20Putt%2029_days.htm

227 famous people who died because they smoked…. (2016, January 11). Clear The Air News Tobacco Blog. http://tobacco.cleartheair.org.hk/?p=12068

1967 Robert Kennedy Tobaccos worst enemy. (1967, October 3). Newspapers.com. https://www.newspapers.com/article/the-courier-journal-1967-robert-kennedy/29877378/

ABC News. (2014, November 21). *5 disturbing things we learned today about Sandy Hook shooter Adam Lanza.* ABC News. https://abcnews.go.com/US/disturbing-things-learned-today-sandy-hook-shooter-adam/story?id=27087140

Abstinence-only-until-marriage programs. (n.d.). Plannedparenthoodaction.
org. Retrieved September 2, 2024, from https://www.
plannedparenthoodaction.org/issues/sex-education/abstinence-only-
programs

Adamczyk, A., Freilich, J. D., & Kim, C. (2017). Religion and crime: A
systematic review and assessment of next steps. *Sociology of Religion*,
78(2), 192–232. https://doi.org/10.1093/socrel/srx012

Airaksinen, T. (2016, August 26). *What I learned in my women's studies
classes*. Quillette. https://quillette.com/2016/08/26/what-i-learned-in-
my-womens-studies-classes/

Al-Anon Family Group Headquarters, Inc. (2015, July 16). *Al-Anon
members say "Al-Anon saved my life."* PR Newswire. https://www.
prweb.com/releases/al_anon_members_say_al_anon_saved_my_life_/
prweb12848614.htm

Aleksandr Solzhenitsyn center — A world split apart. (n.d.).
Aleksandr Solzhenitsyn Center. Retrieved September 2, 2024, from
https://www.solzhenitsyncenter.org/a-world-split-apart

Altimari, D. (2018, December 9). Sandy Hook shooter Adam Lanza's
spreadsheet detailing centuries of mass violence served as a road map
to murder. *Hartford Courant.* https://www.courant.com/2018/12/09/
sandy-hook-shooter-adam-lanzas-spreadsheet-detailing-centuries-of-
mass-violence-served-as-a-road-map-to-murder/

Alvergne, A., & Lummaa, V. (2010). Does the contraceptive pill alter
mate choice in humans? *Trends in Ecology & Evolution*, *25*(3), 171–
179. https://doi.org/10.1016/j.tree.2009.08.003

Amato, P. R. (Ed.). (2010). *Research on Divorce: Continuing Trends and
New Developments* (Vol. 72, Issue 3). National Council on Family
Relations. https://www.jstor.org/stable/40732501

Amato, P. R., & DeBoer, D. D. (2001). The transmission of marital instability across generations: Relationship skills or commitment to marriage? *Journal of Marriage and the Family, 63*(4), 1038–1051. https://doi.org/10.1111/j.1741-3737.2001.01038.x

Anderson, J. (2014). The impact of family structure on the health of children: Effects of divorce. *The Linacre Quarterly, 81*(4), 378–387. https://doi.org/10.1179/0024363914z.00000000087

Andrew, M. (2019, June 3). *Woman shares her regrets two years after divorcing her sweet ex-husband.* Elitereaders.com. https://www. elitereaders.com/woman-shares-regrets-two-years-after-divorcing-ex-husband/

Andrews, E. (2015, September 14). *The mysterious Wall Street bombing, 95 years ago.* HISTORY. https://www.history.com/news/the-mysterious-wall-street-bombing-95-years-ago

Aoki, M. (1970, January 1). *In sexless Japan, almost half of single young men and women are virgins: survey.* The Japan Times. https://www. japantimes.co.jp/news/2016/09/16/national/social-issues/sexless-japan-almost-half-young-men-women-virgins-survey/

Azimy, R. (2020, April 15). *The problem with "feminism" today.* Fearless She Wrote. https://medium.com/fearless-she-wrote/the-problem-with-feminism-today-463493755b96

Barnes, M. (2018, September 5). Lydia Clarke Heston, actress and wife of Charlton Heston, dies at 95. *Hollywood Reporter.* https://www. hollywoodreporter.com/movies/movie-news/lydia-clarke-heston-dead-actress-wife-charlton-heston-was-95-1140095/

Barnes, M. (2019, July 16). Mona Malden, actress and widow of Karl Malden, dies at 102. *Hollywood Reporter.* https://www. hollywoodreporter.com/movies/movie-news/mona-malden-dead-actress-widow-karl-malden-was-102-1224614/

Barroilhet, S., Señoret, C., Mallea, X., Fritsch, R., Vöhringer, P., & Arraztoa, J.-A. (2018). Marital functioning in couples practicing periodic abstinence for family planning. *The Linacre Quarterly, 85*(2), 155–166. https://doi.org/10.1177/0024363918764950

Bayless, K. (2014, January 12). *9 things a stepparent should never do.* Parents. https://www.parents.com/parenting/dynamics/step-parent-boundaries/

BBC News. (2017, January 11). My nightmare on the pill. *BBC.* https://www.bbc.com/news/magazine-38575745

Benson, H., & Azim, R. (2016). *Celebrity divorce rates.* Marriagefoundation.org.uk.

Berkes, H. (2017, October 2). Gambling, guns were mainstay of Vegas shooter's life. *NPR.* https://www.npr.org/sections/thetwo-way/2017/10/02/555088261/las-vegas-shooter-said-to-be-a-restless-retiree-who-liked-to-gamble

Berliana, S., Utami, E. D., Efendi, F., & Kurniati, A. (2018). Premarital Sex Initiation and Time Interval to First Marriage Among Indonesians. *Bulletin of Indonesian Economic Studies, 54*, 1–27. https://doi.org/10.1080/00074918.2018.1440067

Birth Control Has Expanded Opportunity for Women. (2015, June). Planned Parenthood.

Borden, J. (2015, June 22). Dylann Roof's teenage years marked by father's bitter divorce. *The Washington Post.* https://www.washingtonpost.com/news/post-nation/wp/2015/06/22/dylann-roofs-teenage-years-marked-by-fathers-bitter-divorce/

Bradford Wilcox, W., Murray, C., & Barone, M. (n.d.). *The evolution of divorce.* Nationalaffairs.com. Retrieved September 3, 2024, from https://www.nationalaffairs.com/publications/detail/the-evolution-of-divorce

Broken hearts and deal breakers: Reasons why people divorce. (2017, April 9). *Psychology Today.* https://www.psychologytoday.com/us/blog/sliding-vs-deciding/201704/broken-hearts-and-deal-breakers-reasons-why-people-divorce

Brolley, B. (2018, August 30). *The unspoken truth about waiting until marriage*. The List. https://www.thelist.com/132385/the-unspoken-truth-about-waiting-until-marriage/

Brown, J., MA, MS, MS, & MS. (n.d.). *MN psychologist online*. Mnpsych.org. Retrieved September 3, 2024, from https://www.mnpsych.org/index.php?option=com_dailyplanetblog&view=entry&category=industry+news&id=54%3Afather-absent-homes-implications-for-criminal-justice-and-mental-health-professionals&Itemid=186

Buckley, S. (2016, February 27). China's high-speed sexual revolution. *BBC*. https://www.bbc.com/news/magazine-35525566

Burt, S. A., Barnes, A. R., McGue, M., & Iacono, W. G. (2008). Parental divorce and adolescent delinquency: Ruling out the impact of common genes. *Developmental Psychology*, *44*(6), 1668–1677. https://doi.org/10.1037/a0013477

Call, M. (2003, December 18). Those who know Cullen see different sides ** Lawyer, neighbor say he was kind. Ex-wife called him cruel. *Morning Call*. https://www.mcall.com/2003/12/18/those-who-know-cullen-see-different-sides-lawyer-neighbor-say-he-was-kind-ex-wife-called-him-cruel/

Cara, T. (2014, May 15). *In hobby lobby we don't trust!* Ffrfmcc.org. https://www.ffrfmcc.org/in-hobby-lobby-we-dont-trust/

Castañeda, A. J. (2018, October 30). *The truth of the prophecies of humanae vitae III*. Human Life International. https://www.hli.org/resources/the-teaching-of-the-prophetic-encyclical-humanae-vitae-iii/

Chapter 5: Family and personal values. (2012, June 19). Pew Research Center. https://www.pewresearch.org/social-trends/2012/06/19/chapter-5-family-and-personal-values/

Cheng, C. (2015, March 26). The West has it totally wrong on Lee Kuan Yew. *Independent*. https://www.independent.co.uk/voices/comment/

the-west-has-it-totally-wrong-on-lee-kuan-yew-10135641.html

Chetty, R., Hendren, N., Kline, P., & Saez, E. (2014, June). *Where is the Land of Opportunity? The Geography of Intergenerational Mobility in the United States.* National Bureau of Economic Research. http://www.nber.org/papers/w19843

Children who view adult-targeted TV may become sexually active earlier in life. (n.d.). EurekAlert! Retrieved September 2, 2024, from https://www.eurekalert.org/news-releases/845557

Choi, Y., Kim, Y. S., Kim, S. Y., & Park, I. J. K. (2013). Is Asian American parenting controlling and harsh? Empirical testing of relationships between Korean American and Western parenting measures. *Asian American Journal of Psychology*, *4*(1), 19–29. https://doi.org/10.1037/a0031220

Coalition for Divorce Reform. (n.d.-a). Coalition For Divorce Reform | Increasing Awareness of the Negative Impact of Divorce; Coalition For Divorce Reform. Retrieved September 3, 2024, from https://divorcereform.us/

Coalition for Divorce Reform. (n.d.-b). Retrieved September 3, 2024, from www.divorcereform.us

Cockroft, S. (2014, May 19). Virgin schoolboy tells pupils they shouldn't have casual sex. *Daily Mail.* https://www.dailymail.co.uk/news/article-2632611/Sex-without-love-isnt-worth-Virgin-schoolboy-tells-fellow-pupils-not-casual-relationships-wont-make-happy.html

Coffey, L. T. (2019, September 30). *How a bully changed and a victim forgave.* TODAY. https://www.today.com/parents/how-bully-changed-victim-forgave-t160449?icid=related

Collins, R. L., Elliott, M. N., Berry, S. H., Kanouse, D. E., Kunkel, D., Hunter, S. B., & Miu, A. (2004). *Does Watching Sex on Television Influence Teens' Sexual Activity?* Rand.org. https://www.rand.org/pubs/research_briefs/RB9068.html

Conscience. (2020, February 8). Thomistic Philosophy Page. https://aquinasonline.com/conscience/

Cook, M. (2017, October 5). Mass shooters and broken families: The overlooked link connecting these 6 killers. *Intellectual Takeout.* https://intellectualtakeout.org/2017/10/mass-shooters-and-broken-families-the-overlooked-link-connecting-these-6-killers/

Cooper, M. (2009, August 30). *Breaking down divorce rates by religion (and what they tell us).* LoveToKnow. https://www.lovetoknow.com/life/relationships/divorce-statistics-by-religion

Cornblatt, J. (2009, October 27). *A brief history of sex ed in America.* Newsweek. https://www.newsweek.com/brief-history-sex-ed-america-81001

Croteau, J. (2017, June 2). *Things couples should talk about before marriage (but usually don't).* The List. https://www.thelist.com/68394/things-couples-talk-marriage-usually-dont/

Cummings, K. M., & Proctor, R. N. (2014). The changing public image of smoking in the United States: 1964–2014. *Cancer Epidemiology, Biomarkers & Prevention: A Publication of the American Association for Cancer Research, Cosponsored by the American Society of Preventive Oncology, 23*(1), 32–36. https://doi.org/10.1158/1055-9965.epi-13-0798

Dasgupta, A. N. Z., Ueffing, P., & Kantorová, V. (2017). *Sexual Activity by Marital Status and Age: A Comparative Perspective.*

Daugherty, J., & Copen, C. (2016). *Trends in Attitudes About Marriage, Childbearing, and Sexual Behavior: United States, 2002, 2006–2010, and 2011–2013.*

David Hacker, J., Hilde, L., & Jones, J. H. (2010). The effect of the civil war on southern marriage patterns. *The Journal of Southern History, 76*(1), 39.

De Sousa, A., Mahajan, P., Pimple, P., Palsetia, D., & Dave, N. (2013).

Indian religious concepts on sexuality and marriage. *Indian Journal of Psychiatry, 55*(6), 256. https://doi.org/10.4103/0019-5545.105547

Delaney, K. J. (2005, November 26). Big Mother Is Watching. *The Wall Street Journal.* https://www.wsj.com/articles/SB113296733085807076

Divorce rates by occupation and salary, aggregates. (n.d.). Google Docs. Retrieved September 25, 2024, from https://docs.google.com/spreadsheets/u/1/d/1-JVVCiuXBZEpU6_5HsZLYyblVClpEW0ucYBafkNbaYI/pubhtml

Does abstinence-only education work? (n.d.). Upenn.edu. Retrieved September 2, 2024, from https://www.gse.upenn.edu/news/does-abstinence-only-education-work

Doherty, W. J., & Sears, L. W. (2011, October 20). Delaying divorce to save marriages. *The Washington Post.* https://www.washingtonpost.com/opinions/delaying-divorce-to-save-marriages/2011/10/19/gIQAKh0f1L_story.html

Donica, A. (2014, April 3). *Charles Manson.* Biography. https://www.biography.com/crime/charles-manson

Doyle, L. (2012, October 13). 6 Reasons Marriage Counseling is BS. *HuffPost.* https://www.huffpost.com/entry/marriage-counseling_b_1933187

Dunn, L. (2020, February 4). *What my father's infidelities taught me about intimacy.* Aeon; Aeon Magazine. https://aeon.co/essays/what-my-fathers-infidelities-taught-me-about-intimacy

Earp, B. D., Sandberg, A., & Savulescu, J. (2012). Natural selection, childrearing, and the ethics of marriage (and divorce): Building a case for the neuroenhancement of human relationships. *Philosophy & Technology, 25*(4), 561–587. https://doi.org/10.1007/s13347-012-0081-8

Elkins, K., & Kane, L. (2015, August 13). 21 ways rich people think differently than the average person. *Business Insider*. https://www. businessinsider.com/how-rich-people-think-differently-2015-8

Ellis, B. J., Bates, J. E., Dodge, K. A., Fergusson, D. M., John Horwood, L., Pettit, G. S., & Woodward, L. (2003). Does father absence place daughters at special risk for early sexual activity and teenage pregnancy? *Child Development, 74*(3), 801–821. https://doi. org/10.1111/1467-8624.00569

El-Sibaie, A. (2018, February 14). *Marriage penalties and bonuses under the tax cuts and jobs*. Tax Foundation. https://taxfoundation.org/tax-cuts-and-jobs-act-marriage-penalty/

Extrinsic vs. Intrinsic motivation at work. (n.d.). *Psychology Today*. Retrieved September 2, 2024, from https://www.psychologytoday. com/us/blog/creative-leadership/202004/extrinsic-vs-intrinsic-motivation-at-work

Fagan, P. (n.d.-a). *Increasing marriage would dramatically reduce child poverty*. The Heritage Foundation. Retrieved September 3, 2024, from https://www.heritage.org/marriage-and-family/report/increasing-marriage-would-dramatically-reduce-child-poverty

Fagan, P. (n.d.-b). *Why religion matters: The impact of religious practice on social stability*. The Heritage Foundation. Retrieved September 3, 2024, from https://www.heritage.org/civil-society/report/why-religion-matters-the-impact-religious-practice-social-stability

Family values in ancient Rome. (n.d.). Uchicago.edu. Retrieved September 3, 2024, from https://fathom.lib.uchicago. edu/1/777777121908/

Fehring, R. J. (2015). The influence of contraception, abortion, and natural family planning on divorce rates as found in the 2006–2010 National Survey of Family Growth. *The Linacre Quarterly, 82*(3), 273–282. https://doi.org/10.1179/2050854915y.0000000007

Fernandes, A. (2021, May 12). *Who was Norman Lloyd's wife Peggy?*

How love sparked on sets of a play blossomed into marriage of 75 years. Meaww. https://meaww.com/norman-lloyd-dead-at-106-who-was-wife-peggy-lloyd-actress-love-story-on-sets-play-marriage-75-years-535612

Fessler, L. (2017, September 6). *The occupations with the highest and lowest divorce rates in the US.* Quartz. https://qz.com/1069806/the-highest-and-lowest-divorce-rates-in-america-by-occupation-and-industry

Fetters, A. (2018, August 29). Why are STDs on the rise if Americans are having less sex? *Atlantic Monthly (Boston, Mass.: 1993).* https://www.theatlantic.com/family/archive/2018/08/why-are-stds-on-the-rise-if-people-are-having-less-sex/568909/

Finegan, T. (2018, August 24). *What has the Catholic Church ever done for the world? Quite a lot, actually.* TheJournal.Ie. https://www.thejournal.ie/readme/what-has-catholic-church-ever-done-for-us-4199150-Aug2018/

Flurry, G. (n.d.). *A lesson from Rome.* Thetrumpet.com. Retrieved September 3, 2024, from https://www.thetrumpet.com/5360-a-lesson-from-rome

Forbes, S. (2021, June 1). *Time to bust the government's public education monopoly.* Forbes. https://www.forbes.com/sites/steveforbes/2021/06/01/time-to-bust-the-governments-public-education-monopoly/?sh=576574034457

Frostrup, M. (2020, December 20). Now I've had a baby, I resent my young stepson coming over. *The Guardian.* https://www.theguardian.com/lifeandstyle/2020/dec/20/now-i-have-a-baby-i-resent-my-young-stepson-coming-over

Gardner, T. (2001). *Sacred sex: Spiritual celebration of oneness in marriage.* Waterbrook Press.

Garfinkel, I., & Zilanawala, A. (2015). Fragile families in the American welfare state. *Children and Youth Services Review, 55,* 210–221.

https://doi.org/10.1016/j.childyouth.2015.05.018

Gersh, F. (n.d.). *Why I'm one OB/GYN who is not prescribing the birth control pill*. ZRT Laboratory. Retrieved September 3, 2024, from https://www.zrtlab.com/blog/archive/obgyn-not-prescribing-the-birth-control-pill/

Gilbert, S. (2005, April 19). Married With Problems? Therapy May Not Help. *Https://Www.Nytimes.Com/2005/04/19/Health/Psychology/Married-with-Problems-Therapy-May-Not-Help.Html.*

Global Times. (n.d.). *Premarital sex: sinful or sacred in China?* Globaltimes.Cn. Retrieved September 3, 2024, from https://www.globaltimes.cn/content/704610.shtml

Goisis, A., Özcan, B., & Van Kerm, P. (2019). Do children carry the weight of divorce? *Demography*, *56*(3), 785–811. https://doi.org/10.1007/s13524-019-00784-4

Good guys – handsome phin Lyman, 18 – becomes global sensation because he's still a virgin. (2014, July 30). It's the Women, Not the Men! https://kqduane.com/2014/07/30/good-guys-handsome-phin-lyman18-becomes-global-sensation-because-hes-still-a-virgin/

Gordon, J. (2009, July 17). Why I (and, I suspect, many separated women) regret divorcing. *Daily Mail.* https://www.dailymail.co.uk/femail/article-1200225/Why-I-I-suspect-separated-women-regret-divorcing.html

Gordon, L., & Batlan, F. (n.d.). *The legal history of the Aid to Dependent Children Program*. Social Welfare History Project. Retrieved September 2, 2024, from https://socialwelfare.library.vcu.edu/public-welfare/aid-to-dependent-children-the-legal-history/

Granberry, M. (1994, February 15). COLUMN ONE : Backlash to Teaching Chastity : Course in public schools that proclaims safe-sex-is-no-sex draws fire. Backers praise push to stress morality over biology, but angry parents see dangers in a program they call inaccurate and unrealistic. *The Los Angeles Times.* https://www.latimes.com/archives/la-xpm-1994-02-15-mn-23229-story.html

Grant, C. (2003). Teens, sex and the media: Is there a connection? *Paediatrics & Child Health*, 8(5), 285–286. https://doi.org/10.1093/pch/8.5.285

Grazer, G. L. (2011, September 17). Wasbands and wives: Seven reasons to stay married. *HuffPost.* https://www.huffpost.com/entry/wasbands-and-wives-seven_b_967170

Grigoriadis, V. (n.d.). *How the pill changed the world, and the fertility problems it's causing women today -- New York magazine - nymag.* New York Magazine. Retrieved September 3, 2024, from https://nymag.com/news/features/69789/

Grossbart, S. (2021, April 17). The truth about Victoria Beckham and David Beckham's marriage: How they continue to defy the haters. Yahoo Entertainment.

Halbfinger, D. M., & Hart, A. (2003, July 9). Man Kills 5 Co-Workers at Plant and Himself. *The New York Times.* https://www.nytimes.com/2003/07/09/us/man-kills-5-co-workers-at-plant-and-himself.html

Hall, M. D. (2017, May 3). *"let us with caution indulge the supposition that morality can be maintained without religion" - Mark David hall.* Law & Liberty. https://lawliberty.org/let-us-with-caution-indulge-the-supposition-that-morality-can-be-maintained-without-religion/

Haner, J. (1995, January 22). America's most wanted welfare plan. *Baltimore Sun.* https://www.baltimoresun.com/1995/01/22/americas-most-wanted-welfare-plan-2/

Harford, T. (2017, May 21). The tiny pill which gave birth to an economic revolution. *BBC.* https://www.bbc.com/news/business-39641856

Healy, K. (2019, May 19). Not every school's anti-bullying program works – some may actually make bullying worse. *The Conversation.* http://theconversation.com/not-every-schools-anti-bullying-program-works-some-may-actually-make-bullying-worse-116163

Hill, A. (2018, February 13). Couples who argue together, stay together, research finds. *The Guardian.* https://www.theguardian.com/lifeandstyle/2018/feb/13/couples-who-argue-together-stay-together-research-finds

Hirschlag, A. (2021, September 12). *9 things you didn't know about America's first serial killer, H.h. holmes.* Mental Floss. https://www.mentalfloss.com/article/72642/9-things-you-didnt-know-about-americas-first-serial-killer-hh-holmes

Holmes-Greeley, P. (2011, August 8). *Letters: For all those born before 1945.* Mlive. https://www.mlive.com/opinion/muskegon/2011/08/letters_for_all_those_born_bef.html

Holohan, M. (2019, September 30). *How to stop bullying in schools: What works, what doesn't.* TODAY. https://www.today.com/parents/how-stop-bullying-schools-what-works-what-doesn-t-t159669

How having an absentee father can affect a woman's sexuality. (n.d.). *Psychology Today.* Retrieved September 3, 2024, from https://www.psychologytoday.com/us/blog/the-truth-about-exercise-addiction/201711/how-having-absentee-father-can-affect-womans

How media use can affect kids. (n.d.). Kidshealth.org. Retrieved September 3, 2024, from https://kidshealth.org/en/parents/tv-affects-child.html

If my parents are divorced, is my marriage doomed to fail? (n.d.). *Psychology Today.* Retrieved September 2, 2024, from https://www.psychologytoday.com/us/blog/between-the-generations/201902/if-my-parents-are-divorced-is-my-marriage-doomed-fail

Is it illegal to cheat on your spouse. (2019, March 18). Retrieved from Sandiegodivorcelawyer-blog.com. [No longer available]

Israelsen-Hartley, S. (2017, November 22). Ignored or sexualized: How

Hollywood is failing women. *Deseret News (Salt Lake City, Utah: 1964).* https://www.deseret.com/2017/11/22/20636387/ignored-or-sexualized-how-hollywood-is-failing-women/

Jabbour, N., Abi Rached, V., Haddad, C., Salameh, P., Sacre, H., Hallit, R., Soufia, M., Obeid, S., & Hallit, S. (2020). Association between parental separation and addictions in adolescents: results of a National Lebanese Study. *BMC Public Health, 20*(1). https://doi.org/10.1186/s12889-020-09108-3

Jackson, K. M., Rogers, M. L., & Sartor, C. E. (2016). Parental divorce and initiation of alcohol use in early adolescence. *Psychology of Addictive Behaviors: Journal of the Society of Psychologists in Addictive Behaviors, 30*(4), 450–461. https://doi.org/10.1037/adb0000164

Jackson, S., & Vares, T. (2015). 'Too many bad role models for us girls': Girls, female pop celebrities and 'sexualization.' *Sexualities, 18*(4), 480–498. https://doi.org/10.1177/1363460714550905

Jacobson, L. (n.d.). *Does the Catholic church provide half of social services in the U.S.?* @politifact; PolitiFact. Retrieved September 3, 2024, from https://www.politifact.com/factchecks/2013/mar/19/frank-keating/does-catholic-church-provide-half-social-services-/

Jaffe, E. (2007). Mirror neurons: How we reflect on behavior. *APS Observer, 20.* https://www.psychologicalscience.org/observer/mirror-neurons-how-we-reflect-on-behavior

Jang, S. J. (2019). Religion and Crime. In *Oxford Bibliographies in Criminology.* Oxford University Press.

Jemmott, J. B., Jemmott, L. S., & Fong, G. T. (2010). Efficacy of a theory-based abstinence-only intervention over 24 months: A randomized controlled trial with young adolescents. *Archives of Pediatrics & Adolescent Medicine, 164*(2), 152–159. https://doi.org/10.1001/archpediatrics.2009.267

Jenkins, J. P. (2024). Ed Gein. In *Encyclopedia Britannica.* https://www.

britannica.com/biography/Ed-Gein

Johnston, J. (Last Updated: March 21 2019). Stepfather admits he sexually abused his 3 stepdaughters for years. *CBC News.* https://www.cbc.ca/news/canada/edmonton/stepfather-admits-sexual-abuse-1.5063272

Joshua, B. (2011, September 16). *An interview with the authors of "How Far Can We Go? A Catholic Guide to Sex and Dating."* Evangelical Catholicism. https://evangelicalcatholicism.wordpress.com/2011/09/16/an-interview-with-the-authors-of-how-far-can-we-go-a-catholic-guide-to-sex-and-dating/

Kamp, S. (2019, June 14). *Jennifer Lopez reflects on past marriages — including the 2 she doesn't "really count."* TODAY. https://www.today.com/popculture/jennifer-lopez-reflects-past-marriages-including-2-she-doesn-t-t156362

Kay, J. F., & Jackson, A. (2008). *Sex, Lies & Stereotypes.*

Kennedy, S., & Bumpass, L. L. (2008). *Cohabitation and children's living arrangements: New estimates from the United States. 19*(47), 1663–1692. https://doi.org/10.4054/DemRes.2008.19.47

Kent, D. (2019, December 12). *U.S. has world's highest rate of children living in single-parent households.* Pew Research Center. https://www.pewresearch.org/short-reads/2019/12/12/u-s-children-more-likely-than-children-in-other-countries-to-live-with-just-one-parent/

Kessler, S. (2019, December 2). *The rise of birth control & the decline of civilization.* The Imaginative Conservative. https://theimaginativeconservative.org/2019/12/birth-control-decline-civilization-steven-kessler.html

Khazan, O. (2018, October 22). Fewer sex partners means a happier marriage. *Atlantic Monthly (Boston, Mass.: 1993).* https://www.theatlantic.com/health/archive/2018/10/sexual-partners-and-marital-happiness/573493/

King, L. (2014, October 1). Would marriage ruin our happiness? *The New York Times.* https://archive.nytimes.com/opinionator.blogs. nytimes.com/2014/10/01/would-marriage-ruin-our-happiness/

Knausgaard, K. O. (2015, May 17). Anders Breivik's Inexplicable Crime. *New Yorker (New York, N.Y.: 1925).* https://www.newyorker.com/ magazine/2015/05/25/the-inexplicable

Konigsberg, E. (2007, December 8). From 'Troubled' to 'Killer,' Despite Many Efforts. *The New York Times.* https://www.nytimes. com/2007/12/08/us/08gunman.html

Kovner, J., & Altimari, D. (2018, December 9). More than 1,000 pages of documents reveal Sandy Hook shooter Adam Lanza's dark descent. *The Los Angeles Times.* https://www.latimes.com/nation/la-na-adam-lanza-sandy-hook-20181209-story.html

Kundu, T., & Bhattacharya, P. (2018, May 25). *Sex in India: What data shows.* Mint. https://www.livemint.com/Politics/ RC0cvSgItInzrPBjAZ3f2L/Sex-in-India-What-data-shows.html

Langman, P. (2016, May 24). *School Shooters: The Myth of the Stable Home.* ShootShooters.Info.

Langr, C. (2018, July 14). *50 years later: How "Humanae Vitae" predicted the future.* Catholic Dating Online - Find Your Match Today!; Catholic Singles. https://www.catholicsingles.com/blog/humanae-vitae-predictions/

Lavner, J. A., Williamson, H. C., Karney, B. R., & Bradbury, T. N. (2020). Premarital parenthood and newlyweds' marital trajectories. *Journal of Family Psychology: JFP: Journal of the Division of Family Psychology of the American Psychological Association (Division 43),* *34*(3), 279–290. https://doi.org/10.1037/fam0000596

Leefeldt, E. (2019, March 20). *An estimated $10 billion in child support payments going uncollected.* CBS News. https://www.cbsnews.com/ news/10-billion-in-child-support-payments-going-uncollected-according-to-estimates/

Leslie Cane Articles. (n.d.). Lesliecanearticles.com. Retrieved September 2, 2024, from https://lesliecanearticles.com/i-regret-divorcing-my-husband-what-now/

Lickona, T. (n.d.). *Where sex education went wrong*. ASCD. Retrieved September 3, 2024, from https://ascd.org/el/articles/where-sex-education-went-wrong

Living together before marriage may raise risk of divorce. (n.d.). *Psychology Today*. Retrieved September 3, 2024, from https://www.psychologytoday.com/us/blog/sliding-vs-deciding/201811/living-together-marriage-may-raise-risk-divorce

Livingston, G. (2018, April 25). *The changing profile of unmarried parents*. Pew Research Center. https://www.pewresearch.org/social-trends/2018/04/25/the-changing-profile-of-unmarried-parents/

Lyman, P. (2014, June 8). The value of virginity. *The Guardian*. https://www.theguardian.com/lifeandstyle/2014/jun/08/value-of-virginity

Maag, E., & Acs, G. (2015). *The Financial Consequences of Marriage for Cohabiting Couples with Children*.

Maloney, A. (2016, February 9). *Getting a divorce? You could regret that in five years' time*. The Sun. https://www.thesun.co.uk/archives/news/89605/getting-a-divorce-you-could-regret-that-in-five-years-time/

Managing your expectations about marriage. (2016, October 26). *Psychology Today*. https://www.psychologytoday.com/us/blog/so-happy-together/201610/managing-your-expectations-about-marriage

Manhart, M. D., & Fehring, R. J. (2018). The state of the science of Natural Family Planning fifty years after *Humane Vitae*: A report from NFP scientists' meeting held at the US conference of catholic bishops, April 4, 2018. *The Linacre Quarterly, 85*(4), 339–347. https://doi.org/10.1177/0024363918809699

Manson, M. (2014, January 23). A brief history of male/female relations. *Mark Manson*. https://markmanson.net/male-female-relations

Marcén, M. (2012, January 15). *Divorce and the birth control pill*. Munich Personal RePEc Archive. https://mpra.ub.uni-muenchen.de/35955/

Mardenfeld, S. (2012, June 7). *Does sex still sell? What marketers should know*. Business News Daily; businessnewsdaily.com. https://www.businessnewsdaily.com/2649-sex-sells-more.html

Marriage and divorce. (2024, March 13). Cdc.gov. https://www.cdc.gov/nchs/fastats/marriage-divorce.htm

Masci, D. (2018, March 19). *Share of married adults varies widely across U.S. religious groups*. Pew Research Center. https://www.pewresearch.org/short-reads/2018/03/19/share-of-married-adults-varies-widely-across-u-s-religious-groups/

May, K. (2003, May 9). *THE SOAP OPERA SAGA: Soap operas attract a very committed audience*. CampaignUK. https://www.campaignlive.co.uk/article/soap-opera-saga-soap-operas-attract-committed-audience/179634

McDade-Montez, E. (n.d.). *New media, old themes: Sexualization in children's TV shows*. ETR Blog. Retrieved September 3, 2024, from https://www.etr.org/blog/research-childrens-media/

Mckelway, B. (2024, September 2). *Netanyahu asks for 'forgiveness' for not saving Israeli captives*.

McLanahan, S., Tach, L., & Schneider, D. (2013). The causal effects of father absence. *Annual Review of Sociology, 39*(1), 399–427. https://doi.org/10.1146/annurev-soc-071312-145704

McManus, M. (2016, January 10). *Fix no-fault divorce*. Lansing State Journal. https://www.lansingstatejournal.com/story/opinion/contributors/viewpoints/2016/01/10/mcmanus-fix-fault-divorce/78497624/

Miller, E. D. (2012, September 20). *Why the Father Wound Matters:*

Consequences for Male Mental Health and the Father-Son Relationship. Wiley Online Library. https://doi.org/10.1002/car.2219

Miller, J. (n.d.). *The curt jester – punditry, prayer, parody, polemics, puns from a papist perspective.* Splendoroftruth.com. Retrieved September 3, 2024, from http://www.splendoroftruth.com/curtjester/

Mills, E. (2014, May 25). *A virgin takes on the porn demon.* The Sunday Times. https://www.thetimes.com/article/a-virgin-takes-on-the-porn-demon-lfv92kwbtnm

Mitchell, T. (2019, November 15). *Americans have positive views about religion's role in society, but want it out of politics.* Pew Research Center. https://www.pewresearch.org/religion/2019/11/15/americans-have-positive-views-about-religions-role-in-society-but-want-it-out-of-politics/

Montaldo, C. (2014, February 27). *Profile of serial killer Tommy Lynn Sells.* ThoughtCo. https://www.thoughtco.com/serial-killer-tommy-lynn-sells-973154

Moorhead, J. (2014, June 7). Teenagers, it's OK not to have sex. *The Guardian.* https://www.theguardian.com/lifeandstyle/2014/jun/07/teenagers-its-ok-not-to-have-sex-phin-lyman

Morana, J. (2018, July 25). 50 years ago, pope Paul VI predicted #MeToo. *National Catholic Register.* https://www.ncregister.com/blog/50-years-ago-pope-paul-vi-predicted-metoo

Mothers who receive AFDC payments —. (n.d.). Census.gov. Retrieved September 20, 2024, from http://www2.census.gov/library/publications/1995/demographics/sb95-02.pdf

Murray, M. (2019). *Consequential Sex: #METOO, Masterpiece Cakeshop, and Private Sexual Regulation.* https://scholarlycommons.law.northwestern.edu/nulr/vol113/iss4/3

My parents' divorce put me off marriage. (2018, May 21). *BBC.* https://www.bbc.co.uk/bbcthree/article/e3bb0155-f9bf-4ab6-b526-

4ef71dd36b1f

NAMI. (2016, December 21). *The mental health benefits of religion &
     spirituality*. NAMI. https://www.nami.org/faith-community-leader/
     the-mental-health-benefits-of-religion-spirituality/

Next Avenue. (2018, July 15). *The 6 nasty financial surprises for
     divorcing women*. Forbes. https://www.forbes.com/sites/
     nextavenue/2018/07/15/the-6-nasty-financial-surprises-for-divorcing-
     women/?sh=2c6cd02f524b

No surprise: Coed dorms fuel sex and drinking. (2009, November 17). Live
     Science. https://www.livescience.com/5862-surprise-coed-dorms-fuel-
     sex-drinking.html

NPR. (2007, February 15). "unhooked" author warns against "hooking
     up." *NPR*. https://www.npr.org/2007/02/15/7422523/unhooked-
     author-warns-against-hooking-up

NSFG - listing P - key Statistics from the National Survey of family growth.
     (2019, November 6). Cdc.gov. https://www.cdc.gov/nchs/nsfg/key_
     statistics/p.htm

Oakes, K. (2019, June 4). Why is ADHD missed in girls? *BBC*. https://
     www.bbc.com/future/article/20190530-why-is-adhd-missed-in-girls

O'Dell, C., Gill, P., Begrand, A., Stout, B., Ezell, B., Vollaro, D.,
     Kondeusz, S. Z., & Zarker, K. (n.d.). *Who watches these things?: An
     examination of daytime TV's New Era*. Popmatters.com. Retrieved
     September 3, 2024, from https://www.popmatters.com/170869-
     daytime-tv-2495760965.html

Office on Smoking and Health. (2019). Cdc.gov. https://www.cdc.gov/
     tobacco/data_statistics/sgr/history/index.htm [No longer available]

Oreffice, S. (2015, February 6). The contraceptive pill was a revolution
     for women and men. *The Conversation*. http://theconversation.com/
     the-contraceptive-pill-was-a-revolution-for-women-and-men-37193

Osteen, J. (2014, August 29). *Let go of the ashes*. Joelosteen.com. https://

www.joelosteen.com/inspiration/blogs/14998

Pauly, M. (n.d.). The largest–ever survey of campus Sexual assault shows how outrageously common it is. *Mother Jones.* Retrieved September 3, 2024, from https://www.motherjones.com/criminal-justice/2019/10/campus-sexual-assault-survey/

Pavalko, E. K., & Elder, G. H., Jr. (1990). World War II and Divorce: A Life-Course Perspective. *American Journal of Sociology, 95*(5), 1213–1234.

Peck, M. S. (1998). *Further along the road less traveled: The unending journey toward spiritual growth, the edited lectures* (2nd ed.). Simon & Schuster.

Pierce, A. M. (Ed.). (2015). *#Tweeting for Terrorism: First Amendment Implications in Using Proterrorist Tweets to Convict Under the Material Support Statute* (Vol. 24, Issue 1). William & Mary Bill of Rights Journal.

Pinsker, J. (2019, May 30). How successful are the marriages of people with divorced parents? *Atlantic Monthly (Boston, Mass.: 1993).* https://www.theatlantic.com/family/archive/2019/05/divorced-parents-marriage/590425/

Portrait of Adam Lanza and his family begins to emerge. (2012, December 17). *Washington Post (Washington, D.C.: 1974).* https://www.washingtonpost.com/national/portrait-of-adam-lanza-and-his-family-begins-to-emerge/2012/12/17/376759ce-4862-11e2-820e-17eefac2f939_story.html

Premarital Sex is nearly universal among Americans, and has been for decades. (2016, March 1). Guttmacher Institute. https://www.guttmacher.org/news-release/2006/premarital-sex-nearly-universal-among-americans-and-has-been-decades

PTI. (2021, January 29). *Indian Americans household income average USD 120,000 annually: Report.* Economic Times. https://economictimes.

indiatimes.com/nri/migrate/indian-americans-household-income-average-usd-120000-annually-report/articleshow/80573809. cms?from=mdr

Pullmann, J. (2018, February 16). *5 similarities between ancient Rome's decline and today's United States.* The Federalist. https://thefederalist. com/2018/02/16/5-similarities-ancient-romes-decline-todays-united-states/

Quinlan, Á. (2015, April 4). *Step-parents are more harassed than hazardous in the modern 'blended' family unit.* Irishexaminer.com. https://www. irishexaminer.com/lifestyle/arid-20321915.html

Ramirez, A. (2006, August 20). Killer Donated His Kidney, Lawyer Says. *The New York Times.* https://www.nytimes.com/2006/08/20/ nyregion/20kidney.html

Rejecting moral relativism. (n.d.). *Psychology Today.* Retrieved September 3, 2024, from https://www.psychologytoday.com/us/blog/ethics-everyone/201201/rejecting-moral-relativism

Religion and crime. (n.d.). Encyclopedia.com. Retrieved September 3, 2024, from https://www.encyclopedia.com/law/legal-and-political-magazines/religion-and-crime

Religion comparison charts. (n.d.). ReligionFacts. Retrieved September 20, 2024, from https://religionfacts.com/charts/

Retirement Security Women Still Face Challenges. (2012). https://www.gao. gov/assets/gao-12-699.pdf

Rojas, R., & Hussey, K. (2018, December 10). Newly Released Documents Detail Sandy Hook Shooter's Troubled State of Mind. *The New York Times.* https://www.nytimes.com/2005/04/19/health/ psychology/married-with-problems-therapy-may-not-help.html

Rose, M. B. (2018, July 25). *Humanae vitae: Predicting our current crises.* Catholic Exchange. https://catholicexchange.com/humanae-vitae-predicting-current-crises/

Rosenberg, S. (2015, June 2). *Interfaith marriage is common in U.S., particularly among the recently wed.* Pew Research Center. https://www.pewresearch.org/short-reads/2015/06/02/interfaith-marriage/

Rosenbloom, S. (2007, March 1). A Disconnect on Hooking Up. *The New York Times.* https://www.nytimes.com/2007/03/01/fashion/01hook.html

Rozenfeld, M. (n.d.). TV romance can affect real-life marriage. *Scientific American.* Retrieved September 3, 2024, from https://www.scientificamerican.com/article/tv-romance-can-affect-real-life-marriage/

Rubenfield, A. J., & Pandit, G. M. (2019, February 4). *The status of the 'marriage penalty': An update from the tax cuts and jobs act.* The CPA Journal. https://www.cpajournal.com/2019/02/04/the-status-of-the-marriage-penalty-an-update-from-the-tax-cuts-and-jobs-act/

Safranek, L. (2008). Understanding Tragedy: Teen Robbie Hawkins had no remorse, empathy after threatening stepmom's life. *Omaha World Herald.* https://omaha.com/news/local/understanding-tragedy-teen-robbie-hawkins-had-no-remorse-empathy-after-threatening-stepmoms-life/article_5f9366dc-c4da-11e7-b5bc-eb3f5c40ffb2.html

Salaky, K. (2017, August 14). 9 reasons why waiting to have sex may be the best thing you do for your relationship. *Business Insider.* https://www.businessinsider.com/how-long-should-you-wait-to-have-sex-with-someone-2017-8

Sanchez, C. (2017, June 18). Poverty, dropouts, pregnancy, suicide: What the numbers say about fatherless kids. *NPR.* https://www.npr.org/sections/ed/2017/06/18/533062607/poverty-dropouts-pregnancy-suicide-what-the-numbers-say-about-fatherless-kids

Sanchez, R. (2017, October 24). Unsealed FBI docs paint disturbing portrait of Sandy Hook shooter Adam Lanza. *CNN.* https://www.cnn.com/2017/10/24/us/sandy-hook-adam-lanza-unsealed-docs/

index.html

Sanghani, R., Baxter-Derrington, J., Maidment, J., Crisp, J., Sigsworth, T., & Barber, H. (2014, May 19). 'I'm a virgin and I'm glad about that': Are more young people embracing virginity? *Sunday Telegraph*. https://www.telegraph.co.uk/women/sex/10840989/Young-virgins-Im-a-virgin-and-Im-glad-about-that-Are-more-young-people-embracing-virginity.html

Santhya, K. G. (n.d.). *Pre-marital sexual relations among youth in India: Findings from the Youth in India, Situations and Needs Study.* Popconf. org. Retrieved September 25, 2024, from https://ipc2009.popconf. org/papers/92480

Sauer, P. (2015, October 14). *The story of the first mass shooting in U.s. history*. Smithsonian Magazine. https://www.smithsonianmag.com/history/story-first-mass-murder-us-history-180956927/

Schemo, D. J. (2003, February 13). Explicit Sex Education Is Opposed by Most Parents in Survey. *The New York Times*. https://www.nytimes.com/2003/02/13/us/explicit-sex-education-is-opposed-by-most-parents-in-survey.html

Schwartz, A. (2018, December 9). Love is not a permanent state of enthusiasm: An interview with Esther Perel. *New Yorker (New York, N.Y.: 1925)*. https://www.newyorker.com/culture/the-new-yorker-interview/love-is-not-a-permanent-state-of-enthusiasm-an-interview-with-esther-perel

Seese, G. (1987). *Soap Opera Viewers' Perceptions of the Real World.* University of Central Florida .

Serial killers and mass murderers. (n.d.). ThoughtCo. Retrieved September 3, 2024, from https://www.thoughtco.com/serial-killers-4132966

Sexually transmitted diseases. (n.d.). Archive-it.org. Retrieved September 3, 2024, from https://wayback.archive-it.org/5774/20220413182711/https://www.healthypeople.gov/2020/topics-objectives/topic/sexually-transmitted-diseases

Shapiro, S., & Brown, C. (2018, May 9). *Sex Education Standards Across the States*. American Progress. https://www.americanprogress.org/article/sex-education-standards-across-states/

Sharp, R. (Ed.). (2014). *"Incontinentia, Licentia et Libido: The Juxtaposition of Morality and Sexuality during the Roman Republic*. James Madison Undergraduate Research Journal 2. http://commons.lib.jmu.edu/jmurj/vol2/iss1/2/

Sleeper, J. (2015, April 15). *Lee Kuan Yew's hard truths*. Opendemocracy.net. https://www.opendemocracy.net/en/lee-kuan-yews-hard-truths/

Sloan, W. M. (n.d.). *What is the purpose of education?* ASCD. Retrieved September 3, 2024, from https://ascd.org/el/articles/what-is-the-purpose-of-education

SmartMoney. (2012, August 20). *Marriage counselors: 10 things they don't want you to know*. HuffPost. https://www.huffpost.com/entry/marriage-counselors_n_1811685

Smith, J. (n.d.). *Pope Paul VI as prophet: Have humanae vitae's bold predictions come true?* University of Notre Dame. Retrieved September 4, 2024, from https://www3.nd.edu/~afreddos/courses/264/popepaul.htm

Solomon, A. (2014, March 9). The Reckoning. *New Yorker (New York, N.Y.: 1925)*. https://www.newyorker.com/magazine/2014/03/17/the-reckoning

Squires, J. (2009, August 18). Soquel mass murderer John Linley Frazier found dead in prison. *San Jose Mercury-News*. https://www.mercurynews.com/2009/08/18/soquel-mass-murderer-john-linley-frazier-found-dead-in-prison/

Standards and Protocols for the Use of Intimacy Coordinators. (2020, January). SAG-AFTRA. https://www.sagaftra.org/standards-and-protocols-use-intimacy-coordinators-0

Stanger-Hall, K. F., & Hall, D. W. (2011). Abstinence-only education and teen pregnancy rates: Why we need comprehensive sex education in the U.s. *PloS One, 6*(10), e24658. https://doi.org/10.1371/journal.pone.0024658

Stepp, L. (2016, April 22). Alchohol and sex: the culture that absorbs today's girls. *The Washington Post.* https://www.washingtonpost.com/opinions/alchohol-and-sex-the-culture-that-absorbs-todays-girls/2016/04/20/ea70dc5a-fdf1-11e5-9140-e61d062438bb_story.html

Stepp, L. S. (1995, February 26). Youth Say TV Shapes Values. *The Washington Post.* https://www.washingtonpost.com/archive/lifestyle/1995/02/27/youth-say-tv-shapes-values/67de57a6-d215-4e1a-83a5-6255087085d3/

Stepp, L. S. (2003, August 2). Hollywood's Material Girls. *The Washington Post.* https://www.washingtonpost.com/archive/lifestyle/style/2003/08/03/hollywoods-material-girls/10c52315-ab07-4010-8d3d-79573a6046e4/

Stivers, C. (2015, July 10). *Do marriage & family therapists have better marriages?* Psych Central. https://psychcentral.com/pro/do-marriage-family-therapists-have-better-marriages

Stoeltje, M. F. (2015, July 28). The futility of couples therapy. *The New York Times.* https://archive.nytimes.com/opinionator.blogs.nytimes.com/2015/07/28/the-futility-of-couples-therapy/

Super User. (n.d.). *Misquoting Our founding fathers.* Catholiceducation.org. Retrieved September 3, 2024, from https://www.catholiceducation.org/en/culture/history/misquoting-our-founding-fathers.html

Teachings and Practice on Marriage, Divorce and Remarriage. (1982). The American Lutheran Church.

The catholic news you never hear. (n.d.). Restlesspilgrim.net.

Retrieved September 3, 2024, from https://restlesspilgrim.net/blog/2012/10/23/catholic-news-you-never-hear/

The Cross-State Lines Serial Murderer: Carl Watts. (n.d.). Murder Victims. Retrieved September 3, 2024, from https://murdervictims.com/case/coral-watts-serial-killer/

The effects of divorce on teenage daughters. (2019, February 28). *Newport Academy.* https://www.newportacademy.com/resources/restoring-families/effects-of-divorce-on-teenage-daughters/

The peculiar institution [ushistory.org]. (n.d.). Ushistory.org. Retrieved September 3, 2024, from https://www.ushistory.org/us/27.asp

The Twelve Steps. (2017, April 18). Al-Anon Family Groups; Al-Anon Family Group Headquarters, Inc. https://al-anon.org/for-members/the-legacies/the-twelve-steps/

The unexpected legacy of divorce. (n.d.). *The New York Times.* Retrieved September 3, 2024, from https://archive.nytimes.com/www.nytimes.com/books/first/w/wallerstein-unexpected.html?mcubz=1&mcubz=1

The wife's protector: A quantitative theory linking contraceptive technology to the decline in marriage. (n.d.). CEPR. Retrieved September 2, 2024, from https://cepr.org/voxeu/columns/wifes-protector-quantitative-theory-linking-contraceptive-technology-decline-marriage

Thomas, S. S. (2015, June 21). *We asked three experts how to deal with Daddy issues.* VICE. https://www.vice.com/en/article/we-asked-three-experts-how-to-deal-with-our-daddy-issues-236/

Thompson, Z. (2016, October 4). *This is what really happens when you wait until marriage to have sex.* SELF. https://www.self.com/story/waiting-until-marriage

Tuccillo, A. (2019, June 17). *Jennifer Lopez says first two marriages came from loneliness.* ABC News. https://abcnews.go.com/GMA/Culture/jennifer-lopez-marriages-loneliness/story?id=63760173

Tuovila, A. (2008, October 7). *Marriage penalty definition, who gets hit with it.* Investopedia. https://www.investopedia.com/terms/m/marriage-penalty.asp

Universal, N. B. C. (2014, January 12). *50 years of progress halves smoking rate, but can we reach zero?* NBC News. https://www.nbcnews.com/health/cancer/50-years-progress-halves-smoking-rate-can-we-reach-zero-n7621

University of Toronto. (2011, January 26). Parental divorce linked to suicidal thoughts. *Science Daily.* https://www.sciencedaily.com/releases/2011/01/110119084516.htm

Unrealistic relationship expectations: Learning from don Jon. (n.d.). *Psychology Today.* Retrieved September 3, 2024, from https://www.psychologytoday.com/us/blog/the-attraction-doctor/201309/unrealistic-relationship-expectations-learning-from-don-jon

US Census Bureau. (2019). *44 percent of custodial parents receive the full amount of child support.* https://www.census.gov/newsroom/press-releases/2018/cb18-tps03.html

US Census Bureau. (2022). *Cohabiting partners older, more racially diverse, more educated, higher earners.* https://www.census.gov/library/stories/2019/09/unmarried-partners-more-diverse-than-20-years-ago.html

U.S. statistics. (n.d.). Hiv.gov. Retrieved September 3, 2024, from https://www.hiv.gov/hiv-basics/overview/data-and-trends/statistics

Utah State University. (n.d.). *Divorce and parenting courses.* Usu.edu. Retrieved September 2, 2024, from https://extension.usu.edu/divorce/

Vandenbroucke, G. (2015, March 9). *How World War I Changed Marriage Patterns in Europe.* Federal Reserve Bank of St. Louis. https://www.stlouisfed.org/on-the-economy/2015/march/how-world-war-i-changed-marriage-patterns-in-europe

Venker, S. (2017, March 24). *Should it be illegal to be a stay-at-home mom? Why feminists are so frustrated*. Fox News. https://www.foxnews.com/opinion/should-it-be-illegal-to-be-a-stay-at-home-mom-why-feminists-are-so-frustrated

Veteran's view - combat vets much more likely to divorce, separate. (n.d.). Veteransview.com. Retrieved September 3, 2024, from https://www.veteransview.com/news/combat-vets-much-more-likely-to-divorce-separate

Vezzetti, V. C. (2016). New approaches to divorce with children: A problem of public health. *Health Psychology Open*, *3*(2), 205510291667810. https://doi.org/10.1177/2055102916678105

Vogel, W. (2001). The unexpected legacy of divorce: A 25-year landmark study · the love they lost: Living with the legacy of our parents' divorce. *Psychiatric Services (Washington, D.C.)*, *52*(8), 1108–1109. https://doi.org/10.1176/appi.ps.52.8.1108

Wallerstein, J. S. (2005). Growing up in the divorced family. *Clinical Social Work Journal*, *33*(4), 401–418. https://doi.org/10.1007/s10615-005-7034-y

Wamhoff, S., & Wiseman, M. (2007, April). *The TANF/SSI connection*. Social Security Administration Research, Statistics, and Policy Analysis. https://www.ssa.gov/policy/docs/ssb/v66n4/v66n4p21.html

Wang, W., & Wilcox, B. (2020, February 24). *Strong Families Are Living the Dream*. American Enterprise Institute. https://www.aei.org/articles/strong-families-are-living-the-dream/

Ward, M., Akhtar, A., & Lebowitz, S. (2020, September 2). 18 relationship facts everybody should know before getting married. *Business Insider*. https://www.businessinsider.com/facts-about-marriage-2017-2

Waterworth, T. (2020, November 7). *Child's terror of stepfather who allegedly used her as a sex slave*. Independent Online. https://www.iol.co.za/ios/news/childs-terror-of-stepfather-who-allegedly-used-her-as-a-sex-slave-66318a98-3119-4590-aadc-1a81e0f9f1eb

Wenner, M. (n.d.). Birth control pills affect women's taste in men.
Scientific American. Retrieved September 2, 2024, from https://www.
scientificamerican.com/article/birth-control-pills-affect-womens-taste/

*What do you think about this quote by John Adams? "Our constitution
was made only for a moral and religious people. It is wholly inadequa.*
(n.d.). Quora. Retrieved September 3, 2024, from https://www.
quora.com/What-do-you-think-about-this-quote-by-John-Adams-
%E2%80%9COur-constitution-was-made-only-for-a-moral-and-
religious-people-It-is-wholly-inadequate-to-the-government-of-any-
other-%E2%80%9D

What every generation gets wrong about sex. (n.d.). *Time.* Retrieved
September 3, 2024, from https://time.com/3611781/sexual-
revolution-revisited/

What god has joined together: Religion and the risk of divorce. (n.d.).
Institute for Family Studies. Retrieved September 3, 2024, from
https://ifstudies.org/blog/what-god-has-joined-together-religion-and-
the-risk-of-divorce

What If, Like Me, You Regret Your Divorce? (2019, May 31).
Goodmenproject.com. https://goodmenproject.com/divorce/what-if-
like-me-you-regret-your-divorce-cmtt/

What "the pill" did. (n.d.). *CNN.* Retrieved September 3, 2024, from
https://www.cnn.com/2010/OPINION/05/06/pogrebin.pill.
roundup/index.html

What the World Would Look Like Without the Catholic Church.
(n.d.). St. Mary's Catholic Center. Retrieved from http://www.
aggiecatholicblog.org/2016/10/what-the-world-would-look-like-
without-the-catholic-church/ [No longer available]

What women can do about divorce inequality. (n.d.). Ellevest. Retrieved
September 2, 2024, from https://www.ellevest.com/magazine/disrupt-

money/divorce-inequality

Whitehead, B. D. (1993, April 1). Dan Quayle was right. *Atlantic Monthly (Boston, Mass.: 1993)*. https://www.theatlantic.com/magazine/archive/1993/04/dan-quayle-was-right/307015/

Whiteside, T. (1970, December 11). The fight to ban smoking ads. *New Yorker (New York, N.Y.: 1925)*. https://www.newyorker.com/magazine/1970/12/19/the-fight-to-ban-smoking-ads

Whitton, S. W., Rhoades, G. K., Stanley, S. M., & Markman, H. J. (2008). Effects of parental divorce on marital commitment and confidence. *Journal of Family Psychology: JFP: Journal of the Division of Family Psychology of the American Psychological Association (Division 43)*, *22*(5), 789–793. https://doi.org/10.1037/a0012800

Why are so many Indian arranged marriages successful? (n.d.). *Psychology Today*. Retrieved September 3, 2024, from https://www.psychologytoday.com/us/blog/the-science-behind-behavior/201511/why-are-so-many-indian-arranged-marriages-successful

Why it's easier to love a stepfather than a stepmother. (n.d.). *Psychology Today*. Retrieved September 3, 2024, from https://www.psychologytoday.com/us/blog/stepmonster/201106/why-its-easier-to-love-a-stepfather-than-a-stepmother

Wildavsky, R., & Levine, D. R. (n.d.). *Welfare faces: Two moms, too many kids*. Seattletimes.com. Retrieved September 3, 2024, from https://archive.seattletimes.com/archive/?date=19950306&slug=2108537

Will, G. F. (2020, February 21). Elizabeth Warren's misguided approach to charter schools. *The Washington Post*. https://www.washingtonpost.com/opinions/why-warrens-ardent-defense-of-the-teachers-union-monopoly-hurts-students/2020/02/20/fe5aa2b2-5411-11ea-9e47-59804be1dcfb_story.html

Willett, B. (2019, August 13). What fifty years of no-fault divorce has gotten us. *Washington Examiner*. https://www.washingtonexaminer.

com/opinion/2628675/what-fifty-years-of-no-fault-divorce-has-gotten-us/

Williams, V., & Vonow, B. (2020, October 29). *Sex abuse survivor's agony as mom dies just hours after stepfather admits vile attacks.* The US Sun. https://www.the-sun.com/news/1710569/woman-heartache-mom-dead-stepdad-abuse/

With This Ring: A National Survey on Marriage in America. (2005). Fatherhood.org. https://www.fatherhood.org/with-this-ring-survey

Yau, N. (n.d.). *Divorce and Occupation.* Flowingdata.com. Retrieved September 3, 2024, from https://flowingdata.com/2017/07/25/divorce-and-occupation/

Young, C. (1999, January 4). Life Without Father. *The Wall Street Journal.* https://www.wsj.com/articles/SB915255562357531500

Zeratsion, H., Bjertness, C. B., Lien, L., Haavet, O. R., Dalsklev, M., Halvorsen, J. A., Bjertness, E., & Claussen, B. (2014). Does parental divorce increase risk behaviors among 15/16 and 18/19 year-old adolescents? A study from Oslo, Norway. *Clinical Practice and Epidemiology in Mental Health: CP & EMH, 10*(1), 59–66. https://doi.org/10.2174/17450179014100010059

(N.d.). Coursehero.com. Retrieved September 3, 2024, from https://www.coursehero.com/study-guides/wsu-sandbox/stressors/#:~:text=The%20numerical%20scores%20ranged%20from,second%20highest%20with%2073%20LCUs.

ACKNOWLEDGEMENTS

- I thank Almighty God for the ability to write this book.

- I thank all my grandchildren, who motivated me to write this book for their future lives. Thank you, dear grandchildren, for your invaluable contributions.

- Thank you to my children and to their spouses, for building strong marriages and stable families.

- Thank you to my wife, Justice Mary Thangam Thomas, for being an example of a wonderful wife.

- Thank you to my parents, Maria Sebastian and Soosai Maryayee, who raised me with their strong marriage and stable home.

- Thank you to Ms. Amanda Strub, for helping with editing and proofreading.

ABOUT THE AUTHOR

M.S. Thomas was born on February 14, 1937 in Madathattuvilai (city), Tamil Nadu (state), India. When he was 10 years old, his father died. His mother took care of him and his 3 brothers on her own. He attended St. Lawrence High School in Madathattuvilai (city), Tamil Nadu (state), India and then St. Xavier's College in Palayamkottai (city), Tamil Nadu (state), India. He then proceeded to earn his master's degree in Economics at Loyola College, Chennai (city), Tamil Nadu (state), India.

In 1963, he was the first person from his village to travel to America. He travelled by ship and plane from Tamil Nadu, India to Duquesne University, Pittsburgh, Pennsylvania, USA and graduated with his Masters in Business Administration (MBA) in 1968. He married Justice Mary in India on August 17, 1966 by arranged marriage. From 1968 to 1980 he taught Economics at DeSales University in Center Valley, Pennsylvania. In 1980, he joined the Business Department at Saint Francis University in Loretto, Pennsylvania where he taught courses and served as an academic advisor to hundreds of college students. His 37 years of teaching experience in higher education gave him a unique insight into the minds of young American college students. He retired from teaching in 2000 and wrote this book in his retirement while enjoying the blessings of his 2 children and 8 grandchildren.

This is the only picture from the wedding of M.S. Thomas and Justice Mary. M.S. Thomas is seated on the left while the bride, Justice Mary, is seated on the right. This picture was taken inside the church, St. Fatima, during Mass in Kottavilai, Kanyakumari District, Tamil Nadu, India on August 17, 1966.

This is the only picture from the wedding reception of the new Mr. and Mrs. M.S. Thomas. The newly married couple is seated inside the cabana-like structure. Left side is M.S. Thomas and next to him is his new wife, Justice Mary.

Taken in the 1980s in India in M.S. Thomas' native village of Madathattuvilai. Seated is his mother, Soosai Mariyayee. Left to right, M.S. Thomas' elder brother, Soosai Varuvel. Second from left is M.S. Thomas. Third from left is Benjamin and fourth from left is Vincent.

M.S. Thomas and Justice Mary in 1996 in the USA.

M.S. Thomas and Justice Mary taken March, 2024 at the West Deer Township Senior Citizens Center, Pennsylvania, USA.